YOUTH IN CARE CHRONICLES

Reflections on Growing Up in the Child Welfare System

AUTHORS

Ashley, Cassie, Cody, Damon, Jade, Jesse,
Kaylen, Kenneth, Krista, Linda, Megan, Mike,
Patricia, Shay, Shoshana, Theresa, Tyler & Winnie

NOVEMBER 2020   EDMONTON, AB

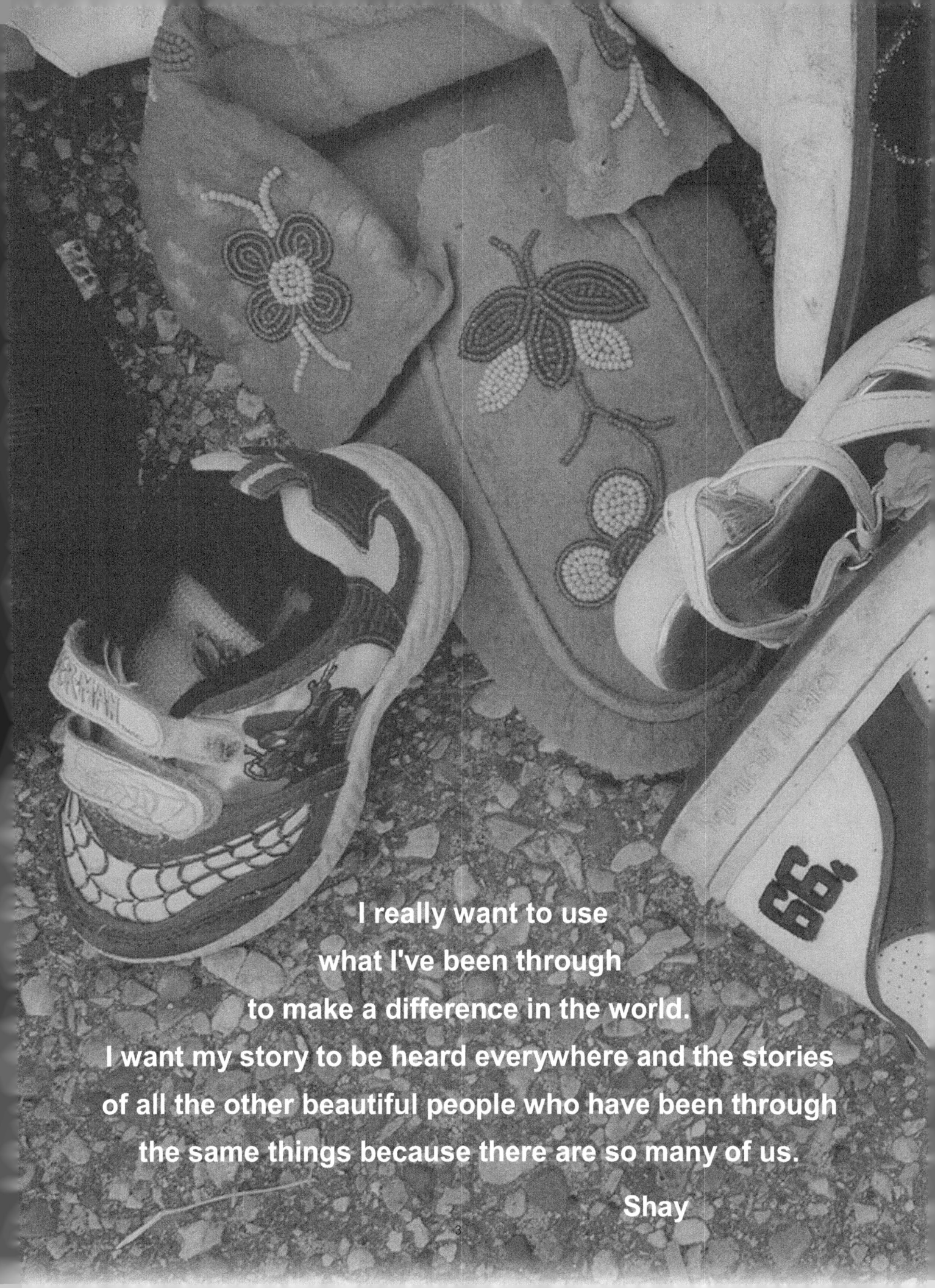

I really want to use
what I've been through
to make a difference in the world.
I want my story to be heard everywhere and the stories
of all the other beautiful people who have been through
the same things because there are so many of us.

Shay

TABLE OF CONTENTS

Foreword 5

Land Acknowledgement 10

Dedication 12

Editorial Team & Acknowledgements 14

Preface 22

Introduction 23

Transitions and Youth in Care 25

Endorsements 31

Help Page 36

Cassie 39

Shoshana 47

Jade 56

Winnie 66

Tyler 74

Patricia 85

Cody 94

Linda 113

Mike 124

Shay 130

Damon 141

Theresa 158

Kaylen 174

Krista 185

Kenneth 194

Megan 216

Ashley 224

Jesse 251

Learning Guide 266

Glossary 277

FOREWORD

It has been a long journey of 31 years working in child protection, but it has gone by very fast. I have been very fortunate as it has been a rewarding journey, especially the last 22 years, which have focused on being involved in the lives of many youth. The youth have taught me so much, starting with how things need to change so the support, help, and services offered to them are relevant, accessible, and involve the youth in all of the decisions made about *their* lives. Moreover, the youth allowed me to be part of their lives, to make mistakes, to ask questions, and to develop a practice that is more meaningful to them. It did not make sense to me to continue doing practice in ways that the youth were telling us is not effective.

Over the years, I have also had the opportunity to share their wisdom and knowledge—consistent with literature and research—whether consulting, training, teaching, writing, or chatting over coffee with those in contact with youth. I learned that youth want relationships with healthy adults, and, despite this, too many workers still default to punitive approaches in their work, which does not result in good outcomes. If a youth feels a sense of shame, guilt, and failure, which is often the case given the way their lives have unfolded, one should ask how heaping more shame, guilt and failure on the youth will somehow bring about positive outcomes. Rather, this type of practice acts as a barrier to relationships often resulting in youth feeling rejected (yet again), and feeling worse about themselves and their situation. They did not choose their lives so would not compassion and understanding make more sense?

It is tough not getting off to a good start in this world. Life can be particularly unpredictable, chaotic, frightening, and there can be times when there is no one to turn to. It is easy to lay blame but the people who are supposed to be caring for their children are often dealing with immense struggles themselves. But, how does a child make sense of this and understand what is happening? Their lives unfold differently because for too many children and youth, sadly, being cared for and looked after in a nurturing way is not part of their everyday experience. These feelings do not go away and for some it takes a long time to make sense of their lives and bounce back from such tragic experiences.

In fact, I have also often asked myself if it is even possible to bounce back from loss, grief, rejection and abandonment. When there is so much pain and when doing whatever it takes to get any kind of relief, can life get better? I have had youth talk about feeling alone, like nobody cares, and not knowing what their futures hold. Wondering if life will ever be different for youth in such a place is very hard as a worker too, as we care for the youth and we just want their hurting to stop. We can feel helpless in trying to help them find some measure of peace. If feeling so overwhelmed by life, I think I would be trying to numb out and escape as well. I have come to understand that, while heartbreaking, the need to check out from reality can be preferred to being alone with nothing but intrusive thoughts about the trauma they have suffered. We know that no one deserves their life to be such a day-to-day struggle, but they are coping the best they can with the little they have got. This is the reality for too many youth and sometimes it can feel that the best we can do at the time is to simply help them be safe on the streets. The *Youth In Care Chronicles* provides a welcome relief from such a narrow and dark view, in that it is made abundantly clear that many do make it despite the difficult journey and having to fight for everything. Some youth are stuck but they still survive, perhaps waiting for a time when it is safe to let go of their pain and let safe people into their lives. The authors, for me, quietly honour the youth who still struggle, while still celebrating those that overcome tremendous odds and are able to control the pain rather than allowing the pain to control them. They are fighting back and giving hope to others.

For youth who grow up "in the system," dreams do not always take hold, but are replaced by just surviving, avoiding the next emotional pain, and smothering the feelings of despair and helplessness. But through all of these coping mechanisms and pushing people away, hope somehow finds its way through, "kicking at the darkness 'til it bleeds daylight," as Bruce Cockburn (1984, 2:53) wrote in one of his songs. Was it one person who saw through their defenses but didn't turn away? Was it someone who saw through the anger and didn't judge them? Was it the family member who reached out and assured them things could be different at a time when the youth was contemplating suicide? Was it a worker who believed in them even when they didn't believe in themselves? Was it the right of passage of becoming a parent and the determination to give their child a different life from what they experienced? Was it the outreach worker who was embarrassed by being tear-eyed thinking that no child should ever be treated this way, as the youth talked about their life? Was it the advocate who would not take 'no' for an answer because the youth deserved better? Was it a fear of running out of time and losing the people who actually do care? Was it to show this "fucking world" that they are not a throwaway kid that will never realize their potential? The authors of these stories you are about to read will answer some of these questions demonstrating their uniqueness, and that we all can respond to life's challenges in different ways. They define their own success in their own unique ways as well. Being in the system and growing up in care is a part of their lives. It does not define them. Their stories define them and tell us about the richness of their lives. Like all of us, the writers in this book will quite possibly face more challenges at different points on their journey. However, life is more than about surviving one day to the next, it can be about those dreams actually taking hold, and about possibilities actually being possible.

This is personal as the authors are allowing you into their world. My work with youth has taught me how difficult this can be. While careful not to speak for this group of contributors, youth can face challenges allowing people into their world, and trusting others, especially if they have experienced trauma early in life. The template of one's world can be that it is a hostile, frightening and lonely place. You may not be able to rely on the very people who are supposed to nurture and care for you. You learn adults are not very reliable, or they cause harm, often because they are in pain and do not know how to heal themselves. However, such troubling experiences can result in children and youth learning to protect themselves from the emotional pain of further rejection and abandonment, building a wall around themselves to keep people out, and hiding their shame, guilt and sense of failure. Keeping people at a safe distance is understandable, but can obviously be a lonely existence. It can take a very long time to find people with the patience and commitment to break through the walls. For some youth the damage and fear can be so great, and their walls so solid, it is a lifelong journey. For others, with caring people who do not give up, they are able to take the risk of allowing healthy adults into their world. For the authors in this book, they are taking this risk a step further and allowing you, as a reader, into their world. This is their gift to us. I have always been struck by how youth want to help and give back, even though life has not given them much. This is what the authors have done. Your gift in return is to honour the risk they took and find meaning in their stories. Whether a social worker; child and youth care worker; working in child protection or in the community; a psychologist, clinical practitioner, or psychiatrist; whether a person who helps people in any way or simply someone who has contact with children, youth, and young adults; or a citizen open to learning more about those among us who grow up in care, the experience of this book will impact you, even just a little bit—your mind, your heart, your spirit, your soul. You will be better off for this experience.

This gift is given not to feel sorry for them or praise them. This *Youth In Care Chronicles* is to educate and to help others learn from their experiences, as well as understand not only the struggles some people in society go through, but how they can overcome, fight, discover themselves, find their spirit, and triumph against the odds. This does not always happen in isolation, and this book further demonstrates how ultimately, we are, indeed, wired for connection, and, as we hear often but do not always respect, that relationships are a big deal!

There are so many uplifting themes reflected in this book you are about to read. A big part of the work with youth must be about amplifying their voices and learning from what we hear to evolve our practice and be better at helping and meeting their needs. Amplifying the voices of young people is what this collection of stories does, loudly, and in a passionate, courageous and heart-felt way.

So, get lost in this book—see, hear, and feel the emotions of their stories and the messages of the authors. Be open to challenging yourself to reflect on your own privilege, your beliefs and attitudes relating to the most marginalized and excluded young people in society. Acknowledge the many labels we attach to children and youth for whom life can be a day-to-day struggle. Appreciate they are also doing the best they can with what they have. Allow their words to make you angry, make you sad, make you frustrated, shock you, help you understand, help you be thoughtful, and see the world differently. But, also cheer on the resiliency of the courageous writers, and the many more youth they represent. Share your experience reading this book with others. Make it a book club discussion. Allow yourself to smile and laugh. Mostly, be inspired!

Peter Smyth, MSW, RSW, MSM
Social Worker, Author, Advocate

Peter has been a social worker for over 31 years, focusing on youth for the past 22 years. He is a sessional instructor with the University of Calgary, Faculty of Social Work (Edmonton), and MacEwan University, School of Social Work. Peter has written articles and book chapters relating to work with youth and child welfare. His book, *Working with High Risk Youth: A Relationship Based Practice Framework,* was published in 2017. In 2020, he was awarded the Governor General Meritorious Service Medal for his service to youth.

References
Cockburn, B (1984). Lovers in a Dangerous Time. On *Stealing Fire*, True North Records.

We respectfully acknowledge that we are located on Treaty 6, Treaty 7, and Treaty 8 territories; the traditional gathering places for diverse Indigenous peoples where the footsteps of the Blackfoot Confederacy – Kainai, Piikani, and Siksika – the Cree, Dene, Saulteaux, Nakota Sioux, Stoney Nakoda, and the Tsuu T'ina Nation, and the Métis People of Alberta have remained imbedded in these lands for generations. This includes the Métis Settlements and the Six Regions of the Métis Nation of Alberta within the historical Northwest Métis Homeland. We acknowledge the many First Nations, Métis, and Inuit who have lived in and cared for these lands and continue to influence our vibrant community.

A mother's wounds bleed into their daughters.
Her life too had been uprooted by "the system" -
and all five of her brothers.
She never got to meet her mother, but
she loved me as if she knew the
love of a thousand
mothers.
I truly believe that it is
the prayers of our
grandmothers
and
aunties
that live within
that allow her to
love
and allow
me
to love
too.

Jade

DEDICATION

This book is dedicated to our authors, Ashley, Cassie, Cody, Damon, Jade, Jesse, Kaylen, Kenneth, Krista, Linda, Megan, Mike, Patricia, Shay, Shoshana, Theresa, Tyler & Winnie. It is dedicated to their pure honesty. It is dedicated to their incredible bravery. And it is dedicated to their sincere desire to make the world a better, kinder, safer place for youth in care by sharing their lives, their stories, and their hope.

To all the families, foster families, social workers, caseworkers, child and youth care workers, teachers, educational assistants, medical professionals, mentors, advocates, police and probations officers, coaches, volunteers, friends, and kind strangers who have crossed the paths of youth in care and provided love, care, understanding and protection, even for just a moment, this book is dedicated to your humanity. It really does only take one person to make all the difference.

The scariest part of being in care is
never knowing what is going on.

Never being sat down
and told why you're
moving because you
just think you're
just a bad kid.

I think just the
sense of longing
is always there;
just not really
belonging
anywhere
isn't a very
good feeling
growing up.

I have an adopted family, now.
I found them very late in foster
care and I'm really glad but in ways,
I still don't feel like I belong.
It's kind of a lifelong struggle.

Kaylen

Lead Editor: Penny Frazier
Project Manager: Penny Frazier
Editorial Team: Cody Murrell
Editorial Team: Dorothy Badry
Editorial Team: Megan Mierau
Editorial Team: Theresa Tucker-Wright
Editorial Team: Erin Leveque
Proofreaders: Megan Henze & Brooke Thomas-Skaf
Cover Design & Photography: Caitlin Varrin www.magichour.ca
Inside Photography: Caitlin Varrin
Inside Photography: Penny Frazier www.pennyfrazier.ca
Inside Graphics: Penny Frazier
Cover Subject: Chasm Frazier

Copyright 2020   All Rights Reserved

No part of this publication may be reproduced, stored in a retrieval system, or transmitted in any form or by any means, electronic, mechanical, photocopying, recording, or otherwise without the prior written consent of the publisher. Permission may be sought directly from Penny Frazier by emailing penny@pennyfrazier.ca or calling 1-780-221-6124 in Canada.

ISBN

Published by Amazon

DISCLAIMER

The ideas, views and opinions expressed in this book are those of the contributors and do not represent the views of the Government of Alberta or Alberta Children's Services. Neither the Government of Alberta nor Alberta Children's Services provided any information in relation to the contents of this book.

PROCEEDS

All proceeds from the sales of the Youth in Care Chronicles will be invested in future projects to benefit youth in care.

Lead Editor & Project Manager

Penny Frazier   www.pennyfrazier.ca

Entering her 5th decade of caring for marginalized youth in her home and in the community, Penny has always believed in the healing power of arts, music, and storytelling. From pioneering youth media projects, to writing and directing plays for students with behavioural challenges, to starting a punk rock band with the residents of a group home, she is known as a revolutionary force in the field. A dauntless advocate, Penny is committed to raising awareness about the experiences of individuals who grow up in care, including the mental health issues they encounter. In the summer of 2019, she was the Executive Producer of *Jesse Jams* – a documentary about a former youth in care she had worked with since 2012 and had been documenting on film since 2016. In collaboration with Trevor Anderson of *Trevor Anderson Films* and funding from *Telus Originals*, she and Jesse were able to see their dream come to the screen and have enjoyed many accolades. Penny has also written professionally for over 20 years and now uses her literary skills to create poetry, plays, and special projects including the *Youth in Care Chronicles*.

Personal Statement

I have wanted to compile a book like this for many years and am so honored and grateful that I was able to connect with these incredible authors and this outstanding editorial team to make it happen. I feel that the stories of children who grew up in the child welfare system have gone unheard and there is so much wisdom we can all glean from their words. Their uncommon lives have required uncommon valour to rise above their adversities and break through the stereotypes they face. I believe that this book will raise awareness and, thus, the level of respect they deserve. I am so happy that other youth in care will be comforted and inspired by reading what is inside, and that people working in the field will benefit from the honesty that has been invested in these pages. I personally want to thank you for taking the time to recognize the importance of this compilation. My hope is to continue gathering and publishing the many stories that need to be shared. As our author, Shay, states: I want my story to be heard everywhere and the stories of all the other beautiful people who have been through the same things because there are so many of us.

Editorial Team

Cody Murrell, BSW, RSW

Cody Murrell is a Casework Supervisor with Alberta Children's Services who works in Edmonton, Alberta. He has been working with children and youth who are in care for the past 7 years in varying capacities. Cody started his career working in the group care sector (multiple specialized group homes) as a Youth Worker. He had also worked as a Child Intervention Caseworker and Generalist before becoming a Supervisor. Cody holds a Diploma of Social Work from Grant MacEwan University and a Bachelor of Social Work from the University of Calgary. Cody has extensive volunteer experience in the Social Work field, which includes volunteering as an Alberta College of Social Worker's Council Member, worker at Amity House, and co-chair of Edmonton Youth Speak Out (a youth in care group, which represents the interests of youth in care and seeks to inform practice through the sharing of the youth's experiences). Cody Murrell is an advocate for youth in care and speaks publicly about his experiences, most notably, at the High-Risk Youth Conference, University of Calgary, and Youth Power. His intense passion for the profession of Social Work and compassion for others stems from his own experience growing up in care. Cody has been happily married to his wife, Shay, for the past 3 years.

Personal Statement
This book represents a deep passion of mine in terms of giving voice to those who may not often be heard and the sharing of their experiences to raise awareness and create meaningful change. It is my hope that this book and the powerful stories contained within it will help change the negative societal narratives that often surround youth-in-care. I also hope that this book will serve to inform practice, act as resource for those who work with youth-in-care and the youth themselves, celebrate the strength and triumphs of youth-in-care, and to let youth in care know that they are not alone. Nothing like this book currently exists, where the stories of multiple people within care experiences exist in one shared place. I believe the value this book brings is astronomical in terms of understanding the diversity of care experiences and outcomes. I feel honored to have been part of this project and to have been brought together with some of the most amazing and inspiring contributors and supports. I want to thank all the contributors for their dedication to this worthwhile project.

Dorothy Badry, PhD, MSW, RSW

Dorothy Badry, PhD, MSW, RSW is a professor in the Faculty of Social Work, University of Calgary. Her research focus is on FASD and child welfare, disability, women's health and FASD prevention, housing and homelessness, advancing knowledge on FASD and loss and grief, and more recently FASD and suicide. She worked in child protection for 16 years in Alberta and continues to deeply care about child welfare issues and those involved on the edges of society and systems. Dorothy has been Child Welfare Research Lead since 2017 with the Canada FASD Research Network. She has received numerous research grants from provincial and national funders, including PolicyWise, the Public Health Agency of Canada, the First Nations & Inuit Health Branch of Canada, SSHRC, and has many publications on FASD research.

Personal Statement

In this new millennium, it is time to hear the voices of those who have been raised in the child welfare system. My connections to the child protection system go back to 1986, when I started working as a child welfare worker in a rural community in central Alberta. I worked there for three years and spent another 13 years in various positions in Calgary, primarily in crisis responses. The lessons I learned were from children – about their need for care and protection and, despite the circumstances, the recognition that, if possible, family connection needs to be maintained. I realized that youth grow up and have wondered about how we prepare them for this inevitability. I have specialized in FASD and deeply appreciate the complexity of this disability and families. Some of the young people involved with this book have FASD, and the CanFASD Research Network is proud to be involved with this work. We thank the youth for their courage in living their lives in the best way possible and for sharing their authentic wisdom in this book. We are incredibly proud of the writers in this book who have become social workers and provide their insightful wisdom, spirit, and resilience in caring for children and youth. As a social work educator at the University of Calgary, I will use this book as a treasured teaching tool for future generations of social workers.

Megan Mierau, MSW, RSW

Megan Mierau is proud to call herself a Social Worker and is currently employed as a Casework Supervisor with Alberta Children's Services. Megan has a decade of experience within the social work field and is a strong advocate for youth in government care. She initially obtained a Bachelor of Social Work degree in 2013 from the University of Regina, and spent time working abroad as a social worker in Australia. In 2015, Megan pursued a Master of Social Work degree from the University of Calgary and, following the completion of her schooling, she was humbled to work on Treaty 7 Territory with children and youth in care. She relocated to Edmonton in 2016 and has worked for the Government of Alberta as both a frontline Social Worker and in a supervisory capacity since that time. As a supervisor of a youth unit within Children's Services, her passions now lie with promoting storytelling for Indigenous youth in care and ensuring youth maintain connections to their home communities. Megan has also supported youth sharing their stories by volunteering with Edmonton Youth Speak Out since 2017. In addition to supervising, this year Megan began teaching as a sessional instructor for the Faculty of Social Work at the University of Calgary and has a passion for education. Megan's lifelong love for learning is continually enriched by her partner, Kieran, and their dog, Yogi.

Personal Statement

For all youth in care, and particularly for Indigenous youth, storytelling is a pathway to healing and a way to control the narrative of which many youth have lost control due to their experiences. It was an honour and a privilege to be a part of the creation of this book, given its overarching goal to provide voice to youth and adults who have experiences within the child welfare system. It is my best hope that these stories will fall into the hands of youth in care who have felt marginalized, afraid, and that they are alone. In reading these stories, youth can realize that, although they have unique stories, they are part of a shared experience and that there is hope beyond what has been lost. There is a saying that stormy seas make strong sailors, and I honestly believe that through unintended adversity, these incredible contributors have become incredible masters of their own destinies. Thank you to the reader, for honouring these stories with your time and attention, and to our brave contributors for sharing your powerful history.

Theresa Tucker-Wright, BCYC

Theresa Tucker-Wright is passionate about working with children, youth, and families. Theresa has worked within the Children's Services field for the past 25 years, including in-group care, supporting pregnant and parenting teens, in child protection, coordinating placements for foster and group care, as an adoption worker, as a permanency adoption supervisor, and as the Adoption Specialist for Edmonton Children's Services. Theresa returned to school as a mature student and graduated from Grant MacEwan's Child and Youth Care diploma program and completed the Addiction Studies certificate from the University of Alberta in 2000. After working for several years within the Children's Services field, Theresa embraced her passion for lifelong learning and chose to obtain a bachelor's degree in Child and Youth Care from MacEwan University in 2015. Theresa has opened her heart and her home to support youth impacted by addictions and, most recently, to a young adult who desired to be a part of a family. Theresa brings a unique lens as a past recipient of Children's Services supports, which resulted in her entering foster care at the age of 13, and ultimately transitioning to independent living. The lack of stability at a young age resulted in frequent moves with her birth family and attendance at 14 different schools. Theresa has strived to create a safe and loving relationship with her husband of twelve years; together raising their blended family of four children.

Personal Statement

I am a passionate advocate about permanency, empowering young people to overcome their experiences, and supporting their voices to be heard. This book represents the journey of many young people's lived experiences, and their bravery in sharing in their experiences is astounding. It is my hope that this book will provide opportunities for youth to know they are not alone in their journey and will provide insight and hope they can draw on, now and into the future. With respect to practitioners, this book will provide awareness about the array of lived experiences of the contributors, which is a fair and accurate representation of the diversity which exists within the Children Service field. As a practitioner, you can impact the trajectory of children, youth, and families in a positive way, as you will see evidence of within the contributors' stories. I feel fortunate to have participated in this project, as I have found healing in writing and poetry, both as a youth and into my adult life. I have worked hard to heal both as an individual and as a family. I hope readers will find inspiration in the contributors' stories, to know that they too can heal from their childhood experiences and trauma. The experience of being in care does not have to define you. It is just part of your journey and, as you grow and surround yourself with healthy and loving people, you can create the life you want as you are the master of your own destiny.

Erin Leveque, BSW, RSW

Erin Leveque is a Social Worker currently working in research at the University of Calgary's Faculty of Social Work. Originally quite opposed to research and its inaccessibility, Erin found a love of using storytelling in research as a tool for social justice and to make research more accessible. The opportunity to witness the vulnerability, tenacity, and courage that folks experience in their everyday lives is a gift that she is forever grateful for, and she is determined to use her skills in research to share stories as often as she can. As an ardent supporter for the representation of lived experiences in the field of social work and beyond, she hopes that this book will provide that little "me too" that makes someone feel connected to community. At this point in Erin's story, she is happily introverting with her husband Jeff, and the two best dogs in the world, Loki and Arya.

The Canada Fetal Alcohol Spectrum Disorder Research Network (CanFASD) has been a proud sponsor of this project and very pleased with the final results. This project had a strong vision from the beginning and will certainly be a valuable resource to teach others about the vulnerabilities and challenges many in our society face. These stories are difficult to tell and hard to convey the compounding impacts of trauma, system barriers, and limited relationships. CanFASD wishes to thank all the participants for their bravery and openness to share these very personal stories. They will have impact and change perceptions.

CanFASD is a research network that likes to work collaboratively and in areas that are going to have the biggest impact for people with FASD, their families and communities. Our work has centered around prevention, interventions, diagnosis, justice and child welfare. We try to be nimble to address areas of interest with our stakeholders and take advantage of new opportunities as they arise like this project. Our research teams, staff, board of directors, family advisory committee and our consultants with FASD all find these personal accounts meaningful and worthy of our engagement and support.

For more information about CanFASD and the work we do check out our blog at https://canfasdblog.wordpress.com, or our website at www.canfasd.ca

ACKNOWLEDGEMENTS

Many thanks to CanFASD for their support of our passion project and the funding to make it possible.

Many thanks to Peter Smyth for his valuable time and consultation.

Many thanks to Jean LaFrance for his help in getting this project off the ground and connecting the right people to make it happen.

Many thanks to Tasnim Nathoo of Grounded Thoughts Therapy & Consulting who conducted the writing workshop with the authors in 2018.

Many thanks to Megan Henze and Brooke Thomas-Skaf for proofreading.

Many thanks to Caitlin Varrin at magichour.ca for her dedication to our cover design.

Many thanks to Chasm Frazier for being the subject of our book cover, dedication page and help page.

And, many thanks to the Adoption Council of Canada for their support and for sharing their postcard collection from Youth Speak Out Edmonton.

Adoption Council of Canada
Conseil d'adoption du Canada

PREFACE

The Youth in Care Chronicles has been a work in progress since 2018 and it is with the greatest pride and pleasure that we are putting it into your hands in 2020. It contains a compilation of the life stories and experiences of 18 former youth in care who have created their own chapters with distinct style. All deliver with an authentic voice and a sincere desire to make a difference.

Our hope is that the reflections shared here will comfort and inspire children and youth who are still in care or who formerly grew up in the child welfare system. We hope their voices will reach a larger audience and spread awareness about the issues youth in care face, help change the societal narrative of youth in care, inform and improve practices that impact youth in care, and influence the government policies that affect them.

Thank you for taking the time to read the stories and reflections within.

INTRODUCTION

It's Time to Listen

While prevalent in our society, child abuse is a phenomenon that survives on secrecy and through silencing the voices of children and youth. This silencing can occur directly and intentionally, but it may also occur through unintended inattention and preoccupation. The sharing of experiences contained within this book are rare peeks past the veil of secrecy that often overshadows them.

Rarely discussed openly within families and communities, child abuse is a topic that evokes great emotion in humans and reactions of blame and shame may further feed the cycle of secrecy that can lead to reoccurrences of abuse. For certain children, the severity of the abuse has come to the attention of others outside the home, meaning that they cannot stay and must come into government care.

Often, being removed from their home is required for the safety of the child, but this child then becomes a member of one of the most marginalized groups in society. Evidence shows that youth leaving the care of child welfare systems have extremely poor outcomes and often experience homelessness, incarceration, addiction issues, poor mental health, and other challenges as a result of their time in care. Abuse may silence children and youth but being brought into government care layers on dimensions of powerlessness and hopelessness that are unparalleled to what most Canadians experience.

Unfortunately, the public is often ignorant to the plights of children and youth in care for the same reason child abuse is often overlooked – it's scary, and we feel more comfortable with its invisibility than its visibility. It leads us to ask a simple question on paper, but a challenging one to actualize: How do we mobilize ourselves to be an ally to children and youth in care and restore their voices? One answer is through allowing the art of storytelling and creating the space to listen.

For all youth in care, particularly Indigenous youth, storytelling is a pathway to healing and a way to reshape the narrative that many youth have lost control of due to their experiences. In sharing their experiences, youth in care can express the feelings of shame, blame, and guilt that have been inherently forced on them by the child welfare system. They are taking some of the power back. While not an easy task, making public the secrecy of child abuse and experiences of the child welfare system opens the doorway to healing, reconciliation, and real societal change. In this book, you will find a collection of stories from former children and youth in care who have been brave enough to demonstrate vulnerability, resiliency, and courage for the world to see. The *Youth in Care Chronicles* was inspired by the storytelling that is already occurring within Alberta, Canada. It is our best hope that these stories will fall into the hands of youth in care who have felt marginalized, afraid, and that they are alone. In reading these stories, youth can realize that, although they have unique stories, they are part of a shared experience and that there is hope beyond what has been lost. There is a saying that stormy seas make strong sailors, and we truly believe that through unintended adversity, these incredible contributors have become masters of their own destinies.

As a reader of this book, you are demonstrating your courage to push the bounds of your comfort. Whether you come already positioned as an ally to children and youth in care or wanting to learn more, we welcome you and invite you to take in the voices shared within these pages. Not only are the storytellers important, but so too is the community, as we work toward being attentive and encouraging to children, youth, and adults in care that are still on their healing journey. We must continue to support them, as storytelling is just one of the ways to restore power and voice to children and youth in care. But first - it's time to listen.

Megan Mierau, MSW, RSW
Editorial Team

TRANSITIONS AND YOUTH IN CARE

Youth in care experience a number of difficult transitions during their lives including placement changes, school changes, family changes, and transitioning out of care. Notably, youth in care experience heightened emotional stress as they navigate loss and grief over important relationships with families, friends, and workers (Chambers, 2020). Youth in care often feel an increased sense of rejection, abandonment, and loss of control over their lives, particularly when they feel their voices are not being heard in relation to important decisions being made about their lives (Chambers, 2020).

While all people will experience transitions in their lifetime, the nuances of transitioning while in care or transitioning out of care are significantly made more difficult when taking into consideration the increased emotional stress and trauma, and the barriers to employment and education (Powers et al., 2018). As evident in research and throughout the stories in this book, youth in care need a significant amount of support as they transition out of care, into adulthood and throughout early adulthood. They need the room to be able to make mistakes like any other young adult and they need the support to ensure that their mistakes are not detrimental to their future. However, Solomon (2010) highlights that "even the most carefully planned and managed ending may feel like yet another betrayal of hope and trust" (p. 176), which means that even though a youth may appear to be ready for the transition and doing well, transition is still an extremely difficult time. The role of child welfare authorities in these transitions are critical as youth in care often have much less supports to fall back on.

Research demonstrates that self-determination; strong relationships with adults in their lives; an intentional way to say goodbye between the youth and worker during a transition; and having knowledge about decisions made by child welfare authorities, including being actively included in making those decisions and allowing time to adjust to changes, are all ways that caregivers and workers can help to improve transitions for youth in care (Chambers et al., 2020; Powers et al., 2018; Mitchell et al., 2010). These recommendations have been echoed by the voices in this book. Many of the youth who shared their stories described the impacts of caregivers and workers in their lives either as someone who was identified as being unhelpful, or someone who was marked in their memory as influential, supportive, and needed at that time and place in their lives. The life course is full of transitions and the role of child welfare in supporting young people to transition from care is critical as it ensures that a strong foundation is in place and that they are prepared to move into adult life.

IN PERSPECTIVE...

Number of Youth in Care

- In Alberta, **16, 210** children and youth received child intervention services in 2019 (Alberta Children's Services, 2020a).
- In Alberta, **71%** of children and youth in care are Indigenous, despite making up **10%** of the population (Alberta Children's Services, 2020b).
- In Canada, **52%** of children and youth in care are Indigenous, despite making up **7%** of the total Canadian population (McKay et al., 2018).

Homelessness

- In a pan-Canadian study on youth homelessness, **57%** of youth overall and **73%** of youth who became homeless before the age of 16 reported being involved in child welfare services over their lifetime (Nichols et al., 2017).

Suicide

- A recent meta-analysis study demonstrated that youth in care were **three to four times more likely** to attempt suicide than the general population (Evans et al., 2017).
- The BC Coroner found that from 2013-2018, **54%** of the children and youth who had died by suicide received child welfare services in the past year (BC Coroner, 2019).

Trafficking

- **85%** of trafficked youth have a history with child welfare (Gragg et al., 2007).
- National Center for Missing and Exploited Children (2014) estimate that **1 in 6** endangered runaways are likely trafficked for sex.

Education

- In 2012-2013, **47%** of youth in care completed high school, compared to 84% of their peers in the general population (Rutman & Hubberstey, 2016). In 2001, the number of youth in care who had completed high school was only **28%**, which means that the policy and program improvements set in place by the Ministry of Education has made an impact in the educational outcomes for youth in care (Rutman & Hubberstey, 2016).

Disability

- During 2012-2013, **46**% of BC children or youth in care were identified to have a disability designation in school, compared to 8.6% of their peers not in care (Rutman & Hubberstey, 2016).
- A 2016 study found that foster children with intellectual disabilities were **46% less likely** to exit foster care than their peers without disabilities and were **5 times more likely** to have died in foster care compared to their peers without disabilities (Slayter, 2016).

Health Outcomes

- In a longitudinal study on the Adverse Childhood Experiences of youth in care, **64%** of youth aging out of foster care rated their health as poor or fair, and this was especially true for youth in care who had experienced significantly more adversity than their peers (Rebbe et al., 2018).
- In an analysis of the 2011-2012 National Survey of Children's Health in the United States, results showed that children and youth in care were significantly more likely to experience poorer mental and physical health outcomes such as being **seven times more likely** to experience depression, **five times more likely** to experience anxiety, **three times more likely** to live with hearing or vision impairments, and **two times more likely** to live with a learning disability or asthma, among others (Turney et al., 2016).

References

Alberta Children's Services. (2020a). *Annual report 2019-2020.* Government of Alberta. https://open.alberta.ca/dataset/476d1e4b-bdfa-4330-a88a-79bdacee1a9a/resource/4ade2575-75c0-4977-bf9c-5b6824c131b7/download/cs-annual-report-2019-2020.pdf

Alberta Children's Services. (2020b). *2020-21 second quarter (September) update.* Government of Alberta. https://open.alberta.ca/dataset/child-intervention-information-and-statistics-summary-quarter-update/resource/1b25536b-6de0-46cc-a95d-4b6d785fd6e7

BC Coroner. (2019). *Supporting youth and health professionals: A report on youth suicides.* Government of British Columbia. https://www2.gov.bc.ca/gov/content/life-events/death/coroners-service/child-death-review/reports-publications

Chambers, R. M., Crutchfield, R. M., Willis, T. Y., Cuza, H. A., Otero, A., Harper, S. G. G., & Carmichael, H. (2020). "Be supportive and understanding of the stress that youth are going through:" Foster care alumni recommendations for youth, caregivers and caseworkers on placement transitions. *Children and Youth Services Review, 108*, 104644.

Evans, R., White, J., Turley, R., Slater, T., Morgan, H., Strange, H., & Scourfield, J. (2017). *Comparison of suicidal ideation, suicide attempt and suicide in children and young people in care and non-care populations: Systematic review and meta-analysis of prevalence.* Children and Youth Services Review, 82, 122–129. doi:10.1016/j.childyouth.2017.09.020

Gragg, F., Petta, I., Bernstein, H., Eisen, K., & Quinn, L. (2007). New York prevalence study of commercially sexually exploited children. *Rensselaer, NY: New York State Office of Children and Family Services.*

McKay, C., Fleming, E., Hamara, G., Powless, B., & Powless, R. (2018). *A report on children and families together: An emergency meeting on Indigenous child and family services. Report prepared for Indigenous Services Canada.* Ottawa, Ontario. https://www.sac-isc.gc.ca/eng/1531151888537/1531152018493#chp3

Nichols, N., Schwan, K., Gaetz, S., Redman, M., French, D., Kidd, S., O'Grady, B. (2017). *Child welfare and youth homelessness in Canada: A proposal for action.* Toronto: Canadian Observatory on Homelessness Press.

Mitchell, M. B., Kuczynski, L., Tubbs, C. Y., & Ross, C. (2010). We care about care: Advice by children in care for children in care, foster parents and child welfare workers about the transition into foster care. *Child & Family Social Work, 15*(2), 176-185.

National Center for Missing & Exploited Children. (2014). *National Center for Missing & Exploited Children 2014 annual report.* Kansas City, MO: National Center for Missing & Exploited Children.

Powers, L. E., Fullerton, A., Schmidt, J., Geenen, S., Oberweiser-Kennedy, M., Dohn, J., ... & Blakeslee, J. (2018). Perspectives of youth in foster care on essential ingredients for promoting self-determination and successful transition to adult life: My life model. *Children and youth services review, 86*, 277-286.

Rutman, D. & Hubberstey, C. (2016). Fostering Success: Improving Educational Outcomes for Youth in/from Care. Victoria, BC: University of Victoria.

Solomon R. (2010). Working with endings in relationship-based practice. In, G. Ruch, D. Turney, D., & A. Ward, A. (Eds.) (2010). *Relationship-based social work; Getting to the heart of practice.* London, UK: Jessica Kingsley Publishers.

Slayter, E. M. (2016). Foster care outcomes for children with intellectual disability. *Intellectual and Developmental Disabilities, 54*(5), 299-315.

Turney, K., & Wildeman, C. (2016). Mental and physical health of children in foster care. *Pediatrics, 138*(5).

Youth who were in care nearly 200 times more likely to be homeless: study

JORDAN PRESS August 9, 2017   THE GLOBE AND MAIL

A first-of-its-kind study in Canada has painted a national picture of homeless youth and drawn a link to the foster care system that researchers say could be playing a more active role in keeping young people off the streets.

The study found nearly three out of every five homeless youth were part of the child welfare system at some point in their lives, a rate almost 200 times greater than that of the general population…………

(To read the full article please click on the headline or type headline into your search bar.)

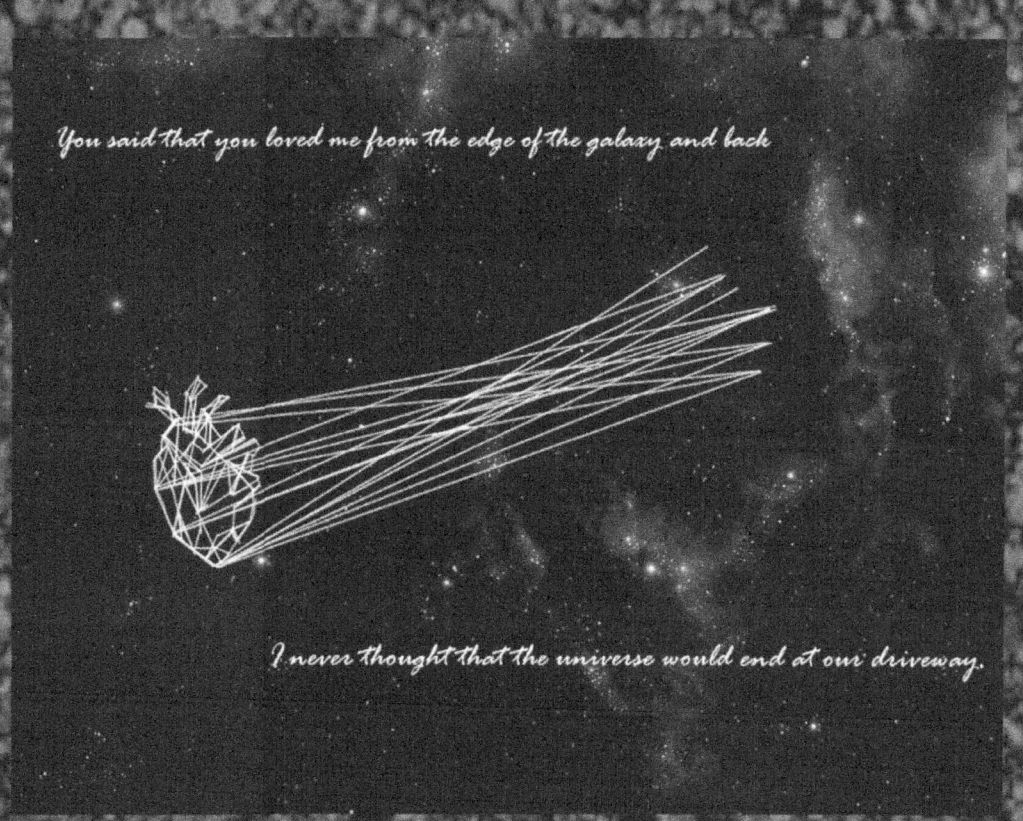

You said that you loved me from the edge of the galaxy and back

I never thought that the universe would end at our driveway.

Postcard courtesy of the Adoption Council of Canada—Youth Speak Out Edmonton

A key message I would like to leave behind is that, in the Child and Youth Care program, we are taught that it only takes one strong relationship with another person to build resiliency. For a lot of foster children, that one person could be someone in their family, so instead of separating family members, try working on keeping them connected with someone who gives them the support that they need, whether that be a family member, a child welfare worker, or a friend.

Shoshana

Youth Leaving Care Five Times More Likely To Die, Report Finds

Lack of supports, money, family creates high risk, coroner reports.

By Andrew MacLeod, 29 May 2018 | TheTyee.ca

Young people leaving foster care in British Columbia were five times more likely than other youth to die, according to a review by the provincial chief coroner's office.

"Although many young people leaving care or youth agreements show great resilience and strength as they transition to adulthood, they also face many more challenges than their peers," a report on the deaths found.

(To read full article please click on headline or type headline into your search bar.)

Postcard courtesy of the Adoption Council of Canada—Youth Speak Out Edmonton

What I've learned is that everyone has their own set of baggage, and everyone is just trying to do the best that they can to get through life. This is my baggage, and I can own it and know that it isn't there because something is innately wrong with me.

Ashley

ENDORSEMENTS

I am amazed when I hear young people talk about their experiences with the child welfare system. I am amazed at their honesty, their willingness to share what happened in their lives, their courage and their insights. I am especially amazed by their generosity in telling their stories; that they might bring comfort and hope to young people who have lived through similar circumstances, and guidance to those who want to help them along their way.

The *Youth in Care Chronicles* tell us about how these young people lived, about being in care, about the traumas they faced, and the many burdens they carried in their young lives. But more than that, they tell us about where they found their strengths, their tenacity and hope, and how they were able to move towards what they really wanted. They tell us about the people who cared about them, and about what a difference the power of relationships made in their ability to transform their lives. And these young people tell us this with the power of their own voices, in a stark, straight up, and unapologetic way…as it should be. It's the best way for us to hear them.

I hope you read this. I hope you are amazed and changed by what these young people have to say.

Del Graff
Child and Youth Advocate of Alberta

The collection of stories shared in the *Youth in Care Chronicles* is a pivotal resource for every social worker that will firmly ground professional practice to human connection. The real-life experiences shared by the writers demonstrate the necessary survival skills needed when kids grow up in care and face uncertain permanency in their lives. The storytellers shine a light on the child and youth care system and expose the importance of the caring relationship between the social worker and child or youth. The social workers role within this system can (and does) make a positive impact, one child at a time. These stories are a testament to show that through trauma, children and youth can not only survive, but they can thrive, especially when shown care and acceptance. It is a stark reminder that every genuine human connection is an opportunity to build trust, love, a sense of belonging and self-worth. As Cassie writes, "…humanity is always necessary."

Jody-Lee Farrah, MSW, RSW
Executive Director (Acting)
Associate Director, Professional Practice & Advocacy
Alberta College of Social Workers

I was involved with this project at the beginning and I am now delighted to have been able to comment on this powerful and moving book.

The Youth in Care Chronicles encourages practitioners to reflect upon their practice, discover their biases, and learn about how their lived experience impacts their perspectives in child welfare work. The hope being that they recognize the absolute value of relationship.

The contributors all longed for a life-long connection with a deep level of respect and trust with someone who accepts them for who they are, and who is there to support them when they need help. One contributor summed this up well as, *"This caseworker impacted my life because she treated me with care and compassion and made me feel loved. She was committed and never made me feel like a burden."*

Another contributor reminds us to acknowledge the resiliency of the ancestors, of family, and the never-ending support from those who have continued to love them. I wish the best for every individual who has lived through trauma and the child welfare system, many of whom will not be so resilient because our systems are flawed. This is why my heart continues to ache. It hurts me to see stories of children experiencing such heartache, especially our Indigenous children which is all too common. We need to do better. *"The folds of the system are deep and mysterious. They can take a child and as the system folds over and over, eventually the child is lost, but the longing never goes away".*

Dr. Jean LaFrance
Associate Professor Emeritus
University of Calgary

Once I started reading *Youth in Care Chronicles*, I could not stop. It was at times painful to read and know that children (through no fault of their own) had to endure so much hurt, rejection and trauma that would last a lifetime. But there was also HOPE throughout – that even though the youth were often dealt a losing hand at a young age, they persevered, survived, and won! I think that *Youth in Care Chronicles* should be a required of ALL people that work in child welfare, and how critically important they can be to help children who they regularly come in contact. They may be the one person in that child's life to make a difference. The book will also be a help to youth currently in care – to remind them that they are not alone, not give up, and believe they can survive and win at life.

Angela Marshall
Director, Wendy's Wonderful Kids Canada
Dave Thomas Foundation for Adoption

I love the cover of the Youth in Care Chronicles. The young man's jacket reads, "The Storm Will Pass", and as a former child welfare recipient of the Sixty Scoop era, my thoughts were so similar, "Everything is temporary."

Seeing children, youth and young adults affected by the separation, displacement of their homes, families, and communities is heartbreaking. Growing up in care is not easy. It is a scary and frightening experience when you walk into your first foster home or group home. There are no familiar faces; you don't have the same bedroom, living room, kitchen, eating habits, and menus are different. The rules and regulations are different in every household. The families you live with may be devoted Christians or come from a diverse ethnic background. Being in the care of child welfare, you have no control over your life.

Social workers can make a huge difference in a youth's life, especially when they take the time to get to know the youth they are working with because culturally, children and youth are the heart of our communities. No matter what age, the child and the youth need to feel that they belong, a chance to be loved, accepted, acknowledged, heard and understood.

Bernadette Iahtail, RSW
Co-founder/Executive Director
Creating Hope Society of Alberta

An engaging collection of meaningful perspectives and lived experiences of those in the child and family intervention system. An essential read for learning about the intimate relational world of social work with resilient youth populations.

Ellen Perrault, PhD, RSW
Dean, Faculty of Social Work
University of Calgary

The authors of this book invite the reader into their intimate lived experiences caught up in the child welfare system. The authors shatter stereotypes and reveal humanity; humanity that was always there which this book reveals with strength and sensitivity. A poignant message and quote from the book, "I want people to know that we are people" demands that readers stop and examine their biases and taken for granted discourses prevalent in society. The authors reveal humanity with words that have the power to change stories and change minds.

The authors affirm with the power of vulnerability and sharp intelligence that every child and youth in care is a multi-dimensional individual with unique attributes and potentials that need to be recognized and championed. This book does just that. This book will be a key addition in Child and Youth Care. It not only deserves but needs to be read with purpose toward change, on individual, collective, institutional, and systemic levels. The authors are experts with heart, agency, and vision for endless possibilities.

Dr. Ahna Berikoff
Associate Professor
Faculty of Child and Youth Care, Grant McEwan University

Powerful! Thank you for sharing youth voices from the Edmonton Youth Speak Out Team. A call to all policy makers, child welfare agencies and permanency families. Lifelong connections and supports are crucial, thank you for highlighting youth voice. Nothing for us, without us!

Cathy Murphy
Executive Director
Adoption Council of Canada

The stories collected in this book are honest, raw, and compelling, offering the reader a glimpse into the experiences of young people in care. It is a must-read for anyone who works with young people and families involved with child welfare. I hope it can be incorporated into required reading material for post-secondary programs such as Child and Youth Care and Social Work. I believe that by daring bravely and sharing their stories the authors will make a difference in the lives of young people.

Michelle Briegel, M.Ed, Certified CCYCC
President, The Child and Youth Care Association of Alberta
Assistant Professor/CYCC Fieldwork Director
Department of Child Studies and Social Work
Mount Royal University

Youth in Care Chronicles is both difficult to read and uplifting in its ultimate message of the power of hope, resilience, and love. Too many of our children not only suffer at the hands of their families, but then within the very systems designed to keep them safe. It is imperative that child welfare system administrators, frontline workers and allied professionals not only read this book, but take action on the failed processes that simply add to the trauma of abuse or neglect, multiple moves, rotating caregivers, separation and loss that children experience in care. Through it all, though, the voice of the amazing and courageous young adults makes the *Youth in Care Chronicles* a valuable resource for any child or youth who is in care or may be struggling with the impact after foster care. The quest for and the right of every child for a safe and loving family and home is the common theme in each story, as is the ultimate message of hope.

Rita L. Soronen
President & CEO
Dave Thomas Foundation for Adoption

Some of the authors in this book talk about times in their lives when they had suicidal thoughts. They want you to know that if you or someone you know is thinking about suicide, self-harm, or just needs to talk, there is help. Please reach out to the resources for your area available 24/7/365. You are not alone.

KIDS HELP PHONE Text CONNECT to **686868** from anywhere in Canada, any time, about anything, or call **1-800-668-6868**

Crisis Services Canada
- 24/7/365 Crisis Line **1-833-456-4566** or text to **45645**
- Online Chat https://www.crisisservicescanada.ca

Hope for Wellness Line
- 24/7/365 Indigenous Crisis Line **1-855-242-3310**
- Online Chat https://www.hopeforwellness.ca

Calgary Distress Centre
- 24/7/365 Adult Crisis Line **403-266-4357**
- Online Chat https://www.distresscentre.com
- 24/7/365 ConnecTeen Youth Crisis Line **403-264-8336** or text **587-333-2724**

Edmonton Canadian Mental Health Association (CMHA)
- 24/7/365 Adult, Family, and Youth Crisis Line **780-482-4357**
- Online Chat https://edmonton.cmha.ca/online-crisis-chat

Association of Alberta Sexual Assault Services (AASAS)
- Alberta-Wide Phone and Text **1-866-403-8000**
- Online Chat https://aasas.ca/get-help/

The hardest part about being in care was having to move just as soon as I got used to a family. I remember packing my teddy bears, dolls, cards, and special things that I had gotten for Christmas and birthdays into garbage bags, then opening them up later and finding things crushed, crumpled, or broken.

I remember being sad because those memories were all I had left of the foster brothers, sisters, mom, and dad I once had.

Patricia

The Sunday Magazine

How former youth in care are working to fix Canada's child welfare system

CBC Radio · Posted: Aug 30, 2019 5:00 PM ET | Last Updated: August 30, 2019

When Ashley Bach first got to university, she tried her best to hide the fact that she grew up in Canada's child welfare system. Eventually, however, she had a change of heart when considering the struggles of her younger foster siblings.

"I realized then that I'd been fortunate enough to finish high school and go to university and ... maybe I could do use that privilege that I had to try to change the system and make it better for my foster siblings and for other kids."

Today, Bach is the president of Youth in Care Canada, and she's part of a network of former youth in care who are drawing on their lived experience to push for change. Ashley Bach, Arisha Khan and Melanie Doucet spoke to *The Sunday Edition*'s guest host Connie Walker about how their time in care informs the work they do today.

(To read full article please click on headline or type headline into your search bar.)

Postcard courtesy of The Adoption Council of Canada—Youth Speak Out Edmonton

It is important for kids in care to know their rights. I didn't know mine and I would have appreciated someone sitting down with me and saying, "Let's talk."

Megan

Cassie

While the road continued spinning by beneath us, I heard: They have dogs. That will be nice huh?
The last statement being the only one to stick in my spinning, little head.

I am a twenty-two-year-old part-time student and worker. I currently work frontline street level at an inner-city organization in Edmonton. I am in my third year of a degree in psychology and have been an active member of Youth Speak Out Edmonton since 2014. I hope to one day use art therapy as a way of helping those seeking trauma counseling and to bring awareness and change to the systemic issues faced by marginalized youth in care in Canada.

I was apprehended in 2003 with my two older siblings and have been in three placements – one foster home for over twelve years and two group homes. I have been to four different schools while in care - two of those were for post-secondary education. For the most part, my apprehension was the most traumatizing thing to happen while I went through the system. A woman in a wheelchair and a large man in a van came and took all of us late in the night from my aunt's home where we had been staying. We had our few collective possessions and dirty clothes shoveled into a small leather suitcase and a black garbage bag and were hustled into the van. We drove through the night and it felt like forever before we were shuffled out of the van. The woman in the wheelchair looked at us kindly and explained that we would be staying at a motel for the night. The remainder of the night and the next morning passed by me in a grey blur. We were led through office buildings and then shuffled to an overcrowded house with a stressed-out middle-aged couple. The couple frantically greeted us and waved goodbye to the child welfare workers at the front door, before turning around and brusquely explaining their house rules while other children ran rampantly around in the dimly lit living room and hallways. We were shown our rooms and glanced nervously at each other when we were informed we would not be sharing the same room. I saw my room and swallowed a growing panic. It was filled with a gaggle of other small girls who glared at me silently when I later made my way into sheets to sleep.

Luckily for us, we were found a placement quickly and were once again being filed into a van, being driven off and being told supposedly placating things like: This is a nice place, you guys are so lucky. While the road continued spinning by beneath us, I heard: They have dogs. That will be nice huh? The last statement being the only one to stick in my spinning, little head. The van finally rolled into a gravel driveway in front of a sunny, beige home nestled in dense, green trees. The door opened, and a blonde woman appeared before us, the sound of dogs barking in the background nearly drowning her out. I stepped inside and glanced around at a house that was much larger and cleaner than I had ever remembered being in during my short few years. I knew some families lived like that but had assumed we would never get the opportunity. Clean clothes? No blood stains or broken glass? No lingering coils of cigarette smoke curling around us?

A round of introductions happened as we were shown around to our rooms. I was once again disappointed I wasn't sleeping with my siblings as we had always done until I saw my room. The blonde woman opened the door and pointed to a freshly made bunk bed with dolls lying in the middle and said: This will be your room, and you have room for lots of clothes and toys. I kept looking around, taking in the softly carpeted floor, the large wooden chest of drawers, the desk, books, and pillows. I couldn't believe this was just for me. We were introduced to the dogs and later the husband, and days began passing by in a blur after that.

The blonde woman was kind and patient, slowly explaining grammar and manners and when we would be going to school and "doing normal children things" again. We went to doctor and dentist appointments – we were emaciated and never taught the importance of oral hygiene before this. We were tested and placed in elementary school. We had a schedule and regular meals and clean beds to come home to. As the weeks and months went on, our biological parents became less reliable, arriving inebriated for visits or ultimately not showing up at all. It was heartbreaking; I would stare at a picture of our mother all the time and tell myself I believed her when she would reassure us she would be bringing us home. We eventually went from a Temporary Guardianship Order (TGO) to a Permanent Guardianship Order (PGO) status and the blonde woman and her husband protected us and tried to educate us.

Eventually, my siblings fell victim to the cycle; caught up in the cycles of anger and addiction. The woman and her husband tried everything to keep me out of the cycle. They even took me to Disneyland for my fourteenth birthday. However, I continued to isolate and perpetuate a deep shame inside my head. It started with self-harm and injuring myself in any inconspicuous way I could until I also began experimenting with drugs in my last year of high school. After years of issues with my own mental and emotional health, I fell quickly into a pit with a few close friends also battling their own issues at the time. My drug use and quickly escalating behavioural issues all compiled and led to my placement breakdown after over twelve years.

I was sent to my first group home in Edmonton and it had one other kid and a chinchilla in it at the time. Two days after I arrived, a worker dropped off another kid who sat angrily in the living room corner until I eventually broke the ice at one of the group home staff's behests. People have always loved to talk to me. There were many questionable things that happened at that first group home which my worker and I have since tried to put in formal complaints about. For example, the supervisor would take my phone and laptop away – but also take it off the property with them when they left. I witnessed face-down, manual restraints, and other aggressive acts from staff against the other children – all younger than 16 at the time. One of the biggest complaints from the other youth about the staff at this group home was that they were not fluent in English and could not communicate properly or de-escalate situations.

Eventually, after complaining enough and pointing out their very flawed system enough, the supervisor decided that I could no longer have a bed at the group home, and I was finally transferred into a Transitional Supported Independent Living (TSIL) group home. Here the supervisor helped me practice driving so I could take my driver's test. I passed on my first try and the supervisor was the one who accompanied me there. I managed to find part-time work and began flourishing amongst my peers and housemates. I had a minimum two-year wait time for a SIL (Supported Independent Living) worker to be assigned to me when I was in the second group home. Once my eighteenth birthday passed, I found an apartment and rented a U-Haul after running everything by my caseworker. Patience has never been my forte. I signed a Support and Financial Assistance Agreement (SFAA) and continued working. Due to the placement breakdown forcing me to move away from my high school in my final year's last semesters, I didn't finish graduating because I was unable to commute to school for the second half of a written diploma exam.

After moving out, I completed modules and received my diploma. Since turning eighteen, I have remained on the SFAA while working and living independently with my cats. For me, the benefits outweigh the devastating parts of being in foster care. I received a better education and continue to employ the advantages of having my post-secondary schooling paid for. My foster parents fought for me to have braces and have always advocated for my best interests. I received many opportunities my biological family would never have been able to offer, and most importantly, I received lifelong connections and support from my foster parents.

However, not everything was great, and I noticed a plethora of issues youth in care face, which continue to marginalize and ostracize them. Issues like caseworkers making unannounced visits to schools and calling kids out of class, issuing vouchers for only specificstores where employees were uneducated in using government vouchers, no contact rules in group homes where a hug can go a long way and the lack of one can speak volumes, and the constant prioritization of bureaucracy over the well-being of actual human beings. When youth make positive and solid connections with group home staff, they are incredibly limited in maintaining that connection beyond the staff's shift time inside the facility. For example, in the first group home there was a no contact policy in place for four years after a staff leaves or is reassigned from their positions. Permanency is crucial to youth in care, but this requires constant consultation with every individual to intentionally accommodate their wants and needs. Permanency is different for everybody, and oftentimes, family is the people we meet along the way who keep us in their hearts. Blood does not mean family. We must remember when dealing with everybody that it is never a matter of category but of degree.

People are people regardless of the behaviour, humanity is always necessary. Be present, be kind, be intentional – everybody has a process and we must respect that. Stop placing policies and paperwork above a human's well-being. All this goes to serve is the perpetuation of hate directed at an outdated and unfair system. It radicalizes children and youth to oppose those service providers and workers rather than assist them in accepting and articulating their needs. We must teach our generation and those who will come after us that it is okay to feel shame, guilt, depression, any of those terrible feelings that we try to avoid, but we must feel it and deal with it. We cannot let those awful things consume us. This only preserves the timeline of the intergenerational trauma we have all inherited. We must feel, accept, learn, and change, and we must do so with love and kindness for ourselves. Hurt people will hurt people; it is time to change.

Now I am learning how to feel and this is the most difficult challenge out of everything that I have faced. I have faced every kind of pain and over time, physical scars heal but it is the feeling of love that really takes me off edge because of its unfamiliarity.

As humans, we always fear what we do not understand.

I don't remember experiencing love until I was almost 19. That's a long time to go without emotional connection and it took a long time to get here and that can be complicated by having two families (my dad's and Theresa's). I have had to learn to navigate struggles with loyalty and worries about if I go with them then you do not love us anymore. I felt pressure from my older sister's and they would primarily make me feel like I had to chose but over time things got easier and I have learned to have both families.

The Universe always balances stuff out.

I think you must be open to take any opportunity, like I did agreeing to move in with Theresa and her family, but now I have a family and I have kids that I love surrounding me and people I can connect with. This is the closest I have felt emotionally in my whole life.

Damon

Life after foster care in Canada
Kids who grow up in the system are not expected to do well. That's a big part of why they don't.

BY Sarah Treleaven   MACLEAN'S   NOVEMBER 12, 2019

Jane Kovarikova spent 10 years in foster care in Ontario, shuffling between a number of homes beginning at age six. At 16, when she dropped out of high school and successfully applied to leave foster care, her social worker didn't discuss options for post-secondary education. "There wasn't a lot of thought about future planning," says Kovarikova. "And after 21, no one has any responsibility for you."

Despite feeling that others had extremely low expectations of her, Kovarikova "had a little fire to fight for more," she says. She stretched her $663 monthly allowance and her paycheques and bought her first house at 19. Kovarikova went on to graduate from high school and then university, to earn a master's degree at the London School of Economics and to enter a PhD program in political science at Western University, which she is presently completing.

(To read full article please click on headline or type headline into your search bar.)

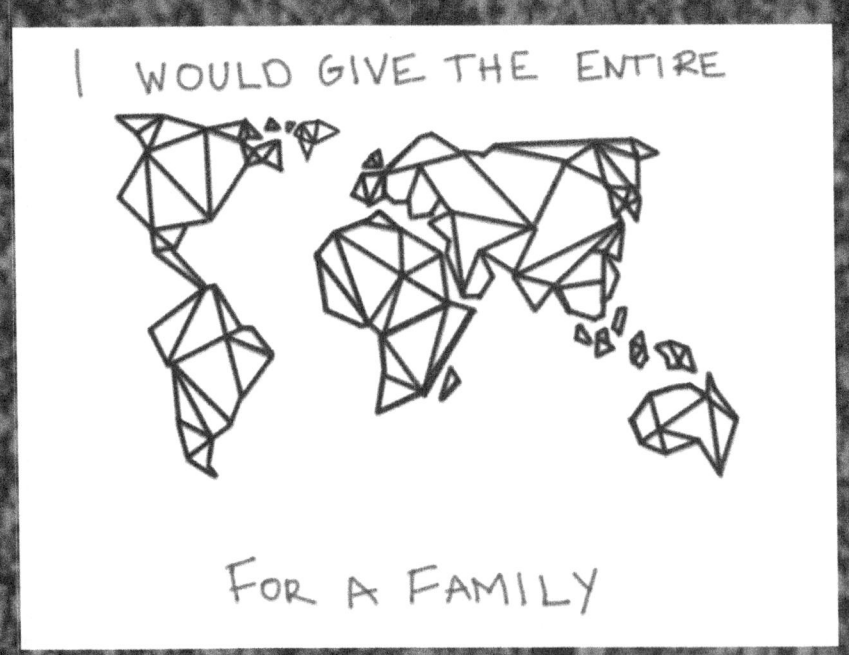

I WOULD GIVE THE ENTIRE [world] FOR A FAMILY

Postcard courtesy of The Adoption Council of Canada—Youth Speak Out Edmonton

> I was very successful the whole time I was in care. I worked part-time and I was saving money. Where most kids have a goal of buying a car, my goal was to build my own life and buy a house and have a family. I told my caseworker what I was doing, and he said they weren't going to be able to keep me on until age 22 because I was doing really well and was able to take care of myself. I told him that I didn't need until age 22. I just needed my file to be kept open until I had everything saved up and was able to make the down payment on a house. So, I got approved for a mortgage and bought my house the day I left care. I was 20 years old.
>
> Tyler

Shoshana

One thing I can say for certain, is that the hardships we experience
in the foster care system leave us with deep wisdom, street-smarts,
and unique personalities with tons of stories to share.

I am 24 years old and I was born in Mayerthorpe, Alberta. I am the second youngest child of ten siblings and I have a fraternal twin sister. I grew up with my biological family for the first four years of my life, and then lived at a foster placement in Morinville, Alberta for 14 years with my twin sister and older sister. My other siblings were placed in different placements throughout Alberta. I stayed in the same foster home for 14 years, graduated from high school, and moved out in 2014.

I have done schooling at MacEwan University and received a diploma in Child and Youth Care, as well as some schooling in Social Psychology and Developmental Psychology electives. Currently, I live with my fiancé and our two cats. I enjoy spending time outside, working in the garden, and I volunteer with Youth Speak Out Edmonton from time to time. I enjoy drawing, dancing, biking, singing, and hanging out with friends and family. My end goal is to get a degree in counseling and help children and youth who have experienced trauma. I want to integrate play, art, and animal therapy because those were the things that helped me when I was growing up in care and going through a tough time.

I also want to break the cycle of intergenerational trauma within my family by being a healthy and positive role model for my future family. I believe it is possible to break the cycle of trauma due to the long-term relationships and the permanency I experienced growing up in care.

MY LIFE STORY

I grew up with nine other siblings and six farm dogs near a small town called Blueridge, Alberta. I have memories of me as a child exploring through the thick forest, walking beside a small stream, or lying in bed with my other sisters. For fun, I remember stacking empty milk crates, playing with my siblings, or trying to catch bugs with my bare hands. I remember a lot of hungry days; however, I remember feeling happy and loved. I was apprehended at the age of four (around October 2000) because of ongoing neglect due to my parent's mental health issues and lack of resources to support my family's basic needs. I don't remember too much about living with my biological family, but I do remember playing with my siblings or driving around with my mom and dad.

Unfortunately, my siblings and I were not always fed, and we didn't receive the cognitive stimulation that we required for regular development. This led to attachment and developmental issues, as well as unresolved trauma. My two sisters and I were placed at a foster home together, while the rest of my family was separated throughout Alberta. This separation caused my family connection to fall apart, because some siblings couldn't always travel or would cut ties with the family for years. When I was apprehended, I remember driving to my 'new home', playing outside, looking over counters for treats, and playing with friends. The foster home was very different from my old home. It was big, warm, and busy, with rules and consequences. It took me a couple of years to adjust to the change in my environment, specifically with school and the increase in structure.

Throughout my childhood, I saw many therapists due to ongoing feelings of anger and distress. I felt bouts of strong emotions about being taken away from my family and didn't know how to properly process the emotions. I received no emotional support from my foster family and was frequently ridiculed and punished for seeking emotional help, which created more unresolved trauma, emotional dysregulation, and avoidance problems. Growing up, my two sisters and I would play games like hide-and-go-seek, home-base, dodgeball, house, and other fun activities. When the foster family and I got into fights, I would go to my two sisters to vent about my frustrations or take a break and have some fun by playing games with them. I believe the support I received from my two sisters helped me through the tough times in my life.

When I was 13, my foster dad was diagnosed with stage 4 terminal cancer. This was a huge blow to the foster home and increased the verbal/physical fighting in the home, which made me feel more unsafe. Around this time, I didn't feel like I had support from the foster home, so I started to smoke and party. Due to my naiveté, I didn't know what a healthy relationship was, so I ended up in an abusive relationship that lasted four years. As things got worse, I started to isolate myself from my friends and family. When I was 16, my foster dad passed away. After that, it was very tense in the foster home so, once I graduated, I decided to move out of town and change my life around.

I decided to upgrade at Centre High until I got into Grant MacEwan University. I distanced myself from unhealthy people and surrounded myself with healthy relationships. In 2015, I was diagnosed with Post Traumatic Stress Disorder (PTSD). Around this time, I started to go through a lot of personal growth; the diagnosis helped me to better understand myself and the things that I needed out of life. Currently, I have been in a healthy relationship for the last three years, and I have made major changes in my life in order to live a healthier lifestyle. I am currently taking a year off school to work on my mental health, and I am returning to the Child and Youth Care program next year to resume my schooling. I have cut ties with my foster family, but still hope to rebuild some relationships with my biological family, and to continue building a resilient future for myself.

MY EXPERIENCE

One of the good things about growing up in a foster home is that I had a sense of permanency. I knew my address, I knew my street, and I knew my neighbors. I had a best friend from elementary school that I graduated with, and I grew up with people I had known for years. I didn't have to worry about being alone or going hungry on holidays (or on regular days), because someone was there to take care of my needs. All of this was possible because I grew up in the same home for almost my entire life. My other siblings didn't get to experience the same permanency I had and grew up living on the streets or enduring abuse from people because they had no other option. The foster family would sometimes include me in events such as camping trips or after school activities. I also benefited from living with my two siblings, as they were a huge support system for me and understood my story and background. Overall, the foster home was safe and more consistent than my biological home.

A lot of positive experiences came from my workers and other professional support systems I had while growing up. Some of the workers that stood out for me were the workers that were personable and honest with me. If I had a question, they wouldn't give me a polite answer just to appease me, they would give me true and honest guidance that I could integrate into my life. For example, I had one caseworker advocate for my educational rights by setting me up with an advocate. With the help of the caseworker, I was able to get my education funded, which helped me get my diploma. By doing this, she taught me that my education is important and standing up for myself can get me somewhere. Another worker that stood out to me was one who wasn't afraid to have genuine conversations with me. They were very relaxed and would answer all of my questions or have casual conversations about what it was like for them growing up and what life had taught them. This was really beneficial to me because it showed me that there is a real person behind the worker, and it helped me build trust.

Some of the challenges I faced in the foster home were ongoing abuse by my foster siblings, lack of proper intervention to maintain physical safety, as well as emotional abuse and neglect from my foster parents. I was continually put down, called names, or humiliated by my foster parents. If I spoke out, they would threaten to get rid of me and send me to a group home if I reported the abuse, or they would laugh at me when I was crying, or send me to my bedroom where I had to deal with my problems on my own. My foster mom over-medicated my twin sister, even when the psychiatrist told my foster mom that my sister didn't need to be on the medications that she was being given. My sister and I later found out that my foster mom was also slipping in another medication with my sister's regular medications without my sister's consent or knowledge.

KEY MESSAGES

A key message I would like to leave behind is that, in the Child and Youth Care program, we are taught that it only takes one strong relationship with another person to build resiliency. For a lot of foster children, that one person could be someone in their family, so instead of separating family members, try working on keeping them connected with someone who gives them the support that they need, whether that be a family member, a child welfare worker, or a friend.

To me, a life-long connection is having a deep level of respect and trust with someone who accepts you for who you are. It's having someone who is there to support you when you need help, and someone who lets you lean on them when you're struggling. It's important to have lifelong connections because it helps the person feel a sense of belonging, love, support, and safety. The life-long connection I have with my two sisters and my fiancé has helped me through the hardest parts of my life. They were always there for me when I felt scared, and they understood my struggles. When I think of the people who have supported me, I feel accepted and like I truly belong somewhere.

I used to maintain contact with some of my siblings because they offered a lot of love and support. I have a relationship with my two biological sisters that I grew up with because they have been long-term ongoing supports for me throughout my entire life. However, I have recently limited my connection with my biological family to undertake some personal growth. I have tried many times to build a relationship with my family, but because of the dysfunction, it tends to be emotionally hard for me to have a relationship with them. Nonetheless, I still hope to try and build my relationship with my family. I hope taking a break will help me have a healthier relationship with them and myself in the future.

I want people to know that youth in care are just like every other person, but we come from tough situations. Youth in care tend to be resilient and strong-willed. Children in care are warriors who are just trying to get through life like everybody else. One thing I can say for certain: The hardship that people in the foster system experience leaves us with deep wisdom, street-smarts, and a truly unique personality with tons of stories to share.

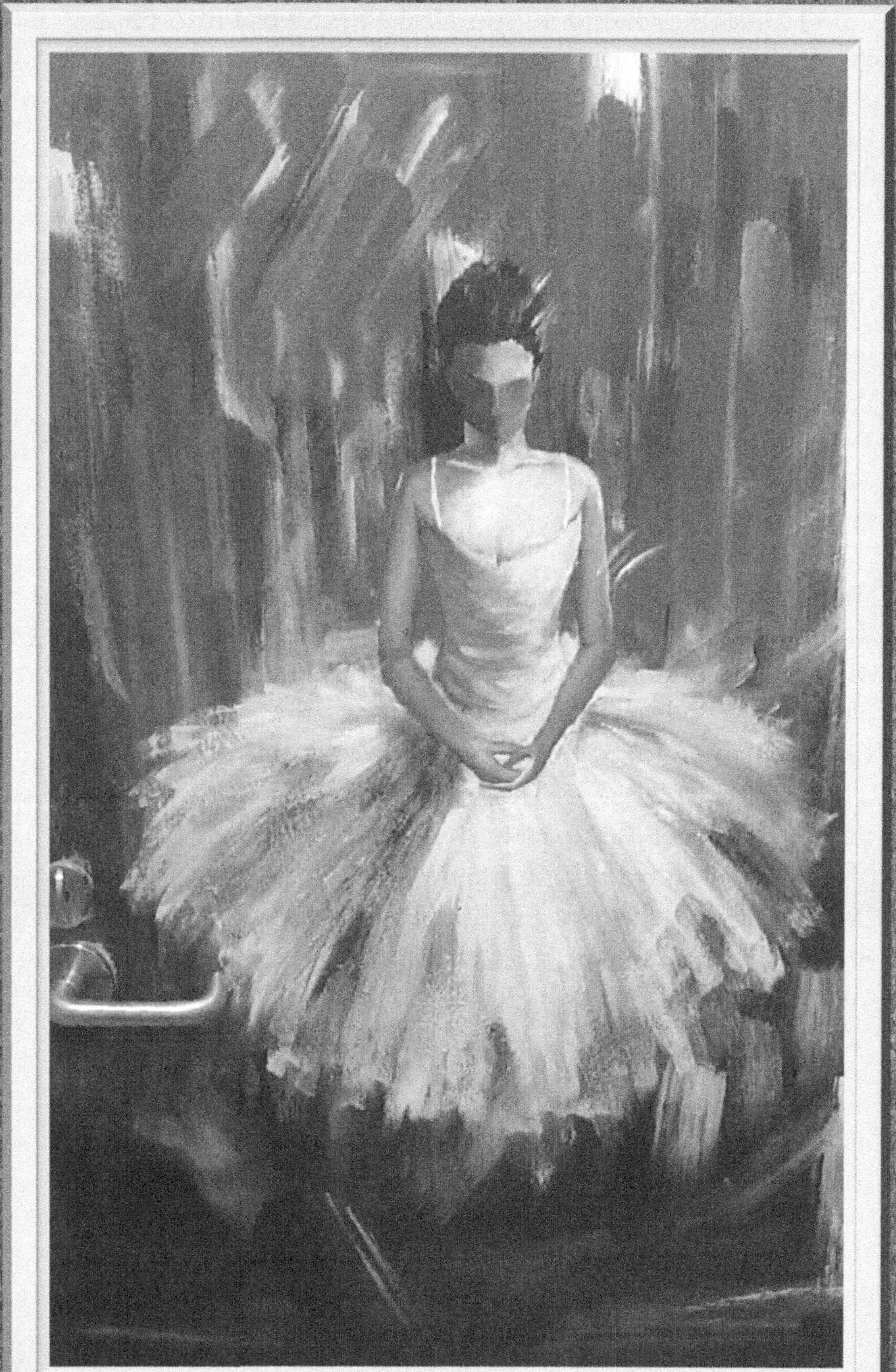

I started drawing a little after I first went into care. My older sister drew a lot and it inspired me to pick up a pencil and give it a go. I loved drawing right off the bat, and would doodle in the morning before school, during class time, and after school. There was something about it that made me feel relaxed and in the moment, and it would give me a break from the stresses that were happening in my life. During therapy, my therapist would ask me to draw different things and I remember sessions flying by. We would talk about what the drawings meant to me which, looking back now, helped me process my story and express myself. During high school I started painting and working with different mediums. I started painting every time I was at school, I couldn't get enough of it. Painting was a major outlet for me, especially during high school when my foster dad passed away and dealing with my abusive relationship. When I needed a break, which was every day, I would go to the art room and draw for a while. The painting of the ballerina was painted on a door inside the bathroom. The harsh lines of the painting and the heavy feel juxtaposes the idea of a 'dainty ballerina'. The painting was done the year my father passed away when I was feeling so exhausted from constantly holding onto different problems. The painting symbolises how I felt; like I had to be strong and graceful while dealing with the chaos. The shadowed face represents the part that I had to hide of myself in order to get through.

The painting of the match with the water was done for a project in art class, and was a little more technical. It was really fun to do overall, and was a very peaceful process.

- Shoshana -

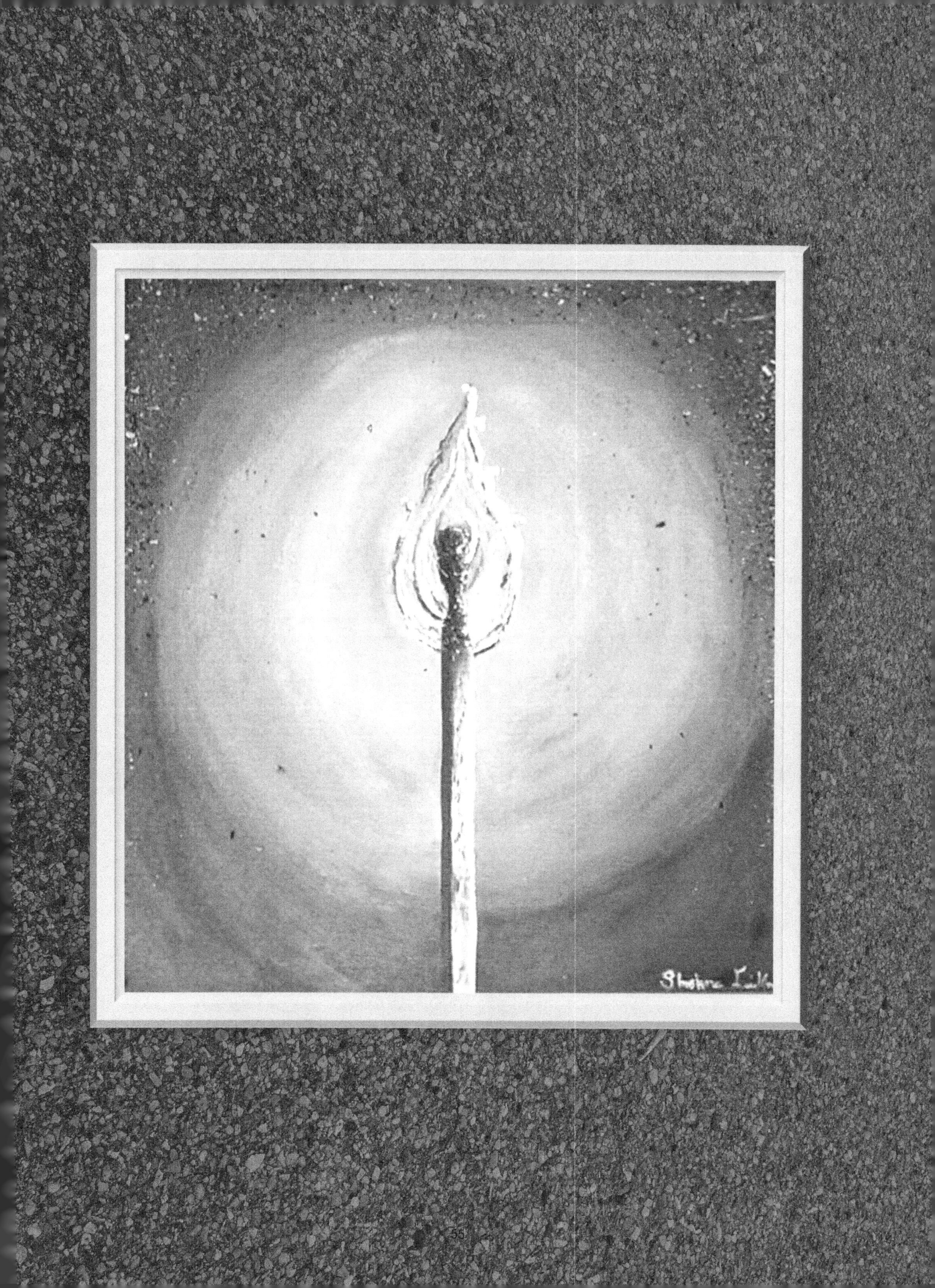

Jade

At 7 years old you don't really understand things; the complexities of life beyond comprehension. But you feel things, I remember that much.
I will always remember the feelings.

THE LESSONS I FOUND WHEN I WAS LOST

The man in the moon, a phrase I'm sure we are all familiar with. I remember always looking, searching, trying to find the man in the moon. But no, she is not a man. It wasn't until ceremony that I learned that the moon is our grandmother. It makes sense. Mother Earth, she is strong, she is powerful, she gives us life here. She keeps us grounded. The moon is our grandmother, our matriarch. It is because of her the tides flow within the ocean. It is she whom our bodies align with in our sacred ability to give life, to cleanse our wombs. How divine a grandmother she is, a silent keeper, forever a matriarch. I remember sitting in ceremony in Red Pheasant. It was morning time and the water woman told us a story of our grandmother, she said that there was no man in the moon but a water woman who sat there and heard our prayers. That night was the brightest moon there had been for a long time. I remember praying to that water woman, to grandmother moon, for strength, for love, for peace. For all the things that my heart so craved. With each phase of the moon, we too align. I wish I knew more. I hope to connect. I hope to feel. I hope to one day sit with wrinkled hands, long gray hair, and a twinkle in my eye and tell stories of grandmother moon. Matriarch after matriarch. Evanescent moments that live within us and through bloodlines. What a beautiful thought.

The summary of a life is a difficult thing to write. How is it that black ink filled within the hollows of forests bring life, depth, and meaning to those who flip the page? To be honest, I'm not sure – but I will try. I remember the day clearly. The memory forever etched within my brain. Being called to the office. I heard my brother's name on the school intercom, and I will never forget the sensation of guilt that rose from within me. At seven-years-old, you don't really understand things, the complexities of life beyond comprehension. But you feel things, I remember that much. I will always remember the feelings. A few weeks prior, I was called to an office. I was tired a lot at school, I was always late, and I often picked up the free friendship lunch from the friendship centre for me and my brother Jacob.

I guess there were a few red flags. So, they called me in. I remember weeks prior in the school counselor's office, the animal crackers and the savory taste they left within my mouth, reaching for another, and then one more. It's funny the things that stick. I can still taste them today, but I can assure you that since that day, they've never tasted the same. The wait in the office was long. The secretary too kind. The principal letting us play in the office with toys long beyond school hours. I knew something wasn't okay – I remember that feeling a lot in my childhood. I remember playing with Jake to make him feel comfortable, he was only a little boy, only four-years-old. I had to comfort him. Yet he had no idea.

Sweet little Jake, so kind and full of smiles when the caseworker finally arrived. I don't remember her face, but I remember the fear I felt in her presence. She told me she heard that I liked chocolate and that she had a chocolate bar for me waiting in the car – that might have been the first moment that I knew what deceit felt like, abandonment too, maybe... where was my mom? Jake had no idea. I remember him running down the hall and the lowering evening sun shining through the double entrance doors as he ran and looked back at me. I could paint you that picture, maybe then it would leave my memory.

It's so strange, isn't it? That this memory, it hurts more than the things that I witnessed that no child should. The fear, violence, sexuality, and substances I was witness to in my home from such a young age. I know those things changed me, made me grow too fast, made me anxious, over-analytical, made me experience my own sexuality much before the time that a young girl should. I can live with things somehow, so cliché to say, but they made me stronger. It's hard to live with being torn from your family though. The matriarch in me – the grandmother, auntie, daughter, and sister – she hurt that day when I got taken away. A hollow wound in the burrows of my soul. One that I would long after stay yearning to fulfill, with love, sex, co-dependent relationships, drugs, alcohol, and a strive for perfection that would forever be insurmountable. It's funny the things that stick. This was my new moon –Not quite visible, but the start of a lifelong journey that I would far from yet to realize. I remember the first time I contemplated suicide. I'm not sure that I grasped the reality of what that meant, but I knew I didn't want to feel anymore. I remember the sensation of wanting so desperately to hurt myself and feel anything other than what I was experiencing. I was only 11. I started crying at the bottle of nail polish and kept thinking to myself – perhaps this will make it go away? I also remember the guilt associated with that feeling. I remember using it against my mom. Begging for her to take me home. It's not like things were terrible though. I had a good life, a good aunt and uncle and cousins, who all cared very much for me. I played piano, soccer, I was a figure skater, and I swam. I attended summer camps and homeschooled but, at the very centre of who I was, I missed my home – my mother, my little brother.

I remember early on after our apprehension; Jake ran away during one of our visits and I chased him down the alley from the little house we grew up in on main street. I found him sitting by a dumpster and he cried looking at me – the face of a broken little boy, telling his sister that he missed when it was just us three at home. He didn't understand why things had to be so different now. I didn't like it either, but I knew that being at home, while it was where we wanted to be, I knew that it wasn't good for us either. It's funny the things that stick. My hurt is so intertwined with that of my mother's and brother's, it's a difficult thing to unravel but maybe it's not meant to. Families, bloodlines, we are connected. To be torn apart, it hurts.

That first thought of self-harm. I wish had known at the time that it was my soul crying for help. My emotional needs were devastated – hard to conceptualize considering I had things "good," but I was still hurting. That hurt would follow me until I was 12 and began to self-harm regularly – until I could have died after a drunken escapade, cutting my arm open too many times to count, and falling asleep, only to awake stuck from dry blood to the mattress in which I slept. The last time I cut was when I was an adult woman, when I relapsed. If only I had known at 11-years-old that what I was experiencing was a cry for help that I was so desperately seeking, maybe then perhaps, I would have found a better outlet – a better way. Instead of drunken outbursts that ended with open wounds on my body, to only later be filled with guilt about the destruction of my own beautiful body. If only I had known.

I don't wish to paint for you such a sad picture. I hope you read these printed lines and can find the beauty within them. I was a happy child, but I was hurt. When I think back on so many things now as an adult woman, a woman reborn in her identity as

Jade Fleury, Nehiyaw Iskwew, from Cold Lake, Alberta, my heart still hurts, but it is also healing. I look back on both sad and happy moments with fondness and gratitude. Each experience molding me to come to the place that I am now. The one thing that hurts me though is that stories of children experiencing such heartache, especially our Indigenous children, are all too common. The folds of the system are deep and mysterious. So easily, they can take a child and as the system folds over and over, and eventually the child is lost, but the longing never goes away. Even if they do not know what it is they are longing for.

I can say that I was lucky. I was the subject of a Temporary Guardianship Order (TGO) and then a Permanent Guardianship Order (PGO) in the care of my aunt, uncle, and cousins; all blood relatives to me. They were wonderful, loving, and kind, but it's with guilt that I still say that in my little heart I didn't feel truly home, especially as I grew older. My brother went to live with his dad. I think the fact that we were separated is one of my deepest wounds. I look at my mom, a strong, beautiful Indigenous woman, and I feel her pain. A mother's wounds bleed into daughters. Her life, too, had been uprooted by "the system" – her and all five of her brothers. She never got to meet her mother, but she loved me as if she knew the love of a thousand mothers. I truly believe that it's the prayers of our grandmothers and aunties that live within, that allow her to love and allow me to love, too. It's true when they talk about cycles of on- going trauma. It's a shame that our system aims to remove children from traumatic situations, but the truth is that it doesn't address the root causes of the issues that families face. The wounds are deep and riddled with trauma, oppression, and colonization. I guess it's a tricky road to navigate, but I also believe the removal of children isn't always the answer.

I moved home when I was 12. I'm not sure that my mother was ready, still struggling with her personal battles and I was rebellious. I was angry. We moved a lot, house to hotel to shelter. I got kicked out of places and I got in trouble with the law. I lived with my mom for two years before moving to Edmonton. I knew I needed to get away. I was drinking heavily and finding myself in situations that I should not have been in. I moved to Edmonton to start fresh. I'm not even sure that our caseworker knew. I don't remember having much involvement with them after moving back to my mom's.

Sometimes, I wonder if that was a good or a bad thing. I'm sure, had they been involved again, that I would have found myself yet again removed from my mother's care and become more rebellious and angrier. But if they had been involved, I wouldn't have found myself moving from family member to family member in Edmonton, co-dependent on a boyfriend who would later hurt me so horribly that I'm surprised I didn't end up in the hospital. I wouldn't have stayed, but I felt like I had nowhere to go. Eventually I did leave though. I knew I needed to graduate. The house that we were living in had no power and we had no food. I was failing high school. Luckily, my father's parents let me live with them. It was there that I found a stable and structured environment, where I was able to graduate high school and leave my boyfriend at the time. Despite this, I found myself continuing to struggle with alcohol and drugs. It seemed they became more and more consuming. They were my outlet. I felt strong and capable. I was resilient and I continuously pushed forward through every circumstance I had lived through, but I've always wondered to some extent, what is resilience? The ability to survive and carry on? Of course, but at what expense? Had I sat with and processed my traumas at the time they were occurring, I'm not sure what would have happened. Maybe it was too much to process and that's why I continued to face forward, no looking back. That is, until it all caught up and I found myself drowning in the deep waters of addiction.

    I started my first year of college kind of as a fluke. I had a tendency to binge and party and I always knew it wasn't healthy, but never realized how quickly it could consume me. I wanted to go to school and I wanted to be in a helping profession and thankfully academics came easily to me. I knew I wanted to do something good with my life. Despite this, in 2015 I fell quick and hard into my addictions and ending upcouch surfing, living out of a van, and attempting to work in a position that I absolutely adored. I had applied for a scholarship at some point within that last year and it was my aunt who suggested I check my email to see and, lo and behold, my first year of tuition was going to be paid for. It was in that moment that I took a leap of faith, took out a massive student loan, moved two hours away, and started my first year of college. It's now five years later, I am sober, I am in love, I have found healing through culture, ceremony, and my family. I have a strong and loving relationship with my momma and my little brother. I don't talk much about my dad, because our relationship, too, has been strained over the years, but this year we have truly rekindled and I'm thankful for his presence in my life. I have nephews and nieces and, most importantly, I am happy.

I graduated from the Social Work Diploma program with a 4.0 Grade Point Average (GPA) and the Bachelor of Social Work program with a 3.7 GPA. My life, every sad memory, every hurt, every joy, every feeling of love or even abandonment has brought me here, to this very place. With knowledge and drive and passion. With the desire to help, to share, and to educate. I would not be who I am without the heartache. I thank the resiliency of my ancestors, of my family, and the never-ending support from those who have continued to love me throughout my journey. I wish the same for every individual who has lived through trauma and the system, but the truth is that there are those that will not, even though they had every potential, because our system is flawed. This is why my heart continues to ache. We need to do better.

We talk so often about anti-oppressive practice and trauma-informed care and if you are a practitioner reading this, I hope you truly reflect on what that means to you. I hope you have done the work to discover your biases and how your lived experience impacts your judgements and perspectives. I hope, in doing so, you are able to recognize the absolute value of relationship with families, with mothers who are fearful of you, and parents going through pain that has been passed on to them throughout generations. In doing so, I hope you can work together to create safe living environments and supports for families. Maybe it's a pipe dream, but I believe it's possible, we just all need to be on the same page. Using our legislative powers togo to court and apprehend or assign a TGO, often creates a lot of barriers and we need to be understanding of that. At least these are my thoughts when I try to look at it from both sides. I know it's hard and, some days, there is no winning for us. But for the people we are working with, it can equal a lifetime of heartache and open wounds that bleed forever, often into the next generation.

As for our youth, they are people and they are resilient. They are truly the definition of strength and survival. They need love and support though they might not tell you that they do. They need a safe place; a constant. I don't think I would be where I am today if it hadn't been for my safe places and the people who stayed consistent in my life. Even if they push you away, to know that you are there and will be always, creates a sense of safety in their mind and in their heart. Providing that type of comfort and meaning, is more than you could ever comprehend. At least it was for me.

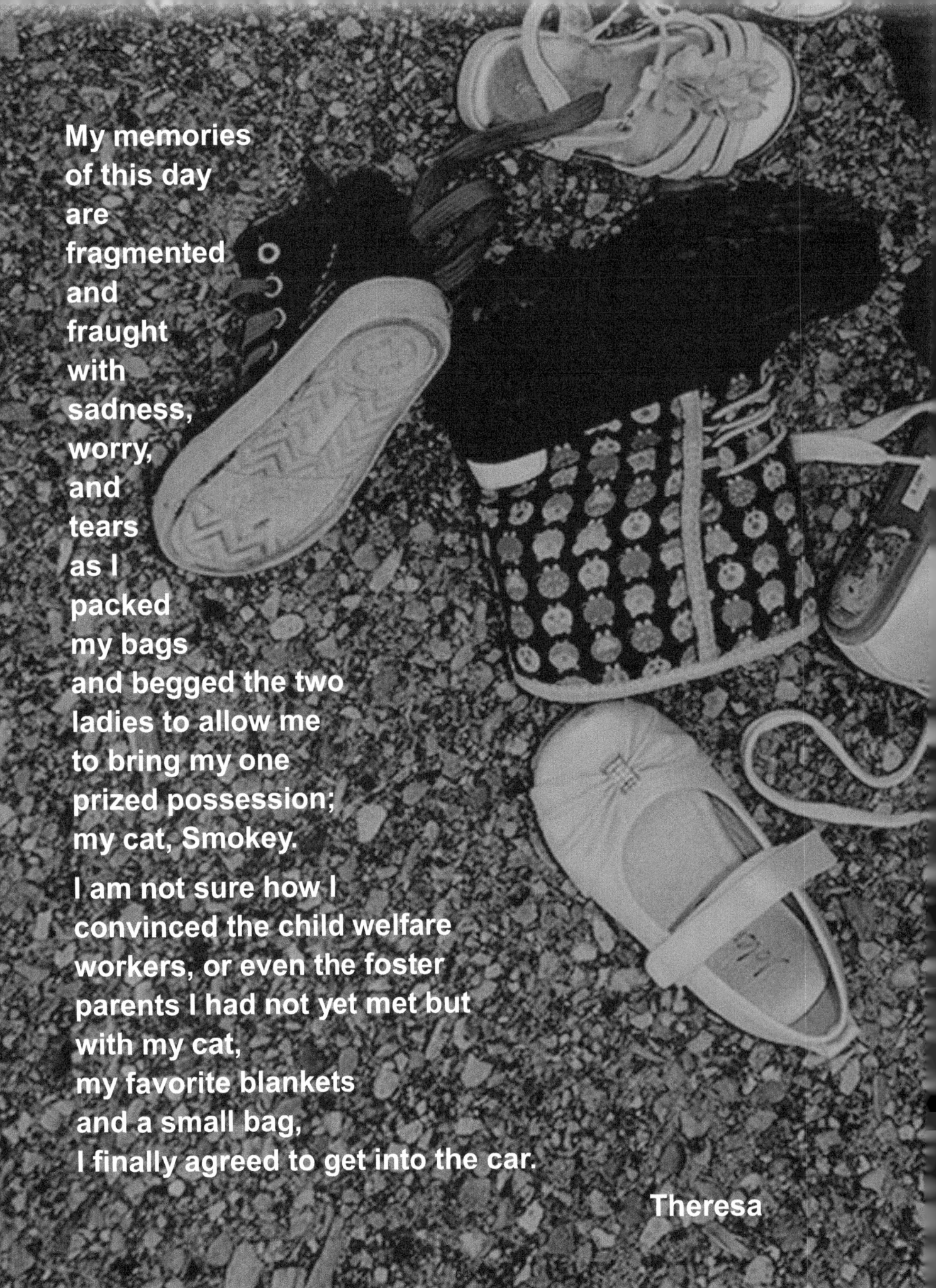

My memories
of this day
are
fragmented
and
fraught
with
sadness,
worry,
and
tears
as I
packed
my bags
and begged the two
ladies to allow me
to bring my one
prized possession;
my cat, Smokey.

I am not sure how I
convinced the child welfare
workers, or even the foster
parents I had not yet met but
with my cat,
my favorite blankets
and a small bag,
I finally agreed to get into the car.

Theresa

Storytelling project sets out to examine experiences of Indigenous youth in foster care

By Taz Dhaliwal Posted June 17, 2020 6:51 pm   Updated June 18, 2020 8:26 am Global News

Using the art of storytelling, a team of professors from the University of Lethbridge is putting together a project to help understand the experiences youth have in southern Alberta when transitioning out of government care.

(To read full article please click on the headline or type headline into your search engine.)

Postcard courtesy of The Adoption Council of Canada—Edmonton Youth Speak Out

My culture saved my life. And the reason that I'm here today is because I have such a deep connection to who I am within my community and I have that love for every single thing that I do in my life. I wake up and I smudge in the morning and even the shawl and I'm wearing and the beaded earrings that my sister made for me, keep me strong. The ceremonies that I go to speak to who I am intrinsically as a two-spirit in Nakota Sioux person from Treaty 6 territory. I can't disconnect myself from that. But when I was in care, I was no longer a Nakota Sioux Indigenous youth. I was a case number so none of that mattered anymore.

                                        Kenneth

Winnie

I lived in the alley behind my mom's house for a while. I am not sure if anyone even noticed me there. My time on the streets was a blur – sleeping in random places like ice rinks, in alleys, under the bridge, or anywhere I could get shelter from the elements.

I am a 23-year-old woman from a small hamlet outside of Grande Prairie, Alberta. I am passionate about all things living and have the passion and drive to excel in the field of Social Work. I have maintained involvement in human services through my continued devotion to public speaking. I am entering my second year of the Social Work Diploma program and I aspire to work as a clinical social worker focusing on Indigenous issues and youth. From what I can recall, Social Services became involved with my family when I was about eight years old, and I formally entered care when I was 12 years old after a period of homelessness. During my years in care, I had over 30 placements and I attended 13 different schools. I dream of owning my own property one day, so I can have a place of my own which is stable and consistent in ways that I can control.

When I was 11 years old, my mother and her boyfriend at the time looked me in the eyes and said they could not have us there anymore – 'us' being my sister and I. We needed to get out and this resulted in us being on the streets. Initially, I left for the night and returned the next day trying to enter the house. At some point, I realized that my mother had changed the alarm code. The result of us trying to enter was that the police were alerted. Unfortunately, my mom told the police that we did not live there anymore, and they came to arrest us. I had nowhere to go because I was too young for the shelter (the acceptable age being 12 and I had just turned 11), so they released me to nothing. My sister was able to go to the shelter, but I was too young to go there. I lived in the alley behind my mom's house for a while. I am not sure if anyone even noticed me there. My time on the streets was a blur – sleeping in random places like ice rinks, in alleys, under the bridge, or anywhere I could get shelter from the elements. Survival was the focus as I had to quickly learn to make it on my own, find ways to feed myself and keep myself warm. On my 12th birthday, I coincidentally ran into my sister. She took me to the shelter because I was now old enough to receive their help. The time I spent at the shelter resulted in a downward spiral for me personally, as I started to help people move drugs and I started to use, too.

After so long, I began to understand how it worked out there and to connect with certain support groups, one of which was a recreation program centered around helping youth who were homeless. The program was run by an older woman who had a passion for youth and their hidden talents. It was a place where you could access musical instruments, art supplies, and there was always a pizza dinner. It was a place I could express myself and feel safe, more so than I had felt while on the streets, at least. One day, I was hanging outside of the youth group and two child welfare workers arrived with police assistance. My sister saw them and yelled for me to run. I instinctively listened to her and ran. The child welfare workers simply waited for the police to retrieve me, as they knew I would not get away. Before long, the police caught up and pushed me and tackled me down on the street. This is a particularly vivid memory of mine, where I was trying to hide while sporting pink skinny jeans and a white sweater. The police brought me back to the child welfare workers to converse about what was happening, most of which I did not retain at that time, nor can I recall now, but I know that, in simple terms, they had apprehended me.

At the time I had no idea where I was going, and the dread was overwhelming. I arrived at an assessment center with only the things I was wearing. I remained in this assessment center for 31 days, during which time I still only had the clothing I had been admitted in, which meant I washed my underwear nightly in the sink with hand soap and hung them to dry. I still cannot understand why they were able to provide me with a journal and crayons, but not a second pair of underwear. In my last week there, a bag of clothes came for me and it was almost immediately after that that I was moved to my first foster home.

Over the next several weeks, I traveled from foster home to foster home almost every day, experiencing a new environment with my belongings in a small bag. The only explanation I was provided could be summed up in the words, 'it was not a good fit.' One of the first foster homes I went to had cameras located all over the home. This made me feel like an animal and I was glad to move after a few days. Eventually, I thought I had found a safe place to stay when I entered one foster home. I recall entering the home and it smelled of fresh baked chocolate chip banana muffins and the foster mother met me with a hug. I remained in this home for two years. I was placed back into school without being held back, my marks improved over time, and I received many awards at school while also eventually maintaining a part-time job. Initially, I enjoyed living in this home; however, I did not know the advances by my foster father were classified as grooming behavior and that he was laying the groundwork for an unhealthy home environment. I still feel angry that they were not prosecuted legally and that the only ramification for his unacceptable behaviour was the removal of their foster licence. I believe that timely counselling would have benefited me to learn to cope with what had occurred. This impacted my ability then, and now taints my understanding and views of what a healthy father- daughter relationship can and should be.

When I was completing high school, I was doing so whilst in an independent living situation which was my own apartment. I would personally attend the parent teacher interviews alone. This was a very belittling situation, as I was the only youth there without adult support. The excuse I would get from my legal guardians or caseworkers was that I was not their responsibility outside of office hours. This comment would continue to give me a complex about my own self-worth for years to come. One particular caseworker found it an easy and necessary decision to support me after hours at my parent teacher interviews. This experience really changed the way I felt about caseworkers and allowed me to feel semi-normal at these events. I would tell my peers that she was my mom. This caseworker impacted my life because she treated me with care and compassion and made me feel loved. She was committed and never made me feel like a burden. I needed support and she was able and willing to provide what I had longed for. This person changed my life in so many ways and I aspire to be like her in my future endeavours to become a social worker.

One of the most scarring experiences I had while in care occurred almost immediately after I was apprehended. My sister and I were being transported to an unknown destination. The driver stopped and my sister got out of the vehicle and, before I knew what was happening, the driver drove away, separating my sister and me. We continued to drive for what seemed like a lifetime, all the while I still had no idea where we were going. After what I know now to be roughly a two-hour drive, we pulled into a medical clinic parking lot. I know that, because of my time living on the streets, the purpose for the following event was to ensure the safety of other youth in the place I was going to be moved. However, I also understand that the way in which this procedure was carried out was entirely unnecessary and unhealthy. The following story is not something I have dealt with lightly and I am sure it will continue to affect my medical health checks for the rest of my life.

When we entered the clinic, I was not given any run down of what was going to occur, but even if I had known, the control of this situation did not lie with me as a youth. I was brought into the doctor's office, where I was restrained while the doctor completed an internal exam while I cried and pleaded for them to stop. There was a male doctor, a nurse, and a worker of some kind. This was a traumatic experience which continues to impact me to this day. I understand that there were many safety concerns associated with me being on the streets and having experienced sexual assault. In this scenario, the health and safety of the other occupants took precedence. However, as important as it is to ensure the safety of other youth, my safety should have also been considered. Now looking back, I wonder how a doctor was okay with doing what they did because, ethically speaking, it was more than questionable. The facts in this situation are that, even at my young age, I could have been warned of what was going to occur and approached like a human. At this point I had been exposed to sexual mistreatment by several men while I was homeless, so the forceful way in which all of this occurred was right in line with an assault. Especially frightening is that a male doctor performed a procedure on a damaged youth. Even in stable, adult lives, women request a female physician. The way this act was carried out was avoidable. It was certainly something I could have prepared for had I been given the opportunity. There is value in transparency.

Moving around so frequently from home to home impacted my ability to envision myself in long term or stable relationships with anyone. It has impacted the way I view myself and my confidence level. It has created a mindset that I was, and am, a burden. Most importantly, this turn of events greatly affected my relationship with my sister, as we were separated at a very vulnerable time in our lives as youth. Before everything in our lives went to crap (for a lack of better words), we were very close. We were like sisters, but after all of this we were two people trying to learn who each other had become over the years. Only now do I feel like I have a sisterly bond with her, and that sensation had been gone for just over ten years now.

The most beneficial part of child welfare's involvement for me would have to be when I transitioned into an independent living arrangement. This arrangement for me meant that the stability of my living arrangements was dependent on my own actions. During this time, I proved to myself that I could be independent. I blossomed as a person and truly became the strong, independent, and courageous woman I am today. My experience as a young 'do it yourselfer' pulled down all my walls of emotion and showed me how to be happy on my own, so that I could grow to nourish healthy relationships in all areas of my life. I am thankful for my life experiences so far because they made me into a more resilient and hardworking individual.

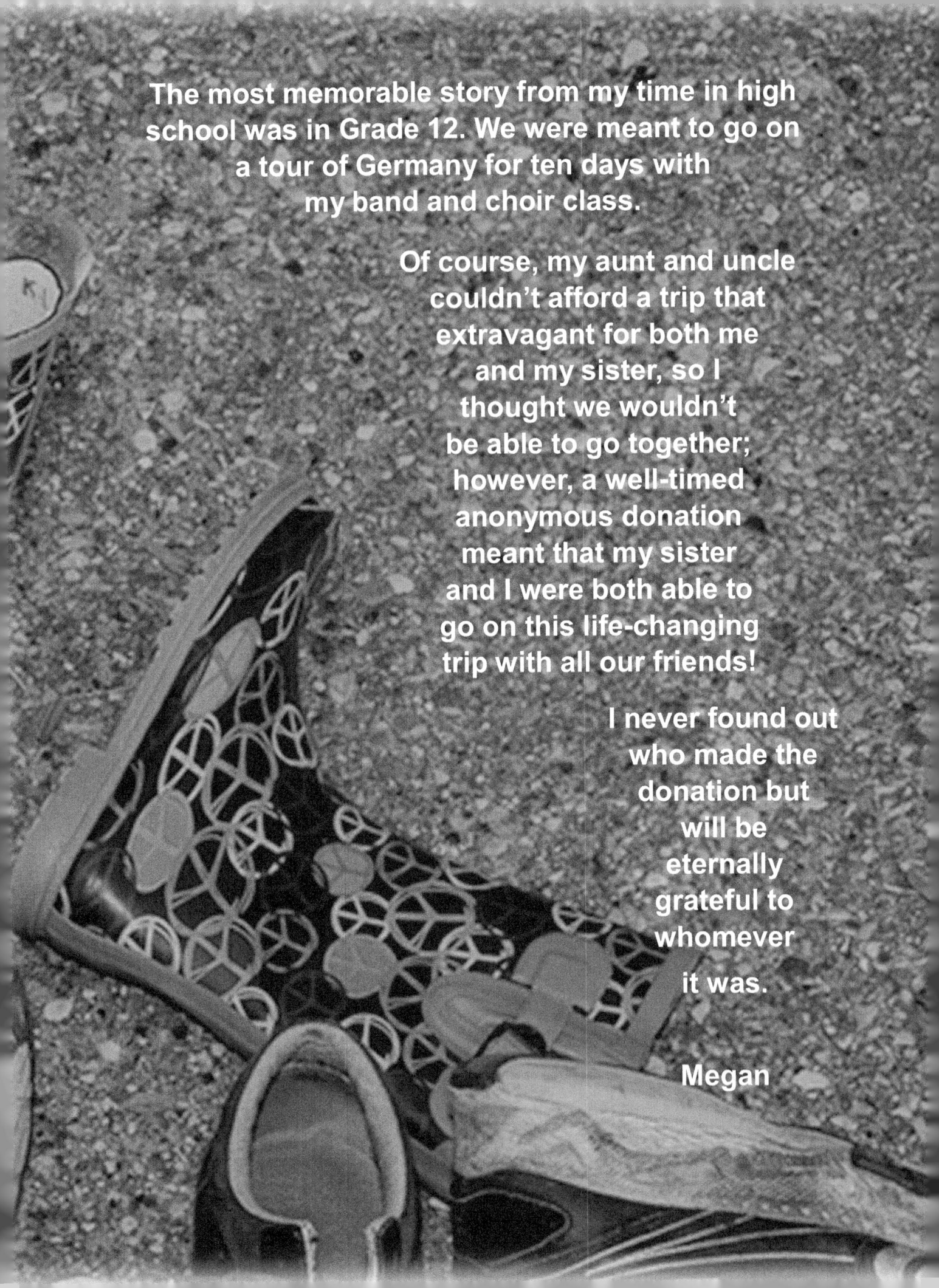

The most memorable story from my time in high school was in Grade 12. We were meant to go on a tour of Germany for ten days with my band and choir class.

Of course, my aunt and uncle couldn't afford a trip that extravagant for both me and my sister, so I thought we wouldn't be able to go together; however, a well-timed anonymous donation meant that my sister and I were both able to go on this life-changing trip with all our friends!

I never found out who made the donation but will be eternally grateful to whomever it was.

Megan

Canadian Journal of Behavioural Science/Revue canadienne des sciences du comportement

Sex Trafficking of Women and Girls in a Southern Ontario Region: Police File Review Exploring Victim Characteristics, Trafficking Experiences, and the Intersection With Child Welfare

Kyla Baird, Kyla P. McDonald, and Jennifer Connolly Online First Publication, October 10, 2019.

Domestic sex trafficking is a growing crime in Canada, with the majority of victims being children and youth. Youth involved with Child Welfare (CW) are vastly over-represented among sex trafficking victims..........

(To read the full article please click on headline or type headline into your search bar.)

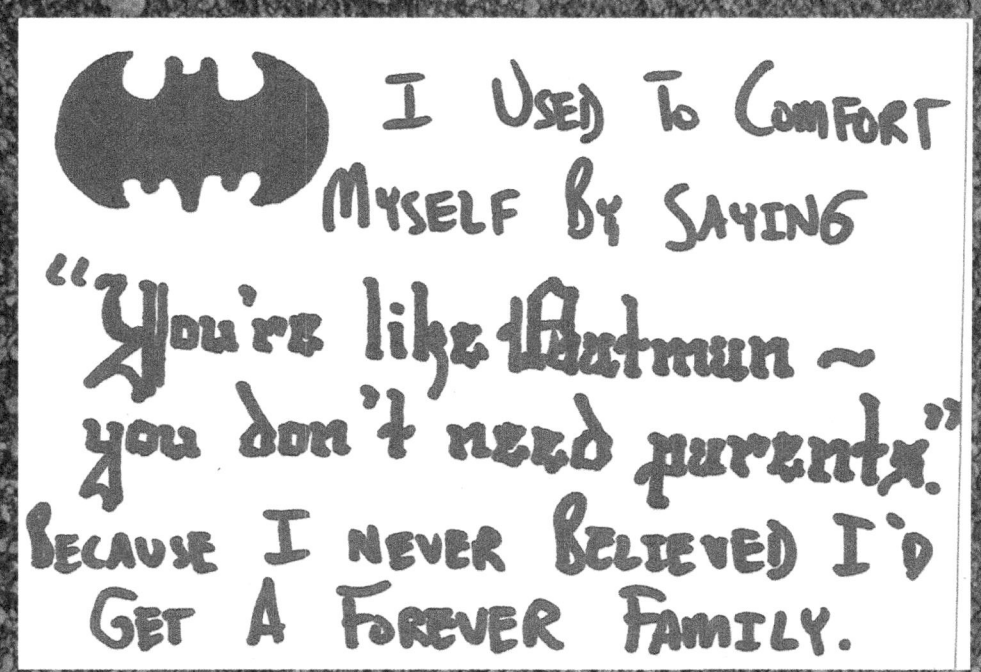

> I used to comfort myself by saying "You're like Batman — you don't need parents." Because I never believed I'd get a forever family.

Postcard courtesy of the Adoption Council of Canada—Youth Speak Out Edmonton

I want to leave the government people who are reading this with some hope, too. Youth in care need easier access to arts and music programming. Edmonton needs a big arts and music center where any of us could go and find a forever community. It would make a big difference so many of our lives. A lot of us struggle academically because we have learning disabilities, or we move around too much. Lots of us aren't good at athletics. We may not have a lot of family or friends. We have trouble fitting in most places we go but there is a place for everyone in the arts. They don't care if you are a person of color or LGBTQ2S or have disabilities or are poor or look weird or whatever. You can really grow because you are accepted and supported. I guess you kind of heal through whatever kind of creative expression you use and. It not only changes lives—it can actually save them. I am living proof of that.

Jesse

Tyler

My stubborn streak is good in that way because now I am driving the world's biggest trucks – the ones I dreamed of driving when I was playing with Tonka trucks in the sand.

I started out in care when I was around 10 years old. I had anywhere from 10 to 13 placements, and I went into an independent living program by the age of 16. My placements were mostly group homes, and I also did a lot of shifting between my mom and my dad and my grandparents.

I went to two junior high schools and I went to one high school. Even though I moved around a lot, my worker always made sure that I never had to change schools. That was big. Even if it was in a different city, they made sure I got to go. They would have cabs or youth workers take me all the way to Spruce Grove from Edmonton or to Leduc from Edmonton. I think not moving around from school to school really contributed to my academic success. I enrolled in the Registered Apprenticeship Program (RAP) there, graduated 6 months early, got paid to work while I apprenticed, and left high school with 140 credits. I took the Culinary Arts Program at Northern Alberta Institute of Technology (NAIT) and went on to work in that industry for a few years; I loved it, but I knew I needed to make more money to reach my goals, so I went into business management and security, and started my own painting business. I did that for quite a while, but after my divorce, I knew I had to do something different. So, I asked one of my best friends, who had also grown up in care, what he thought I'd be good at and he suggested heavy equipment operating. He reminded me that I could still qualify for a bursary for children who grew up in care, but I only had one year left before I no longer qualified. So, I got the funding, took the advanced course, and went on to work in the fracking industry, driving semi-trucks all over Canada. It was getting hard to find work after a while, so I looked at other job opportunities and saw my dream job – driving the world's biggest trucks. I applied, got the job right on the spot, and have been there since. I have benefits, a pension, and I love what I do.

I only had two child welfare workers. The first one wasn't good, but my second one was great and I fought hard to keep him with me long-term. At that time, workers were only supposed to stay with kids for two years, but he kept getting approved for more and he ended up having me on his caseload from the time I was 12 until I was 20. We had built a relationship and I told him that if he stayed, I'd do a lot better because I have abandonment issues. We still maintain contact today. I drove to

Lethbridge to see him two years ago. He was a great worker because he fought to keep my file and stay involved in my life. He always tried to get me anything I needed and was always concerned with my stability. When I went to school, he was the one who would make sure I stayed in the same school and he figured out how to get me there and back. I felt like he looked at me more as a family member and he did meaningful work. He'd tell me how much he loved coming to visit with me and say that it wasn't even a visit. He said it was like hanging out with a friend and taking a break from his stressful job.

I was very successful the whole time I was in care. I worked part-time and I was saving money. Where most kids have a goal of buying a car, my goal was to build my own life and buy a house and have a family. I told my worker what I was doing, and he said they weren't going to be able to keep me on until age 22 because I was doing really well and was able to take care of myself. I told him that I didn't need support until age 22. I just needed my file to be kept open until I had everything saved up and was able to make the down payment on a house. So, I got approved for a mortgage and bought my house the day I left care. I was 20 years old.

I sold that house and bought my dream home at age 22. I was also married and had a little girl by that time. I always wanted to have a family because that was something I never had. Our marriage only lasted a year and I gave her everything when we separated. I just said she could have the house and everything in it, because I wanted my kid to grow up in a home that I knew that was safe and stable. Fortunately, I have a good relationship with my former wife so I get to see my daughter all the time. On special occasions like Mother's Day, I take my daughter to pick out flowers for her mom. I respect her mom all the time and, even though we're separated, I want my daughter to see that this is how a guy should actually treat a lady. She's a really good mom and I am really grateful for that. Right now, I am saving up the down payment for another house and I am looking at buying one in the spring of 2021. I've been pretty much single since we separated in 2015 because I needed to work on myself and understand why I couldn't get attached to people, why I'd push them away. Anytime somebody would start catching feelings, I would start pushing them away to protect myself. It took a long time to get over that, but I have finally started seeing somebody now and it's great.

Before I was even in care, my mom and my dad were separated. I had emotional issues because my parents weren't together. My mom and I didn't see eye to eye, and we ended up getting in fights all the time. Consequently, she didn't want me and gave me up to my dad. It was good for a while, but it turned out that my dad's new wife made him choose between me and her kids. I wasn't supposed to know that, but I heard it while I was eavesdropping in the middle of the night. The next day, I was being driven back to my mom's, and I never really saw my dad much after that. I started to become violent with my mom and the police got called and took me away. She charged me and I spent a couple days at a youth detention centre. From there, I went to court and the judge asked my mom if she even wanted me and my mom strictly said on the stand that she had never wanted me.

From there, I went to live with my grandparents, but I was still dealing with my feelings about my parents not wanting me and constantly being moved from home to home for all those years. I was with my grandparents for six months to a year and then I left my keys at school one day and was locked out of the house. I was scared and I didn't know how to react, so I broke the door down. My grandparents thought I was starting to act like I had with my parents and couldn't handle me anymore, so they gave me up to a group home. From there I started shifting around to different group homes. I was a very hurt and angry kid by then, and I didn't know how to voice what was going on inside.

When I moved into care, I got that first child welfare worker who would just come and go and didn't listen to me. It was just, "Here's the rules and sign this paper and here's your next new home." That was it. It was when I got my new worker that things began to change. He asked me a lot of questions about what I liked to do and what kind of youth worker I would like and he matched me up with a great one who I would hang out with a couple of times a week. A key moment in my life came when my youth worker told me he wasn't going to be able to work with me anymore. I was so sad thinking that he was just another person who was going to come and go in my life.

I was so happy to find out that he just didn't want to be my worker anymore because he said he would rather be my friend and we are still best friends to this day. We'll have dinner together. We'll go to his house and we'll have a fire. He's doing renovations on his house right now, and I have a painting company, so I was helping him out with that. The greatest feeling is knowing that we are family to each other and are like brothers and can tell each other that. Family is not really people that you were born into, but the people that stick around no matter what. No matter how tough times get, you'll always be there for each other.

It's been difficult to build relationships with my biological siblings. My one brother is very jealous of me because he thinks I was lucky to go into group care. He got into drugs for a while but, when I had my daughter, I convinced him to get cleaned up or he would never see her again. Today, he is sober and doing well. My other brother I really don't have much contact with and he kind of went on his own way, trying to figure out his own life. He changed his name and everything, and I think he just wants to do his own thing. I also have a sister and a brother on my dad's side. I have never met that brother, but we have been communicating by text and building a relationship. He just had a little girl last month, so I'm going up in two weeks to go see her and meet him, so that is pretty great. I met my sister but, because of her mother's instability and her expectations of me, I had to distance myself from that relationship at that time. But now that she is older and I reached out to congratulate her on graduating, we may be able to build a relationship now.

As for my parents, when I had my daughter, I actually reached out to my family and told them that if they wanted to be involved in her life, they would have to build a relationship with me again. So, I built a relationship with my dad and my mom, and then I saw them for who they truly are, and I had to distance myself from my father until I completely cut him off. I still maintain a relationship with my mom, mainly because I have a child. She's not very involved with me, but she's a good grandma. My grandparents have always stayed involved in my life and are still involved with me and my daughter.

I think if child welfare didn't come into my life, I wouldn't be as successful as I am today. I think I would have gotten there, but not as well. I'm the most successful person in my whole family. They didn't really have much for life skills. We were a welfare family growing up – not goal-oriented. In care, there's a lot of planning and structure and routine, which was good for me. The group homes would do courses and try to help you build life skills and build relationships with people. I built a lot of relationships with other youth in care that I'm still really good friends with. One of them is basically my brother.

I don't think being in care impacted me negatively. Moving from home to home maybe wasn't the best, but each home had an opportunity for different learning experiences. I ended up meeting a staff member that taught me how to play football and I joined the football team at my school. That was not something I had thought about doing before. So, each place had their own little opportunities. In one group home, I won a big award for being a role model for other youth in care.

The scariest part of child welfare involvement was thinking that my family was giving up on me and I had no idea what was going on. Suddenly, they tell me I must sign this paper that says my parents are no longer my guardians, the government is, and then you're in a new home. I didn't really see my mom very much after that and didn't see my dad at all. He became obsolete and, eventually, so did my mom. We went anywhere from six to eight years without speaking.

There definitely are stereotypes about kids in care. People look at them and think they are not going to go anywhere or be successful and they're all going to end up on the streets or whatever. You shouldn't be judged by the fact that you grew up in care. Every kid deserves the same thing. I think a lot of youth become the way they are because of the stereotypes. They don't want to have goals because they're constantly getting judged and bullied.

I want people to know that we are people. We have been through a lot more in life than the average person. We shouldn't be treated like any less of a person or be given up on. Everyone has potential, but people sticking around to help us out a little more makes a huge difference. Everyone that came into my life, whether it was my caseworker or youth worker or staff, a lot of them stuck around and they became big parts of my life. And that's part of the reason I am the way I am today. The continuity of relationships is really important – somebody to stick with them long-term, like a family should. Kids in care have already had everything taken away from them. Everything is gone. Then they move around from home to home with a backpack full of whatever is most important to them, so people need the opportunity to stay connected.

I wouldn't change too much about the child welfare system. I was pretty happy with my care. The only thing I would change is a way to figure out what a kid is like and figure out what the most suitable home is for them. What are they like? What do they like? Who would they be most compatible with and who could they share the most experiences with because they have the most things in common? They need a better way for workers to match people. They do it on dating sites. When you are in care, you always see psychologists and psychiatrists; they could administer that compatibility assessment. I think kids in care would be more successful in the right place.

If I could leave workers with some advice, it would be to maintain their relationships with their youths as much and as long as they can because, later in life, it's really nice to have those people that you grew up still in your life. Don't treat your youth like a paycheque. At the end of the day, if you feel like a youth is your paycheque, then maybe you need to find a different youth to work with. You should wake up and want to be like hey, I want to go hang out with this kid. If a kid is acting up while they're out in public with them, it may be because they feel you don't want to hang out with them. If it's true that you don't think they are special and don't want to do things they like doing, then they sense that and are feeling hurt all over again. Workers should feel like it is more than a job. It has to be a passion, where you are building relationships with the youth that you're working with. That's what good workers do. I had lots of youth workers and the ones that I kept in touch with were the ones I had bonded with because they treated me like family. Also, a lot of our friendships with other youth in care are made at camps and other special events, so those experiences are important, and we need to stay connected when we find someone we can bond with. Workers can help make that happen. Maybe they could even look at placing friends together in the same group home if possible. Those relationships are so important.

I am not very interested in looking at my file. It's the past. I'm living in today, every day. I'm achieving goals and building my future and doing so well. I don't want to open up stuff that doesn't need to be worried about. What happened 10 years ago doesn't matter. I'm focused on the now. In fact, I've been holding onto a lot of stuff since I was a youth – just like little trinkets and stuff – and just recently I have been starting to get rid of all that stuff. Even a small thing that was bought at the dollar store, I just wanted to keep it because I was scared to let stuff go. I'm 27 years old now, and I'm finally starting to release some, and I'm growing every day. I didn't really get to be a kid growing up. I missed out on a lot, so I am making sure that my kid has got the dream life with her dad. I work in Fort McMurray a lot, but we keep in touch every day and when we are together, we have fun. We go quad riding. We go fishing. We go boating. We go floating down the river. She's a little nervous and anxious about bugs and stuff, but I help her along the way, and she loves all the things we do. She's always so thankful and grateful for everything. Everyone remarks about what a great kid she is and how her manners are the best and I am really proud of her.

If you are in care or grew up in care, I want to tell you to never give up. Set goals. Don't listen to anybody telling you that you can't do it, because you can. Don't let anybody get you down. Whatever you want to achieve, you can be successful if you want to be.

A lot of my success is because a lot of people were telling me I couldn't do it and so I wanted to prove them wrong. That really motivates me to be better and to be more successful. My stubborn streak is good in that way because now I am driving the world's biggest trucks – the ones I dreamed of driving when I was playing with Tonka trucks in the sand.

I found it odd one time, when I was speaking on a Youth Speak Out panel, I told the audience that I had a positive upbringing and that being in care was beneficial and that I wanted to be a social worker to keep the positive circle going. Everyone started clapping and I was like: Wow! It was just kind of a moment of clarity that I can be the change I want to see in the world. The only way it is going to happen is if I make it happen.

Mike

Dan Carter: From the streets to the mayor's office

By Kate Wheeler   LOCAL LOVE   January 22, 2019

Oshawa's new mayor once struggled with addiction and homelessness; now, he's changing the way his city handles those issues

Dan Carter, a man seemingly tested since birth, was on trial once again.

His struggles began when he was just a baby. His mother died weeks after he was born and the family was too large—five girls and three boys—for his newly single father to manage. Newborn Dan and his toddler brother, Tommy, were sent to foster care. The boys were separated; Carter was eventually adopted and found unconditional love, but his new life wouldn't be easy.

(To read the full article please click on headline or type headline into search bar.)

Once you find yourself belonging, you find a sense of your humanity and what you could have been earlier. Who you could have been, who you are – it just still brings out your humanity and replaced some of my identity. It replaced some of the bad parts with a good part. I think I have a lot of Theresa's personality now, and I'm starting to adopt some of her drive. It's given me a sense of identity and belonging. It's beautiful. Humanity gives you back your humanity.

Damon

Patricia

She told me she was going to help me and I wouldn't need to worry from this day forward. That night, we made a plan to change my story from 'foster kids can't make it", to proving that they can, and that became my motivation from that day forward.

I have been in foster care my entire life, but foster care is not who I am, and I choose not to let it define me today.

My mother has a mental illness called schizophrenia and my biological father was not present at my birth or throughout my life. My sister and brother's dad adopted me at a young age and taught me all about the sacred Aboriginal ways of life and practices. I remember him as funny – full of life, lessons, and love. Unfortunately, when I was around 14, my father became a homeless person after his father passed away and he was beaten by two teenagers who thought it would be fun to harm homeless people. He died from a slow brain bleed. I often think if only those teenagers had known the wonderful person he was, or the fact that he had a family that cared for him and needed him, that I needed him, maybe things would be different.

I have a beautiful sister and I had a charismatic brother who grew up by my side for most of my life, from home to home. We were an inseparable trio. My brother was everything to me and I would do anything to keep him safe and have him be happy in his life. I remember when we were kids, we all buried him in a snow pile, and I dug him out as soon as everyone went inside because I didn't like that prank. He thanked me for that.

We were separated when my foster mom fought for me to stay with her, while my sister and brother were too old and reckless to stay in the same home. They started to get into street drugs and moved from group home to group home. My brother began to go in and out of jail, while my sister got heavy into her addictions. He developed schizophrenia three years ago and that's when I decided to care for him, as I had aged out of care and was in charge of my own life. I remember carrying him around in my old van because he had nowhere to sleep. This is when I started to realize that we had no one but each other. I helped him get on a permanent disability pension, signed him into a group home, and got him in to see a specialist.

By that time, school had started to become heavy and I had to focus on myself. It started to become very difficult taking care of my brother. Schizophrenia was a lot more complicated than I thought. My brother would be in and out of the hospital and told me he didn't like the lack of freedom at his group home. I became overwhelmed with school and couldn't visit him at the hospital. He started to call me more often and I would try to be there, but my course load was heavy. He told me he felt alone in the world, like a freak, and wondered if there was any help. He wanted to get a job and start working out. I told him he had to really try to be independent, and that I would help him with those things as soon as I finished my exams.

My goal was to eventually have him live with me. My brother could not cope with the voices in his head and the isolation that followed. Soon after a hospitalization, around the Christmas season of 2018, my brother took his own life. I struggle with that pain every day; it is like a stab wound in my back as I try not to spiral into depression. I still need to make it through school. I need to be successful. I have to find my way and live the life I have dreamed of. The pain of losing my brother has never gotten better, so I try not think about it for now. I feel very sad for him and have heaps of regret. I remember having to plan my brother's entire funeral. As for my sister, she is struggling to make her way through life battling addictions. These are the very real struggles that I face today.

I had many experiences growing up in foster care. I had four main families, one of whom I still call mom and dad. Foster care was confusing and scary for me at times, and I would describe it as a big rollercoaster of emotions. The hardest part about being in care was having to move just as soon as I got used to a family. I remember packing my teddy bears, dolls, cards, and special things that I had gotten for Christmas and birthdays into garbage bags, then opening them up later and finding things crushed, crumpled, or broken. I remember being sad because those memories were all I had left of the foster brothers, sisters, mom, and dad I once had.

Having to figure out a new routine, a new school, and make new friends over and over was difficult and confusing. Visits with my biological mom were hard because sometimes she wouldn't know who I was or was going through psychosis on the visit and I would have to leave early. I remember I would worry about my dad a lot when I didn't see him for a while. I would wonder where my brother and sister were and if they were okay. I didn't know who to talk to because new homes and new people were scary and, honestly, a lot of them were strict and unapproachable.

I remember being moved to a new home a few weeks after my dad's passing and having a field trip one night for the theatre club I had joined as an extracurricular activity to get me out of my head. My foster mom made me go about 45 minutes early and I remember walking to the bus by myself. It was dark, but not too cold, and as I started to walk across the big open field towards the bus, I started to cry. I found a big pile of snow to sit on in the middle of the field and put my face in my arms. I not only cried about my beloved father, but my life. I missed my foster family. I missed my dog, Fiona. I missed my brother and my sister, and I missed my best friend, Trina. I thought about being bullied at school and having no friends now. I thought about my life in care and why I had to move all the time and I wondered why I didn't have anyone to talk to. So, I started to pray to God, as my father had told me to do when I felt sad. I told God that I hated the life he gave me, that it was too much for me. I told him I wished he could talk back to me or give me a hug, and I was angry with him because he couldn't. I asked him to give me a sign that he was even there for me. When I looked up, I saw the northern lights and a sky speckled with sparkling stars. It was the most beautiful thing I had ever seen in my life. I started to laugh and smile because I felt like God had heard me. I started to run in the wind with my hands out, spinning in circles under the beautiful sky. Life can only be beautiful after pain.

I had a similar experience at the age of 22, when nothing was going right. I had applied to university many times, my brother had just been diagnosed with schizophrenia, and I had just gotten fired from my job for being too nervous to speak to customers. My boyfriend at the time told me he didn't want to be with me because I was awkward, and he was afraid I would become schizophrenic like my mom. My caseworker tried to push me off of funding, and I didn't know how I was going to make it. I lost all hope. I took it upon myself to buy a rope and write a letter that stated foster care is not meant for people to grow up in and become successful. I wanted to prove that you could not make it no matter how hard you tried. Another worker who was covering for my child welfare worker at the time, got in contact with me that week. One night after a long conversation with her, I admitted to buying a rope and writing a letter. Soon after, there was a knock on my door, and I was taken to the hospital under a Form 10, which meant I could be detained for up to one month under the Mental Health Act.

After talking to the psychologist at the hospital, all I could think was that he was using really big words but was really cute and how ugly the scrubs I was wearing were. I heard a silly woman coming down the hall, yelling, "Hey! Do you know where a young, pretty girl is? Her name is Patricia!" Around the corner came that wonderful child welfare worker, with big balloons and flowers. I was so happy and embarrassed to see her. She told the psychologist that he could leave now and held my hand telling me how much she believed in me, and how much I would miss out on if I took my life. She told me she was going to help me, and I wouldn't need to worry from this day forward. That night, we made a plan to change my story from 'foster kids can't make it,' to proving that they can, and that became my motivation from that day forward.

She became my child welfare worker shortly after that night. She took one look at my file and said it was hard for her to believe what they were writing about the girl in front of her, and said we are going to start over. She asked me about my goals and what I wanted to see happen in my life. I told her I wanted to go to school and support myself. She would tell me stories about her children and how many times they applied for school. She told me about times that she felt sad in her life and that everyone feels this way. She told me that I was not stupid; I was just going through normal adulthood. I felt heard for the first time in my life.

Soon after, I saw a neurologist and got a complete reassessment of my cognitive functioning. This neurologist told me that there was absolutely nothing wrong with me and that I was functioning at a university level. The impact that news had on me was immense, because it allowed me to stop listening to what people told me. I knew myself and that I was smart and capable. I started to trust myself and walked with my head held a little higher after that day.

Soon after that, I saw a psychologist every week who specialized in working with kids in care. He taught me that I was reacting perfectly normal for the circumstances I was given. I finally could voice and figure out why I was so afraid all the time, and why I gave up so easily on things. We worked through and figured out complex things that I never knew I had in my subconscious mind, like the feeling of having 'foster kid' taped on my forehead, and that everyone thought I was worthless and would give up on me.

He told me, "Nope. Nobody knows that about you or needs to know that about you. You keep that to yourself and walk with your head held high." I learned that people could make it in life without the notion that you needed a mom and a dad and that, in fact, many people who didn't grow up in care don't have moms and dads, and have parents who are divorced, and that people with families have lots of issues. He taught me that being successful was about my mind and my choices and that I was just as capable as anyone else to make it in life.

I learned to surround myself with people who made me feel good about myself and cut out people who made me feel bad. I learned about bullies and how to stand up and advocate for myself appropriately. I learned how to be my own parent. I would look in the mirror every morning and encourage myself to get up at a decent time and ignore the negative voices in my head. I started to become kind to myself and become aware of my surroundings and tell myself I was safe. I started to walk out of that office with self worth and dignity and with hope. I will never forget that psychologist, because he cleared the storm of confusion and chaos in my head. I still use the coping mechanisms, tips, and tricks he gave me to this day.

My new child welfare worker also got me into a group called Youth Speak Out that I went to every Tuesday. In this group, we spoke about our experiences growing up in care to audiences of social workers, teachers, and even legislators who have requested to have us come and speak. I was told by a supervisor that my story about the garbage bags had really touched him and that he was working on getting suitcases for kids in care to pack their things in when they move. Youth Speak Out not only gave me an outlet but allowed me to make a difference for those struggling in the foster care system. It made me feel like I had a purpose. It also allowed me to meet people that were successful in care, which was a very important step. I met people who graduated from university or were enrolled in post-secondary. They looked confident and sure of themselves and they were smart and articulate. I made lifelong friends with some of these people. They were people I called to talk about what I was going through, because they were people who understood and went through the same thing. They were my true role models.

I started to think that if I don't see foster care plastered on their heads, then people don't see that on me. I admired them for going through what they had and making it through to a successful life. I started to take off that label completely and felt free and proud. I started to volunteer at an Edmonton hospital, St. John's Ambulance, and the Hope Mission, and gained more experience to become more competitive for school. I applied for the youth worker position at an Edmonton youth shelter and got hired.

I finally got into my Emergency Medical Technician (EMT) program and became a primary paramedic. I am now a registered primary-care paramedic and an advanced care paramedic student on my intermediate practicum. I work as a youth worker now, helping kids in need, and have just been promoted to be the CPR instructor for my company. I live on my own with my boyfriend in a beautiful home and practice meditation, mindfulness, and listen to motivational speeches often. I would like to be a motivational speaker one day and share my story to inspire others. Life does get easier if you try hard every day, you can become your own parent and live a life that you chose with stability and love.

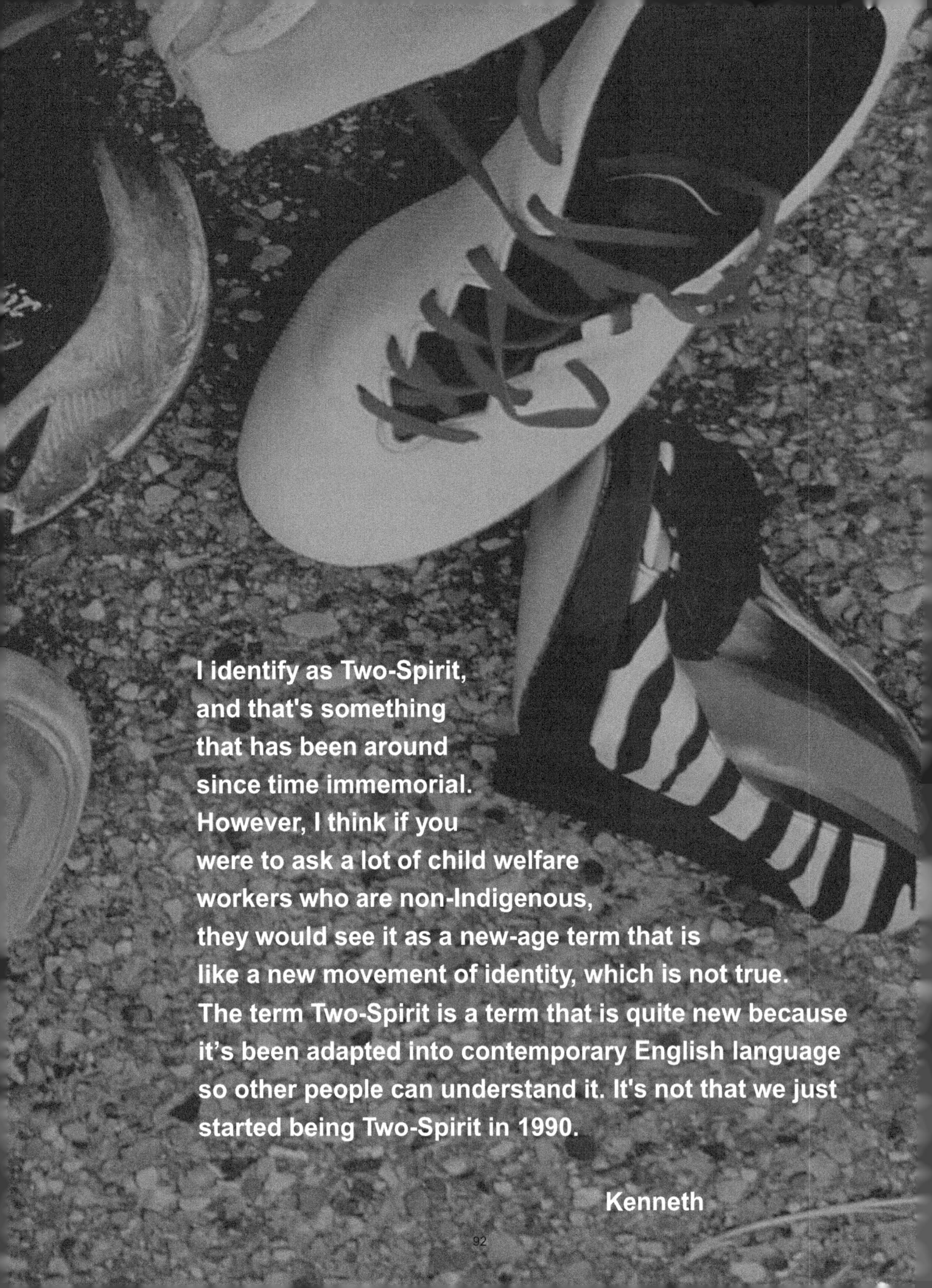

I identify as Two-Spirit,
and that's something
that has been around
since time immemorial.
However, I think if you
were to ask a lot of child welfare
workers who are non-Indigenous,
they would see it as a new-age term that is
like a new movement of identity, which is not true.
The term Two-Spirit is a term that is quite new because
it's been adapted into contemporary English language
so other people can understand it. It's not that we just
started being Two-Spirit in 1990.

                                                  Kenneth

Ontario to overhaul child welfare system, will focus on keeping children linked to their family

The reforms seek to change one of the assumptions that has animated the present child welfare system: That some people aren't cut out for raising children.

Tyler Dawson July 29, 2020 NATIONAL POST

Under Ontario's child welfare changes, funding will be shifted to new initiatives "to better serve Indigenous, Black, racialized and 2SLGBTQ children and youth."

(To read full article please click on headline or type headline into your search bar.)

Postcard courtesy of The Adoption Council of Canada—Youth Speak Out Edmonton

After so long, I began to understand how it worked out there and to connect with certain support groups, one of which was a recreation program centered around helping youth who were homeless. The program was run by an older woman who had a passion for youth and their hidden talents. It was a place where you could access musical instruments, art supplies, and there was always a pizza dinner. It was a place I could express myself and feel safe, more so than I had felt while on the streets, at least.

Winnie

Cody

Don't let your past or others define who you are and who you will become.
There are lots of other youth in care and former youth in care
who are extremely successful, and you can be too.

I am 27 years old and I have been lucky enough to be happily married to my best friend, Shay, for the past three years. We bought our first home two years ago and live in Edmonton. We have an orange tabby cat named Nacho, with future plans of having our own children. I hold a Diploma of Social Work from Grant MacEwan University and a Bachelor of Social Work from the University of Calgary. I am currently working in one of my dream jobs as a Casework Supervisor with Alberta Children's Services. I have two families: The Murrells (my biological family) and the Schafers (my adopted family). On the Murrell side, I am the oldest of four siblings (two sisters and one brother) and on the Schafers side, I am the youngest of four siblings (two brothers and one sister). My life journey has been tremendously challenging at times and to get to where I am now has required a lot of perseverance and a lot of support along the way. My story is one that few know, and I hope that by sharing it some good might come from it.

I first came into government care when I was six years old and left care when I turned 20. While in care, I attended ten different schools and lived in nine different placements (four foster homes, two group homes, an adolescence residential treatment program and two semi-independent living apartments). I had hundreds of workers who worked directly with me over the years including caseworkers, youth workers, health care workers, medical professionals, advocacy workers and foster parents.

Some of my earliest memories that I can recall start when I was around five years old. At that time, I was living with my mom (Linda), my dad (Richard), and my little brother. My dad was an interesting character. He'd been to jail for several years before he started his own car lot. He had been a bit of a troubled kid but was trying to get on the right path and was trying to overcome his challenges. He managed the car lot and my mom stayed at home with us. I was a busy kid with lots of energy – some might even say a bit too much. Life was pretty normal, simple, and happy up until this point. Gradually, my parents began to fight more often, and this eventually led to them separating. My dad moved into an apartment with a pool because he knew how much I liked to swim, and I saw him mostly on weekends. I was sad and confused about what was happening with my parents, but I loved spending time with both of them.

About two months after my parents separated, I was called to the office from my kindergarten class to find my mom crying uncontrollably. I had never seen her cry like that before and knew something was very wrong. My mom told me that my father had died, which I later learned was from a drug overdose, and that he was not coming back. I remember not understanding what it meant that he had died, but very clearly understanding that he was not coming back. I was instantly heartbroken, grief stricken, and struggled to cope. I soon developed some severe behavioural problems, became very difficult for my mother to manage, had gotten kicked out of my first school, and was placed in a specialized behavioural school program.

My mom continued struggling to care for me with my increasingly difficult to manage behaviors, her developing addiction to crack and alcohol, and her struggles with mental health. Living with my mom was like a free-for-all; I did what I wanted. I looked after my younger siblings because my mom was often locked in her room using drugs for hours and sometimes days at a time. It was a lot of responsibility. I had almost no childhood. I can't remember a time that I was living carefree, other than maybe before my dad died, but my memories are quite limited. It was often pretty scary. I never knew who was going to be in our home. There were nights that my little brother and I slept in the basement and I would nail the door shut so it would be hard for someone to break in. Sometimes, there were physical fights between us and she would be so fed up she would sometimes have to call the police or she'd call child welfare on herself. The chaos eventually caused me to develop some major mental health problems and distorted thinking. There was little to no stability and we moved a lot. I moved with my mom more than I actually moved around in care.

When I was six years old, the child welfare authorities were alerted and became concerned about what was occurring in our home. Shortly after, my brother and I were apprehended and placed in our first foster home. I remember being taken from my home by someone who I only knew as a stranger and being told that I was going to be living with this other stranger, my new foster parent. I remember feeling extremely scared, unsure about why I had been moved here, and the worker leaving me in this new home only minutes after dropping me off. Sadly, almost every move thereafter was similarly abrupt, seemingly cold and confusing. Every move after only reinforced the idea in my head that no one wanted me, that I didn't belong anywhere, and that I wasn't loved. These feelings had a profound impact on me growing up and some of their remnants still impact me today.

Being in this new home, I remember having to get used to a lot of new things – new rules, new routines, and a new caregiver, which I found very difficult having already been comfortable with all these things at my home. I remained in this foster home for several months but was quickly removed and placed in a new foster home with my brother, following an incident where I punched my foster parent after witnessing her restraining my brother. At the time, I thought she was hurting him and I had grown increasingly protective of him, having been separated from all of my other family.

I was seven when I went into my new foster home, which seemed pretty good for the first while. My new foster caregivers had their own children, so we played with them a lot. Over time, it started to feel like I was less important than their biological children, as they seemed to get some preferential treatment, but it did not overly bother me until my brother had been blamed for destroying a TV that one of their children had destroyed. The day after the TV was destroyed, I remember coming back to the house and not being able to find my brother. I remember asking where my brother was and being told by my foster caregivers that he had been moved to a group home. I remember a deep sadness totally engulfing me, which quickly evolved into extreme anger. I began destroying the house and only stopped when I was physically escorted to the basement where the lights were turned off and the door was locked. I slept on the floor until I was woken by my worker the following day and was immediately moved to my third foster home.

I lived in my third foster home for about a year and remember feeling very cared for, and maybe even loved, by my third foster caregivers. When I was eight years old, I was returned to the care of my mom and her partner at the time. My mom quickly began using drugs again and my brother and I were apprehended soon after. I returned to my third foster home, where I stayed until being returned to the care of my mom and her partner at the age of nine. He and my mom had just had my little sister. At the time, I remember being OK with her dad and even feeling cared for by him. However, he and my mother broke up shortly after. Since then, it appears that he has developed what I can only describe as an apparent hatred of me. During this time, I was temporarily placed in a residential mental health program to help stabilize me, and this is where I was diagnosed with Attention Deficit and Hyperactivity Disorder (ADHD) and Oppositional Defiant Disorder (ODD).

My mom quickly began using drugs again and began prostituting in the home. My mom would often lock herself in her bedroom for days and could not be woken up. I would look after my brother and sister, ensuring that they had food and that they had someone to go to when they needed something. My mom began bringing more people into our home that I did not know and did not feel safe around. I remember a time when we were giving one of her 'friends' a ride home and my mom asked him to pay her what he owed her and he postured towards her. I remember grabbing a knife out of my pocket (which I had grabbed from the house because I felt unsafe with this friend) and threatening him with it until he left the car. I became increasingly protective of my siblings and often slept with them downstairs in a locked room. I remember feeling so scared some nights that I stayed up all night until the sun came out, just to make sure my brother and sister were safe.

Just prior to my 12th birthday, I became the subject of a Permanent Guardianship Order (PGO) which, simply put, meant that the government had taken on a sole parent role in my life. For me, this represented a point of no return, where my mom could never get better, never get me back, and that I was just going to hurt for the rest of my life.

Shortly after that event, I had started spiralling out of control and got put in my first group home, where I entered into the darkest chapter of my life and complete hopelessness consumed me. During my stay there, I often ran away, broke things, threatened others, and tried to hurt others. I felt that there was no way out and that life would not get any better. I had often dreamed of dying and not having to feel the pain and hurt that I had. On several occasions, I tried taking my life, but thankfully staff intervened and stopped me from making this irreversible mistake. Ironically, while I was living in the group home, I began to discover that I had the potential to succeed academically, which was previously unthinkable, as I believed I was stupid. A teacher worked on setting some academic goals with me and, although I struggled greatly, I began to make significant progress. During my stay there, I rarely saw my mom as she often missed our scheduled visits and I was only seeing my brother about once a month.

Due to my challenging behaviours, I was moved to an adolescent residential treatment centre at the age of 13 and stayed there until I was 15. There, my behavior escalated for a while but after several months, I began to stabilize a bit. I was given several things to work towards, and lots of guidance and strong role models (several staff members who I looked up to and felt strongly that they cared for/believed in me). I was able to start working on my emotional and behavioural issues. It was there that I got my first real work experience and had the discussion about what I was going to do with my life.

I had a fantastic key worker (a staff assigned directly to support me) and I originally told her that my plans for the future probably consisted of me going on welfare and playing video games. She encouraged me to think critically about what I wanted to do and pointed out that I seemed to have great relationships with my peers and thought that I may make a great Social Worker one day. At this point, a seed was planted and, although I didn't have the knowledge or the skills, I had a genuine belief that I could be more. I started to think about what kind of life I wanted and what I needed to get there. In hindsight, it made an incredible difference to have someone else believe in me when I didn't fully believe in myself. I began studying incredibly hard and working towards my independence.

During my stay there, I rarely saw my mom, as she often missed our scheduled visits and I was only seeing my brother once every few months. With the help of my key worker and counselor, I was able to recognize the negative impact my mom was having in my life and I was able to put some stronger boundaries in place with her, which resulted in me not seeing her for several years. After this, I started making some significant improvements with a lot of help. I started attending a community high school, as opposed to the specialized behavioural schools I was previously attending.

Shortly after I turned 15 years old, I moved into a transitional group home and began working on various life skills that would help me prepare to live independently. It was there that I first met my best friend, Tyler, who remains my best friend to this day. Tyler and some of my other friends at the time had become the closest thing to family for me. The bonds with my friends were strong and because I considered them family, they had a significant amount of influence over me – either lifting me up or bringing me down. It took me a while to understand what healthy relationships were and how to set boundaries with the friends that may not have had my best interests at heart. I got a job at a McDonald's and started working, making and saving money, and learning new skills. I joined my school's football and rugby teams and made some good friends, including my soon-to-be adoptive brother, Connor. One of the most significant turning points that set me on a clear trajectory for success was becoming part of the Schafers family. They showed me what it was like to be a part of a healthy family, which was difficult for me to get used to having lived in many institutions. They also helped eliminate all the extra barriers that I had which would have made my life a lot more difficult.

It started off as a mentor relationship, where Mrs. Schafers saw something in me. She became someone I could check in with and she would check in on me. If I needed a ride somewhere for football/rugby practice or if I needed anything, she was there. This quickly evolved into me being invited to their house and celebrating holidays with them. They were the first ones to help out when I really didn't know what to do or didn't have anyone there for me. When I was 16, I moved into my own apartment, which was supported by child welfare, and the Schafers helped me move all my stuff. Mrs. Schafers and the Schafers family (including Mr. Schafers, my adopted brothers, Connor and Clayton, and sister, Courtney) were always there for me and I knew I could rely on them for anything. When I decided to skip a few days of school, Mrs. Schafers found out and was at my door to get me to school, even though she lived 45 minutes away from me. She made sure I stayed in school. Someone caring about me in a different way was life changing. There weren't a lot of people who were interested in my well-being, including myself at times, until I wasn't doing well. It's all the little things that made me feel like I mattered and, through the Schafers family, I learned what a family could be.

Living on my own with some financial support under a Supports and Financial Assistance Agreement (SFAA), I began learning how to manage a household while attending high school. I was lucky enough to have several teachers in high school that were patient with me, allowing me to make mistakes and grow, despite me being a bit rough around the edges. Many of my teachers stood out to me, as they invested in me and my learning. I was lucky to have a teacher that took enough of an interest in me to take me shopping to buy my grad suit, to ensure that my grad day would be that much more special. I had often imagined that I would never graduate or live long enough to.

At 17 years old, I graduated from Sturgeon Composite High School with Honors. I had decided at this point that I wanted to be a Social Worker and try to make a difference in the child welfare system. I found a new job that was more related to what I wanted to do and offered the skills that I wanted to build. Immediately after graduating, I applied for a general studies program to knock off courses that I needed, as I was not able to get into the Social Work program because of my young age. Registering for post-secondary school was difficult and scary to navigate and I would have struggled to do so without the help of Mrs. Schafers. At the time, I was lucky enough to have the cost of my post-secondary education sponsored by a bursary designed to help children who had grown up in care to pursue further education. Without this program, I would not have gone to post-secondary school and would likely be in a much different place. Everyday, I am extremely grateful for this bursary as it helped change my life and gave me a way to break out of my family cycle.

At 19 years old, I had completed two full years of general studies and was accepted into the Social Work Program at Grant MacEwan University. There, I grew a significant amount both personally and professionally. Through post-secondary schooling and the help of some amazing professors, I was significantly expanding how I thought about and understood myself and the world around me. For that first few years, I often felt as if I was an imposter and that, somehow, I was able to sneak into the program – I thought to myself that 'they don't let people like me in'. I am so glad that I was so wrong about that.

At 20 years old, I applied for and got hired as a relief Child and Youth Care Worker and began working in several group homes. I began to develop my skills and worked towards my goal of becoming a Social Worker. I had developed an immense passion for child welfare work, as I deeply understood the impact it had in my own life. I wanted to help others who were in similar situations, use the lessons that my own experience taught me to help others, and help improve the system that I was a major part of for so long. At the time, I had taken an interest in business. I started a small business and became a partial owner of two others. It was also at this time that I completed my second Social Work practicum and was introduced to Jim Campbell. I was able to be open with him about my experiences growing up in care and I always felt accepted. Jim soon became my most important professional mentor in the field and, shortly after, he and the Campbells became family to me.

At 21 years old, I graduated with my Diploma in Social Work. For me, this was one of the proudest moments in my life, as it signified that I would not be just another statistic, that I would be taken seriously, that I truly made a major change in my life, and that I had broken my family cycle. When I got my Social Work Diploma, Mrs. Schafers helped convince me to pursue my degree while I was young and had the funding. Without her sound advice and persuasion, I may never have finished my degree.

Once I had been accepted into the Bachelor of Social Work program, I got an entry level position working in child welfare as a trainee. This was also the year that I met my amazingly beautiful soon-to-be wife, Shay. Between the ages of 22 to 23, I graduated with my Bachelor of Social Work and was promoted to a caseworker working within child welfare. At 24, I got married, was promoted to an investigator in child welfare, and began serving as a board member for the Alberta College of Social Workers. At 25, my wife and I bought our first house. At 26, I was promoted to a supervisor in child welfare, which really brings me to where I am today. My life is settled now and the hardships I experienced throughout my journey have had less and less of an impact on me with each year that passes. I can more fully enjoy life and help others, which ensures that my life is full of things that I am passionate about and that provide me with fulfillment.

I love what I do, and I feel my life has prepared me well for my role working in child welfare. Some things I just instantly understood. A lot of the terms and protocols I was already familiar with. Having a lot of meetings was normal for me, having been a kid in care. You have lots of meetings when you're a kid in care and are often expected to be articulate and clearly advocate for yourself, which can be challenging and is not normal, but it was normal to me. I remember having a conversation with my old worker and we both laughed, as he said that he remembered me coming to my case conference fully prepared with my clipboard and my notes at 13 years of age. He was a good worker and helped make the difference for me by being a strong advocate. I felt that he really wanted what I wanted, which was good things for me, and he met me where I was at. He was the only consistent worker I had while in care (having worked with me for nearly ten years), which was quite an anomaly.

My interest in the field really comes from my personal experiences. I lived with hundreds of other kids in care and, although we were all somewhat different, there was a similar and general theme to our stories. So, I wanted to work in the field to help make a difference and I thought how cool it would have been to have a worker who knew a little bit about what I was going through – someone who had the understanding and was able to have real conversations with me, knowing that they knew what it was like. Growing up in care has given me a deep passion for the work I do, with an immersive level of compassion for all those that I work with. I like to think I can contribute significantly to the field and make a difference for people with a level of understanding that you can't get somewhere else – the kind of education you can't get in school.

When I was 13 years old, I remember having a fight with one of my workers and telling him that I could do his job better than him. He told me that it was harder than it looked and, although I did not believe it at the time, he was right. He really was a good guy and I really was a difficult kid, but he kept trying to work with me. At a separate time, we both shared another good laugh, as he told me that I was one of the most difficult children he had worked with. This made me very proud, as it highlighted where I used to be in my life and where I am now. How dramatically my life has shifted from then to now has given me a firm belief that change is so possible.

I could probably write a chapter on how my childhood diagnosis affected my life. I was OK with the ADHD and the ODD labels, but I was also diagnosed at the age of ten with a mood disorder, a personality disorder, and a mild mental retardation (what they called it back in the day). The former was very troubling and actually absurd when I look back. I have read my whole file and I know I was misdiagnosed. I was diagnosed with these during some of the worst stages in my life and when my world was extremely chaotic. I think what they were seeing were behaviors that were materializing because of my life circumstances and then slapped a label on it. I was a very troubled kid, even needing to go to an intensive behavioral program in a local hospital. I'm not sure that there's a better way, but it is quite clear that I didn't have some of these diagnoses or, at least, I don't anymore. I think it can be very easy to give a kid in care a diagnosis and those labels can be harmful because they can stick.

Aside from my own journey, another part of my life that has reinforced the possibility of change is seeing my mom's journey and recovery. It was around the time when I started my post-secondary education that I began talking more with my mom. At the time, she had been several years sober with my soon-to-be stepfather, Conrad, and had given birth to my little sister, Armoni. I feel incredibly lucky that my mom actually started getting healthier in my adult years. It seemed highly unusual for someone to go from heavily using multiple substances and living a high-risk lifestyle for over a decade, into full recovery. It helped me to see her progressing in her life. My mom and I don't have your traditional parent/child relationship. We started rebuilding our relationship when I was about 16, but we have really only had a stronger relationship for the past four years. It's been an extremely hard journey.

At first, we struggled. I think my mom was hoping that rebuilding our relationship was going to result in a return to a traditional mother/son relationship, to pick up where it was with no interpersonal work involved. I was not on that page. In terms of trying to rebuild a relationship with my mom, I had a lot of expectations of her. Having thought a lot about what I needed to move forward in our relationship, I knew I needed her to take responsibility, at least in part, for how her actions impacted me. There were a lot of times that we had very intense arguments and our relationship could have ended at any of those points. These intense arguments often ended in multiple hang ups, walk outs, and taking breaks from each other for extended periods of time. I think it took a long time for my mom to admit and fully appreciate the pain that I felt, but I am thankful that she kept trying to make amends. It is something that I strongly desired and has helped me move forward in our relationship. Eventually, one of us would phone the other, apologize, and we would start trying to work through stuff again. During the rebuilding phase in our relationship, things were a bit awkward, as we did not have a typical mother and son relationship. The type of relationship we had at the time is difficult to describe and would most closely resemble a mutual friendship, but eventually our relationship grew with mutual respect and blossomed into a more mother and adult son type relationship.

For a long time, I held my mom solely accountable for what happened. But as I matured, I could not blame my mom or my upbringing forever. I had to also hold myself accountable. There's only so much blame you can point at someone without having to say you're part of the problem too. What really put it in perspective for me was understanding that she had grown up in group homes and correctional facilities. Then, I started looking at my grandparents and found out that they had a history of generational hardships, abuse, and trauma. It became clear that my anger was a little bit misdirected towards my mom and was a much larger issue spanning across generations. My mom and my grandparents had similar experiences and, at a certain point, you can't continue to blame them – you just need to make some changes and break the cycle. It often just takes one person to do this, and it can have ripple effects. I am happy to say that, through a lot of hard work on both sides, me and my mom have built back a strong relationship. I am also proud to say that 2020, the year of Covid-19, was also the year that I was the officiant at her marriage to my stepdad. I feel proud of her and I think we both feel lucky to have each other.

I have a diversity of relationships with my biological family – some good and some lost. My brother is walking a different path than I am and is struggling with severe addictions issues, mental health issues, and criminal activity. He has spent more of his adult life in jail than not, but at this point, he does not want any help from anyone. This is very sad for me, as I tried to be his protector when my mom struggled to do so, and he was the closest thing I had to family growing up in care. We were close growing up and I feel that he has drifted away and disconnected. Because of the struggles I had growing up and, although I loved him very deeply, I know that I had caused him some pain and likely played a role in denying him some happiness by encouraging him to misbehave in different placements that he was doing well in. I could write a book about how being separated from him in care impacted me and likely impacted him. At the time, it was reasoned that due to my aggressiveness, he was at risk being around me. Although there may be some truth to this, it was nonetheless one of the most difficult things I experienced. I wanted him to have a good life and it's really hard to see him swing so far the other way.

I also have an adult sister, who never came into care because her dad raised her. I don't think her dad wanted her to know too much about us and so our relationship is quite skewed, nearly non-existent, and she doesn't speak to us much. I believe that she is struggling with her own mental health issues. I have tried to reconnect and develop a better relationship with her, but my efforts have been unsuccessful. I believe that this is because she is still likely hurting from her own experiences of trauma and the influence of her father's apparent hatred of my biological family. This is very sad for me, as I tried to be her protector when my mom struggled to do so, whether she will ever know it or not. I have a fantastic relationship with my youngest sister and I am really happy that she has got to experience the joys of having a healthy family and a healthy bigger brother. I still have a strong relationship with my Aunt Karen and did throughout most my life growing up in care. While growing up in care, she was the most consistent family member I had and, to this day, I am grateful for her and for what she did for me even if, at the time, I couldn't fully appreciate it. Over the years, I have developed a stronger relationship with my grandparents and my dad's side of the family and have regular contact with them.

I didn't realize until I was a little older how growing up in care had impacted me, my concept of the world, of what family was, and what their role is. Growing up in care, I really only had people who were paid to care looking after me. I often lived in homes where staff rotated on a schedule and, every 8-12 hours, there was someone new looking after me. This was something that was normalized for me and really impacted how I often saw relationships as very temporary. Growing up like this taught me that my relationships with everyone – my mom, siblings, foster parents, group home staff – were all short-term. When you think about relationships like this, it gives you a very dim view of the world and a feeling that no one is there for you. I don't know if there's a better way to do it, especially given the behaviours I had, but the staffing situation in group care sets you up to become institutionalized at a young age. I hate to use the word 'institutionalized,' as I have many great memories from the homes I lived in, but my days became so structured, my view of relationships became a bit warped, and how I acted in these settings made it difficult for me to interact with people outside of them.

I really started realizing this when I started going to community school and was seeing how some of my interactions were being perceived as strange. I realized that I was being housed with other youth who had the same or worse issues as me, and living that way for so long made me think that some of the things that happened regularly at these homes (such as seeing daily restraints, fighting, my bed being bolted to the ground and having to always lock my room door to prevent stealing) were normal. You become used to things like the five-second rule, which, in the homes that I lived in, meant that someone was being restrained and everyone had five seconds to get to their room. In one of my placements, I got used to bathrooms with no doors. Having grown up in an unhealthy family and in care, I developed a high degree of intuition. I became acutely aware of how everyone around me was feeling and how they might react. I also developed a deep level of understanding and empathy through the pain I experienced and lived though. I believe that my experiences have made me better able to tune into someone else's pain and has made me more sensitive to their struggles. Having had the experiences I did, I developed a bit of a knack for sensing if someone had grown up in care themselves. I often found that by simply talking to others about their family life, those who grew up in care or had a tough upbringing got a little weird in their answers around this topic. I always appreciated meeting others who grew up in the same way I did and often felt that, just by talking about shared experiences, an instant connection formed.

Some of the stereotypes I faced growing up in care were that I was damaged, broken, unstable, bad, and untrustworthy. One of many examples from my life was from when I was going to junior high and I had a friend that I used to play with. I noticed that he started avoiding me and stopped hanging out with me. One day, he told me that his mom said he couldn't play with me anymore, as I was trouble because I didn't have a family and I was causing problems at that school. This really made me feel like I wasn't good enough to play with other kids at school. Some of the stigmas attached to growing up in care became internalized. Hearing that people thought I was damaged made me think and feel that I was damaged. Over time, I have had to slowly peel these labels off and fight against them, so that I did not let them define me. I began to believe that only me and my actions could define me and that seemed to help a lot One of the most significant and positive impacts of having grown up in care was that it helped give me a second chance in life – one that I did not think I would have. Although my experience of growing up in care is best described as chaotic, it also gave me many opportunities, like the opportunity to go to post secondary school, to get mental health support, to live in a stable environment, and to develop some positive role models. Some of these opportunities afforded to me, having grown up in care, were beneficial in many aspects, but, alone, they would have still left me stranded and incomplete. It was really the relationships I had with those outside the system that made the most significant difference in my life. These relationships extended far past my involvement with the child welfare system and are still critical to my success today. Without these outside relationships and the opportunities afforded to me by the child welfare system, I am ultimately unsure where I would be right now.

Growing up in care, I did not have many role models. I also did not know a single person who had grown up in care and who was not just getting by in life. For the longest time, I thought that there were no other successful people who had grown up in care and was determined to be the first one. It was not until my adulthood that I learned there were many successful people who had grown up in care, but that you just don't hear about them much. They don't tend to be very vocal about their childhood experiences. Perhaps this is due to them being worried about the stigmas that may be attached to them if people found out or them just wanting to put it behind them, but I remember thinking how much of a difference it would have made for me even knowing one person when I was younger who grew up in care and was successful. I will always remember a story from Rick Mercer, who helped put this in perspective for me. During one of his shows, he talked about being largely secretive about being gay until he decided to come out publicly. He talked about his reasons for coming out publicly and said that it was important to him for gay youth to be able to identify with others like them who are successful and not feel they need to be ashamed of who they are.

What he said resonated with me so strongly, I began to apply this thinking to my own life. I decided that I was not going to apologize or feel embarrassed for how I grew up or over something I really had no control over. For a long time, I was reluctant to share my story because I was afraid that all those labels would be attached to me again and that I may be treated differently. Now, I hope that other youth in care can learn from my experiences, know that there are many others who have grown up in care who are successful and not let their pasts or others define who they are.

Dear Mom Poem

Dear Mom I know that life hasn't always been
What we had expected it to be
But I've always loved you very dearly
And you mean the whole world to me

Dear Mom our lives have always been a mess
I'm sure you know that, that's no contest
But I've always loved you very dearly
And you mean the whole world to me

Dear Mom I know we don't always see eye to eye
I know we don't so I'll continue to try
Cuz I've always loved you very dearly
And you mean the whole world to me

Dear Mom I know I'm not the perfect son
So I will always try to please
Cuz I love you very dearly
Since you were the one to give birth to me

I wrote this poem
Just for you

Love
Your Son,
Cody xoxo

A poem Cody wrote for his mom as a gift when he was 16.

Linda & Cody 2017

Know what day this is?

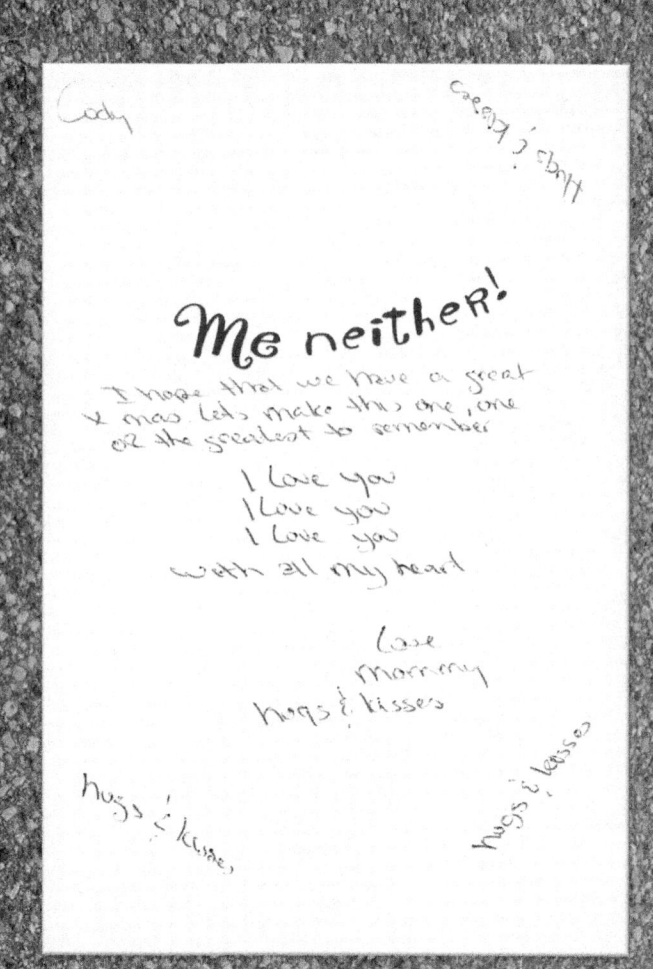

Me neither!

I hope that we have a great x-mas. Lets make this one, one of the greatest to remember

I love you
I love you
I love you
with all my heart

Love
Mommy
hugs & kisses

Cody

hugs & kisses

hugs & kisses

Cody, I am sending you this card to let you know that you are important to me even though I know it doesn't seem that way many of times. You came up with some good ideas tonight (about telling the staff so they could talk with _____) I am going to do that. You are a very smart boy and I know that you do try everything possible to help me. You are very thoughtful, caring, loving and I could just go on and on. You also bring so much joy to my life. I am so grateful to have you as my son.

I am going to try to get my life in a better order, please pray for me because a lot of times I forget to pray for myself.

I know I need to change a lot of things in my life. It is very scary.

Please continue to be the boy that you have turned out to be. I knew you had and have so much potential. I love you Cody. You guys (you and your brother) mean the world to me. You are the best. And keep continuing to work hard and stay on the path.

Monday, December 11, 2004

A card Linda gave Cody when he was living in a group home.

Linda

I moved to Red Deer on May 3rd. I was so sick. I slept for seven days.
When I woke up I realized that I didn't want to die because I had kids.

I was taken into care at the age of 12 and was done at 18. I started out in a group home and that led to many more. I was first placed in a regular group home, but then they switched over to a placement for kids with severe mental health issues and I started running away as I didn't feel I belonged there. I was trying to get my point across for them to get me out. I don't even know how many times I ran away. It's hard to nail down how many placements I had, because they would place me, and I would run away over and over again. Sometimes, I got into trouble which would land me in open custody placements.

School was tough for me because I was bouncing around so much. The first school that I went to passed me to grade 8 with the condition that I didn't go back to that school. They would register me in another school and I'd walk in the front and walk out the back. I did correspondence for a while. I just didn't have much interest in school. I know now that I struggled with Attention Deficit Hyperactivity Disorder (ADHD) and so it was extremely difficult for me. I would be the class clown and often felt that teachers just didn't want me around.

When I started running away at age 13, I started smoking lots of pot, drinking alcohol, and skipping school. That is also when I started hanging out with men in their twenties. The next thing I knew, I was living with them and, soon after, the one I considered my boyfriend pimped me out. I worked the streets for quite some time, but I got smart really fast. I wasn't giving any man my money and I was going to work for myself. That was empowering and I learned how to manipulate people for all kinds of things and just led this bad-ass life.

I got picked up by the authorities between ages 13 and 14. My parents were kind of involved in that for some reason. I remember listening to the guy that was the overnight judge talking on speaker phone to my parents and they're like, "No leave her there." After that, I started hanging out with criminals and committing crimes and returned to prostitution. When I was 15, I got picked up by the police and charged with seven charges because I had beaten up a trick who didn't want to pay me. I got 11 months in custody.

At this time, I had a boyfriend. He was in jail for armed robbery when I met him and I liked that blonde-haired, blue-eyed, tough-guy type. My child welfare worker had found out and she tried to keep us apart. She sent me out to Strathmore to live in an open custody facility but, of course, he and I found ways to keep in touch. I used to call that worker every day to tell her how much I hated her and then, about nine months in, I phoned her one day and told her how much I loved her. I wanted a different life and she was just so awesome. We planned for when I got out of jail and she supported me in every way. I got a placement, but it was terrible, and so she offered to have me live with her. I know her bosses tried to dissuade her, but she took me in anyway and I became part of her family.

When I was with her, I got a job and I started working in a clothing store and had really started to turn my life around. I was doing so well with my new family, until my boyfriend got out of jail. I was 17. We started living together and the heavy drug use started again. When I turned 18, I told him it had to stop because I wanted to have kids and so we both quit using and drinking. I went to a lot of counseling and we started a used car lot together, which was pretty successful. I got pregnant with our first son, Cody. While I wasn't perfect, I was changing a lot and my husband wasn't. I wanted him to get help and move forward, but he wouldn't, and we were dysfunctional. He was at the car lot all the time and I decided to go back to school and found out through upgrading that I was smart. I wanted to pursue a Social Work Diploma and was accepted and put on a waiting list. His behavior didn't change, and I remember distinctively thinking that my life is either going to stay like this or I'm going to get out now, so I left him. He died of a drug overdose less than three months later.

After that, my life started falling apart. School was out of the picture. I started drinking heavily and then I got into drugs. It was a really tough time. Even if my partner wasn't good for me, he was terrific with the kids and they were devasted – especially Cody, who was five at the time. He had already been diagnosed with ADHD and a few other things, and he really started to act out. I started getting help with the kids, because I wanted to be the best mom I could be and did not want to be like my parents were to me. Then I ran into an old friend at the grocery store, and she was looking good and wearing all brand names. She told me she was working in a "massage parlor" and so I started working there. The downward spiral did not take long to manifest in my life. I was used to a certain lifestyle because we had made good money at the car lot, and now I didn't know how I was going to put food in the kids' mouths. So, I resorted to my old line of work for a really long time. During this time, I started smoking crack and my life became very dark. It was a very bad situation for my kids.

I had gotten together with my eldest daughter's dad at this time. He was a client and we ended up living together and having our baby. He is probably the worst person I have ever met to this day. I was with him for four years and then I decided to leave and try to stay clean. My kids had been taken away a few times and then I got them back, but it was a huge struggle. You never plan to get high again, but the first big thing that happens, you do. You think it's just going to be one time, which in my case, led to four whole years. Cody was 12 by then and had gone through a lot with me and my addictions. It was a really sick situation. I tried to hide it, but I was in my room for hours on end getting high and I was working in the sex trade and it was so dysfunctional. Cody's anger started to build. I remember reaching out for help and they started sending somebody to my house, like three times a week, to help me with the boys, to get them to bed, and provide other supports. Then one day, Cody beat up his brother and his brother was laying on the floor, not moving. I got into a fight with him and he started running away from me, around the kitchen table, and I couldn't catch him. I told him, "When I catch you, I'm going to kill you." I felt terrible and I told child welfare that I needed some help because I felt like spanking him and if I started, I might not stop. They knew that I didn't believe in spanking and I still don't to this day, but they came and got him the next day but left my younger son with me. Cody was very hurt and angry, and he would talk to his younger brother and encourage him to misbehave (which he did), so he was taken away as well. Once that happened, my daughter's father refused to bring her back. At that point, I was heartbroken and went completely off the deep end.

I just numbed out. I was already into drugs heavily and got back into prostitution. To not feel that pain, I just stayed high all the time. My addiction was so bad that I didn't go to bed at night. I would pass out after many days of being awake because my body couldn't go anymore. I would have supervised visits with my kids and I would go to the bathroom and get high, then come back to finish my visits. I missed a lot of visits with all my kids completely and still cry about that sometimes, but that was the way I lived. I was over-the-top messed-up. I lost my house. I lost all of our personal belongings – my kid's pictures and videos of them with their dad. I feel so sorry about that, too. It's so sad to say that, as much as I loved my kids, I was just so messed up and so addicted to drugs that nothing else mattered but that next high. I loved them so much and I wished I could straighten out, and I tried so many times. I have been to almost every detox in Alberta (some of them multiple times) and I have been to treatment a total of four times. My turning point 12 years ago was when I was 118 pounds soaking-wet, my teeth were falling out, my bodily functions were leaving me, and I was schizophrenic, so I didn't know if I could ever carry on a conversation with anybody, even if I got clean. And, I knew I was dying.

My now husband and I were in addiction together and we would talk about getting clean. I would say that I was going to go to church. He would say I could go to church, but he would rather go for a motorcycle ride. We went to detox together, but I couldn't stay. I left him there, but I kept talking to him and then he went to Henwood Treatment Centre. I even went to see him there just totally messed-up. He would phone me and I remember thinking he was coming through the ceiling while we were talking. When he called me to tell me he was moving to Red Deer, I thought I either have to let this guy go because he's on the path to being straight or I have to get straight and be with him. He registered in a program there on April 7th, and I came to Red Deer on May 3rd. I was so sick. I went to detox and slept for seven days and, when I woke up, I realized I didn't want to die. I knew I didn't want to die because I had kids. While in recovery, my husband came across an old friend that he failed grade one with, who was going to church, and then they went together. I wanted to go, so we started going together and that's where we still go to church today. I connected with the pastor and he helped me get a place. It was a bad environment for me, as one of the guys living there smoked crack and was always inviting hookers up, so I ended up getting my own apartment to get away from all those triggers. I kept going to church and I just gave everything over to God and said, "Here I am - help me. I'm a broken mess." And he did. My husband and I were reminiscing not too long ago and were laughing about getting our first library cards when we got straight. We were skipping down the road because we were trusted with a library card 12 years ago and look at us today. I was telling my friend how I got started in recovery, and that I can't believe I'm a foster parent now. My friend proceeds to say that she doesn't leave her kids with very many people and I am one person that she does. I like to say it all started with a library card and I worked my way up.

I started intense therapy in 2008 and continued until 2012. Now, I go when I need to. I came in really broken and got as much help as I could and got better. I did a lot of work on myself and just started changing with God's help. Not too long ago, we were sitting in our foster parent training program and they were teaching us about kids in care and it hit me that I'm a miracle! I was blown away. A lot of people don't come out of the experience that I had, positively.

I have been incredibly lucky to repair my relationship with Cody. It has not been an easy road, as he was angry at me for many years and I don't blame him. He was really hurt and so we couldn't even talk about me being forgiven. It was very intense, and it was a lot of hard work. He was a teenager going into his twenties and he had a lot of harsh things to say to me, which were fully understandable. He was expressing himself and I had to accept that. He was really argumentative and would love to argue with me, but it was about being willing to listen to him and, sometimes, it was really hard. Excruciating, really. But we made it through all of that. A lot of times now, we just agree to disagree, and we try to respect one another. Cody and I are a lot alike in that we are up front and tell it like it is. Because I had many boyfriends andled the lifestyle that I did, Cody had a hard time accepting my husband, but he has always been a really thoughtful person and, for the past few years now, he and my husband have a wonderful relationship. We got married this summer and Cody was our officiant, so it doesn't get better than that. We have come a long, long ways. Relationships are ongoing work and I am always trying to do better. I have forgiven myself and I know whatever choices I make today affect tomorrow. If I make good choices, they will have a ripple effect. I've always been a person that I knew was going to rise above. Whenever I had my boys and was doing well, people used to say to me, "Wow, you came from that upbringing and look at you, now."

If I hadn't gone into care, I think my life could have been far worse. I come from a long line of intergenerational trauma. My mother was taken into care as an older teen because her mother had serious mental illnesses and her father was a very abusive alcoholic who beat my grandmother all the time. Her younger siblings went into foster care and she was placed with someone in the community because, at that time, she was too old to be under government care. So, we have three generations of history with trauma, family violence, family dysfunction, and child welfare.

I was super excited to leave my house. My mom and stepdad were really abusive. They didn't talk to me for a long time after I was taken into care and, to this day, my mom has never told me that she loves me and will still say that it was my fault that I got taken away. I guess maybe she has to deny the truth because she can't face it. My real dad had nothing to do with me and I didn't meet him until I was 14. My stepdad told me he loved me on his deathbed this year and one other time on the phone – the first time I went to treatment. It almost seemed like it was accidental. When I entered care, I was a very vulnerable young girl, desperately wanting to be loved and, because I didn't have that from my family, it is not surprising that I went down the road I did.

At one point, I wanted nothing to do with my parents. Then I had the boys and I kind of wanted my kids to know their grandparents, but I didn't trust them and had to set clear boundaries. From the very beginning, I informed them that they could never hit my kids. That was hard because my parents believed that everybody deserves a smack, a spanking, or whipping. I tried their kind of discipline for two weeks and it was a big mistake. I went back to my own beliefs and Cody was the only child who ever got spanked. Maybe I just had to prove it to myself that they were wrong. I was spanked by them all the time and it was wrong.

The most impactful memories I have from care are being pimped out by my boyfriend at the age of 13. Being put on the streets really wrecked me. I was so young and didn't know any better at the time. It was so traumatizing. The other time of my life in care that I will never forget was being taken in by my caseworker. She was amazing and it was life changing. She truly cared for me and accepted me for who I was. She was the most significant person for me growing up in care. She just really loved me unconditionally no matter what I did. I knew she was that one person they talk about – that one person who makes the difference. Unfortunately, she didn't know I was using and cosigned a car loan for me and, because of my addiction, I wasn't making the payments. It got repossessed and went against her credit, so she was really mad at me and we don't talk as a result. I was in the wrong and will always feel bad about that. She was a big part of my life and helped me in so many ways. She helped me write my application when I decided to go into the social work program, wanted me to move to Fort McMurray after my first husband died, she would help me take care of the kids and so much more. Those kinds of workers are rare.

Where I am at now is pretty amazing. I am married to my wonderful man and we have a 10 year old daughter and I am a proud foster parent. I volunteer at the Pregnancy Care Centre. I also volunteer on the board of the Dream Center in Red Deer, which is a faith-based addictions treatment facility being built right now by our church. A building became available and the church bought it. The pastor said that they bought it, but had no idea what they were going to do with it. I clearly heard God say to me that the building is supposed to be a Dream Center and, when I told the pastor and his wife, they felt the same thing and here we are. It's a really big miracle story. To think that was me in recovery 12 years ago, and now I am doing this! So, when that dream was getting started, I pulled up to a red light after dropping my daughter off at school and I clearly heard God tell me that I needed to be a foster parent. Before the light turned green, I knew I had to do it. I talked to my husband and he was so on board, he didn't even hesitate. I am 46 now and life is really good, but it still has its challenges. Cody is doing really well, but my younger son is heavily into his addictions and I am not sure where he is. He doesn't talk to any of us. My 18-year-old daughter and I don't have a very strong relationship either, and I could stay stuck there or realize I have no control over this. I love my kids and I reach out to them and let them know I'm here. I can't make the decision for them, so I just pray. You must live your best life and then, if they want to join you it can be great. The more time we all get to spend together, the better.

Life isn't a basket full of roses, but it's where you choose to go that can make it better, I take care of me, look after my mental health and live my best life. I know there's a plan for every person and we don't know what it is, so we just have to do our best and have faith.

When I was completing high school, I was doing so whilst in an independent living situation. I would attend the parent teacher interviews alone. This was a very belittling situation, as I was the only youth there without adult support. The excuse I would get from my legal guardians or caseworkers was that I was not their responsibility outside of office hours. This comment would continue to give me a complex about my own self-worth for years to come. One particular caseworker found it an easy and necessary decision to support me after hours at my parent teacher interviews. This experience really changed the way I felt about caseworkers and allowed me to feel semi-normal at these events. I would tell my peers that she was my mom. This caseworker impacted my life because she treated me with care and compassion and made me feel loved. She was committed and never made me feel like a burden. I needed support and she was able and willing to provide what I had longed for. This person changed my life in so many ways and I aspire to be like her in my future endeavours as a social worker.

Winnie

What people just don't get about homeless youth in Canada

By Anne Theriault, April 23, 2020   LOCAL LOVE

Street kids are not just rebels without a cause—and they want (and need) your help.

(To read full article please click on headline or type headline into your search bar.)

Postcard courtesy of The Adoption Council of Canada—Edmonton Youth Speak Out

I haven't done drugs for three years; I quit when I got pregnant. I didn't abuse any substances when I was pregnant because I wasn't going to mess with my daughter's life just because I wanted a 50-minute high. It's really sad when that happens to a baby. I have a baby brother who's three and I see the effects of my mom's drug use in him all the time. It's a lifelong struggle for those kids.

Shay

Mike

Maybe nobody knows how to answer the questions that they have, but you need to try and answer it the best way you can without judgment or dismissing them entirely. It's important that kids in care be treated like they would treat a normal kid, because that's what we are.

I went into care when I was 12. I only had one placement because I went to live with my auntie and her son. We lived in Edmonton until I finished grade 5, and then we moved to Sherwood Park. I went to grade 6, Junior High, and then graduated from Salisbury High School there. I also started working part-time jobs after school and on weekends from the age of 14 and gained a lot of good experience. I would have to say that my experience in care was pretty positive overall because I only lived in one place where I knew the people really cared about me.

I had a few workers before we moved to Sherwood Park and then I had a really good worker who stayed with me from around age 12 until I turned 19 or 20. I have my caseworker and my auntie to thank for how good my life turned out and for why I have good values and know my priorities. They were always there for me, and my caseworker also helped my auntie and I have better communication when I was in my teen years. My worker really took the time to find out how I was doing and always wanted to know what I needed. I want to be a social worker because of her; I want to do that for someone else. If I can change someone's life for the better, like she did for me, that's what I want. I feel it's important give back. I like the saying about leaving the world a better place than how you found it.

Whether you're a foster kid or not, you need lifelong connections. You need a support system that is always there. If you fall on hard times or you're having personal doubts or personal problems, you have someone you can talk to that has either experienced it or is just there to listen. That is what I call family – whether that be blood-related or not. I have a few people that I'm blood-related to that I would call family, but there are so many people that aren't blood that care about me. For example, my close friends' parents treat me like family. I made some good friends in high school that I still have to this day, that I now refer to as my family, since they kind of informally adopted me.

I have a relationship with my biological family, and it's important to me to keep in touch with my mom, dad, and sister. I have two nieces and a nephew between the ages of 18 months and nine years, and they are really important to me. Before I was taken into care, I wouldn't necessarily say I felt unsafe, but there were times when it was 'iffy.'

I never really wanted to be formally adopted, but I think workers should try to find permanent or adoptive homes for older children. Just because they're older does not mean that they don't have the same needs. They are still kids. You age out of care at 18 and when I think of myself at 18, I was still pretty much a kid.

My culture isn't a huge part of my life. I am somewhat distant from my culture a lot of the time, but it wasn't because of my placement. My auntie would ask me if I wanted to learn about my band or go to find out more about my culture, but I never really gave it much thought. To a certain degree, it's important because you should know where you come from, but it was just never a big priority for me.

I would have to say that my experience in care was overall positive. The most impactful experiences I had during that time were having the same caseworker for many years and graduating from high school. I think being in care impacted me for the better because I have had a lot of opportunities that I might not have had, otherwise. Right now, I am receiving the Advancing Futures Bursary to continue my education, and that is very beneficial. When I am done university prep, I will be going to Grant MacEwan University to get my Social Work Diploma and then see where I want to go from there. I may go on to get my degree.

What I want people to know about kids in care is that we are all human and everyone deserves to be treated as such. I think anybody who meets any kid in care needs to understand that they need to have an open mind and a high level of understanding. Every kid is different. They need to listen and be patient, because the kid may not be where they want to be at the moment. Nobody wants to open up to someone who already has a preconceived notion. Maybe nobody knows how to answer the questions that they have, but you need to try and answer it the best way you can without judgment or dismissing them entirely. It's important that kids in care be treated like they would treat a normal kid, because that's what we are.

What I would change about the child welfare system is some of the rules. I guess there are rules put in place because there needs to be but, for example, when I was younger, they told my mom not to be emotional when we would visit, which is a pretty tall order. I think it can hurt the process of having a kid integrate into a different life.

There is still a lot of emotion and I think going into therapy, where it can be controlled and kind of directed to a more positive outcome rather than just a lot of grief and sadness, would be a better way.

I would also probably change the process of people becoming child welfare workers. I think there needs to be a bit more extensive look at their past. At the university level, I think an earlier practicum would help or maybe shadowing a worker. It seems that there are a lot of caseworkers that are just in it for a paycheque which is terrible. I think everybody should have a career that they're passionate about. Maybe if more people would do that and take up appropriate professions, more positive change could happen.

I hope to have my own family one day. At that time, I hope to be a well experienced social worker, and maybe even be someone higher up, where I can affect some real change. I might be lucky enough to be in a position to change things at the University faculty level. Right now, I can influence change through the Youth Speak Out Edmonton group. I found it odd one time, when I was speaking on a Youth Speak Out panel, I told the audience that I had a positive upbringing and that being in care was beneficial and that I wanted to be a social worker to keep the positive circle going. Everyone started clapping and I was like: Wow! It was just kind of a moment of clarity that I can be the change I want to see in the world. The only way it is going to happen is if I make it happen.

My name is Jesse and I have Fetal Alcohol Spectrum Disorder, Post Traumatic Stress Disorder, Major Depressive Disorder, Severe Conduct Disorder, Schizoid Personality Disorder, Authority Defiance Disorder, Generalized Anxiety Disorder, Schizophrenia and other stuff.

I have had 46 placements and hundreds of workers. I have contemplated suicide hundreds of times and have hundreds of scars from self harm on my arms, legs, stomach and face. I am what they call a complex case. In the past I was called a hopeless case, but I am not anymore.

I play guitar and sing and have a mumble-punk band called *Jesse Jams & The Flams*. We play and record all original songs. Last year, *Trevor Anderson Films* made a documentary about me called <u>JESSE JAMS</u> that has been shown at film festivals around the world and has won awards. I have a nice girlfriend and my bandmates are true friends that stand by me in my dark times and now I live in my own apartment in a great community. I still struggle with my mental health but I am doing better than I used to. I think the big reason I am so successful is that I don't abuse drugs or alcohol, and a couple of years ago, I started to believe in myself. I hope you can believe in yourself, too. Good things can happen.

Education key to success for youth in foster care

By LAURIE MONSEBRAATEN Social Justice Reporter   TORONTO STAR   OCTOBER 3, 2018

Jane Kovarikova knows exactly when her troubled life in foster care took a turn for the better. "A friend studying at community college let me have a try at one of his assignments — and to my surprise, I received a solid grade," she said.

"That moment sparked the confidence I needed" to apply to post-secondary education, said Kovarikova, 34, who left foster care after 10 years at age 16 and dropped out of high school. But she eventually went on to earn a Master's degree at the London School of Economics and is currently a doctoral candidate at Western University.

(To read the full article please click on the headline or type headline into search bar.)

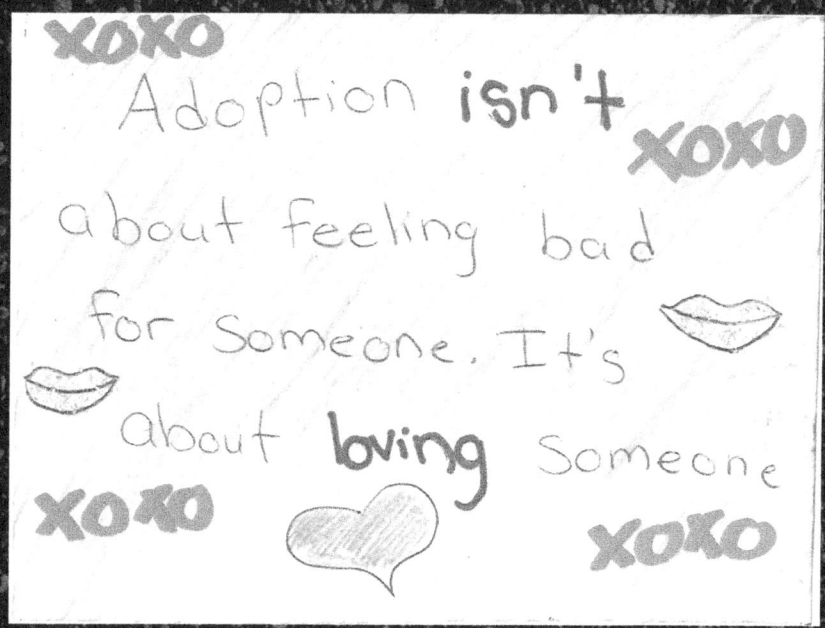

Postcard courtesy of The Adoption Council of Canada—Edmonton Youth Speak Out

I attended 12 elementary schools. I went to three different schools for Grade 3. That is when my twin brother and I got separated. I went to two schools for junior and then I moved to a group home for the summer and a couple months in the fall. I went to Ross Shepard High School and then I moved back home and then I finished high school at J. Percy Page. The impact of going to so many schools is that there is no stability. I had no friends. I was bullied a lot, especially when the teacher would tell the class that I was in foster care and then I'd be called an orphan. I'm sure it was an accident on her part, but you get a lot of dirty looks from other kids after that.

Kaylen

Shay

I have had a lot of workers. A lot of them would tell me that I was a star and that I was going to do amazing things. No matter how bad I was doing, No matter how many times I was getting arrested—some would say that I was still shining, That's something that kind of stuck with me.

I advocated for myself to come into care around the age of 12. No one advocated for me. I called this amazing youth worker in Edmonton and he gave me the steps and told me what to do. I did all that, but six or seven months later, I was still not in care, so I was sleeping on couches everywhere at the age of 13. I was basically homeless because I was not going back to the place that ruined me in the first place. It was not safe there. My parents were separated. My dad would get so drunk that he would just sit there and tell me that he wanted to kill himself and my mom was so abusive. She would hit me so hard I'd have bruises on my face so I wouldn't go to school. I told workers what was going on inside my home, but no one took me out because my mom was a functioning addict at the time. I was raising my brothers and I would try to tell the authorities that, but they just weren't listening.

I think it took over a year from the time I advocated for myself to come into care. I was 14 when I was actually apprehended. So, from around age 14 to 18, I lived in about 25 different places – not just group homes, but also couch surfing and correctional facilities. I was charged with armed robbery at the age of 13 and, after that, I got numerous assault charges. I was never in a foster home, but I had a kinship placement. I was in group homes and, a lot of times, I was just kind of allowed to be homeless and sleep at friend's places. I lived with my boyfriend off and on from the age of 13. That relationship was terrible and so toxic. It was so abusive but I didn't know any better, so I just stayed or would break up and then go back. I stayed at the Youth Emergency Shelter sometimes, too.

I didn't know how hard it was to get a Temporary Guardianship Order (TGO) so I was angry. I would go inside my caseworker's office and beg to be taken out of my home. I would tell them that I was slowly dying because I had to steal to get food and I'm getting arrested. I ended up getting a TGO when I was 14. I advocated for my youngest brother to come into care with me because he was like six or seven months at that time, and I was raising him. He came into this kinship placement with me, but there was active addiction in that home as well. The mom was amazing, but the boyfriend was a serious alcoholic, and my brother and I were kind of stuck there. I would voice my concerns to the family support worker, who just wanted to hear the good because I would tell her about it and she would just start telling me about some other kid who had it worse than me and I was like, OK, but I am trying to tell you about my situation right now. Finally, they figured out what was going on and I signed a SFAA (Supports and Financial Assistance Agreement). I want people to know that SFAAs are an absolute lifesaver for youth in care. I don't know where I would be if I hadn't had that support.

We got a small, one-bedroom basement suite and my dad slept in the living room. There continued to be a lot of emotional and physical abuse by my boyfriend, and it got worse. He ended up wrecking the whole bedroom. He destroyed the wardrobe we had, ripped my daughter's crib part, smashed our bed to pieces, and then he was gone. He was so difficult to deal with. He would just break little things or he would smash something my grandma gave me right in front of my face. Then he would disappear for days. He would take my bank card and my phone and leave me there for weeks at a time by myself with my newborn child.

Finally, there was a situation where he was at his sister's house and I went to see him, and he ended up beating me very badly. He locked my daughter inside the house and started taking videos of me being crazy outside because I wasn't leaving without her. Then, he knocked me out and I fell. When I came to, I got in through an open door, got my daughter and got on the bus. My face was all bruised up and my nose was bleeding. My daughter was only three or four months old at the time. The bus ended up getting pulled over by the police and I told them everything, including my boyfriend's name. That's when I decided I wasn't going to see him anymore. Of course, he called me crying and trying to apologize and threatening to kill himself, but I was at a point where I was just done. He was risking my child and everything to do with me. I told him that he wasn't what came first in my life now. My daughter was the most important person to me.

I proved to everyone that I wasn't going back to him and I just started moving forward from there, but at first, I went through a dark time when I was partying alot. I never had a proper mom, so I had never learned how to respect my body and myself and know that not everyone deserves me. I didn't treat it as a temple, like I should have.

I gave it to whoever gave me a look. This phase of my life led me to being raped numerous times, which was hard to come to terms with. I had a hard time sorting out my feelings and would think that maybe it was my fault, but I know now that it's not. The last time it happened, I was given alcohol shots until I passed out and then I was raped. The guy went around after and was laughing and telling everyone. I did talk to the police and they said there's no point of even trying, because there's no proof. It's all about evidence, sadly. I've heard stories that he has raped other girls and women since then, so I wish he could be stopped.

After that, I partied a bit more, but then I got my job. I started working at Starbucks and I started to turn my life around. I moved again. I stopped having people coming over to my house. I haven't done drugs for three years; I quit when I got pregnant. I didn't abuse any substances when I was pregnant because I wasn't going to mess with my daughter's life just because I wanted a 50-minute high. It's really sad when that happens to a baby. I have a baby brother who's three and I see the effects of my mom's drug use in him all the time. It's a lifelong struggle for those kids.

I have a lot of supports for my daughter, but I don't really have a lot of supports for myself. My dad got sober after I had her and he's doing better. He's a good grandpa, but we don't have that good father-daughter relationship yet. My brother and his girlfriend have been together 13 years and they don't have any kids yet, so they're all over my baby. It's like everyone is there for my baby, and that's so good, but then when it comes to me, who's there? I went through postpartum depression and I didn't take care of myself at all and there was no one to help me. Also, because of my life experience, I know how not to raise a child, but no one teaches you how to raise a child. My daughter is Métis, so I want to help change a lot of perceptions about Aboriginal people. I want to learn a lot about Métis culture, so my daughter doesn't just know the stereotypes. I want her to be proud of who she is.

I don't have a therapist right now, but I had a therapist while I was still on probation because I was arrested a lot of times before my pregnancy. I was on about three different probation orders. I was also on house arrest and then two different probation orders. My therapist was so amazing. I absolutely loved her, but she ended up shattering her leg and had to go on leave for several surgeries. She is the one counsellor that I've actually liked, and I have to try to find a new one, but they are all so busy.

Special occasions can be tough in care. I was in the TSIL placement on my 17th birthday. There were just a few people from the group home there, but it was really kind of sad because I didn't really have any friends there. My birthday is December 19th, so Christmas came, and I was pregnant. There was only me and one staff member, so there was no dinner. She drove me around to try to find food, but everything was closed.

Another impactful moment was when I met this one police officer who came to a domestic dispute call involving me and my mom. She called the cops on me because I started hitting her back. A policeman saw what was going on and I told him that she'd been doing this to me my whole life. He told me that his dad was a severe alcoholic who would come home and you're going to move next. I kept all my stuff packed up. I was always ready. Finally, in my TSIL placement, they forced me to unpack.

The scariest part of being in care is not knowing when you are going to move next. I kept all my stuff packed up. I was always ready. Finally, in my TSIL placement, they forced me to unpack. I would say my experience in care impacted me for the better and the worse. There are a lot of things that I am traumatized by from care and living with my parents was not ideal. I just wish I had left them sooner. My mom would abuse me physically and say she wished she would have got an abortion and things like that stay with me. I look at my daughter and I don't know how anyone could ever say that to a child. I don't want my daughter to go through what I went through. I brought her into this world, and she is not going to have to go into care. While in care, I was thankful to meet a lot of people that were going through the same thing as I was. At the same time, it wasn't a good thing, because I got into gangs and I was doing a lot of drugs. We would compare jail stories and things like that. Trauma attracts drama, right? People that have been in care seem to have the most personality. Just like the ones who have been to jail. Kids that have been in care long-term and have been bounced all over the place crack the most jokes and have that sense of humour.

I have had a lot of workers. I just stopped counting at around 25. A lot of them would tell me that I was a star and that I was going to do amazing things no matter how bad I was doing, no matter how many times I was getting arrested, some would say that I was still shining. That's something that kind of stuck with me. I've had child welfare workers and youth workers come to me and talk to me about their other kids because they don't really know what to do to get the kid to work with them. Those kinds of things really stuck with me and I felt like I was doing well. I must have been because they were coming to me.

I have an amazing youth worker; I absolutely love her. She's transitioning from being a youth worker into a family support worker, but she wanted to hang on to my youth file. It's important that workers stick with us long term, because no one else has stuck with us. I had an older brother that could have taken me, but he didn't. I had my parents that could have gotten sober for me, but they didn't. I have had so many people in and out of my life, which is why I can't holda friendship. It's hard for me to even make an emotional attachment, especially after my experience with my former boyfriend. I've even struggled trying to make an attachment to my daughter, because I feel like everything is temporary. We need to have a good worker who is with us long term and who is there when we trip up. I need someone who can advocate for me, so I don't always exhaust myself trying to get what I deserve on my own.

A good child welfare worker or youth worker is someone with empathy. Someone who is not afraid to bend the rules. Someone who will go over and above. Someone who doesn't only have textbook knowledge. And, if you don't like your job and you're going home angry at the end of the day and you're not treating your kids the way you should, don't be afraid to leave. Just quit and do something else. If you don't feel like you have a connection with a certain kid, that doesn't mean you're a bad worker. Just try to find someone who is more compatible with that kid, otherwise you're not going to get anywhere and it doesn't help the kid. In fact, It can make things worse and the kid may not want to trust anyone after you. It can make them think, "I'm impossible to work with or nobody wants to work with me."

Family is important, but I was sat down in a room full of people with my parents sitting there saying they would not change for me. They said, "Take her. I don't care." That really messes a kid up. Eventually, I got to where I didn't show emotion. I showed anger – my secondary feeling. That's how you show your pain because you don't want to seem weak. It's self-preservation. You don't want other people to see your vulnerabilities because then, they can really hurt you. Now, I have a relationship with my dad because he quit drinking a couple of years ago when my daughter was born, but I have nothing to do with my mom. She's addicted to heroin, crack, methamphetamines – anything she can get her hands on, pretty much. I witnessed her do it when I was younger. When I was 15, she tried to run me over with her car because she thought I stole her drugs. So, I have completely cut her off. She has seen my daughter once. My dad still talks to her all the time and I try to explain to him that I don't want to know what she is doing. This way, when she dies from an overdose, because she's died numerous times and been brought back, that's my way of detaching myself. That way I don't have to be sad when she dies.

What I want people to know about kids in care is that they have been through a lot. They've been through more than most people at age 50, 60, 70, or even 80. I can't speak for everyone, but from a young age, most of us have already been betrayed by the very people that were supposed to be there for us and love us forever. Most of us are experiencing intergenerational trauma, which is so incredibly hard to break. We deal with so much on a daily basis, and to not fall into the intergenerational trauma cycle is really difficult every single day. I just want people to know that we're just hurt, and anger is a secondary emotion. We mask everything else because we've been hurt so many times. We will try to overpower you, because that's who we are. We have our pride, which is really high because we've been broken so many times. You can't tell us you know how it feels if you don't.

If I could change the child welfare system, I would change the amount of funding that's put into it and I would put good counsellors in every single group home consistently five days a week. I would change the way that kids are brought into care. I would like counsellors on deck, ready to help these kids deal with the trauma they went through in order to get there.

There are stereotypes that every kid that's in care is bad – that they're going to end up like their parents. That their parents couldn't handle them because they were bad kids. That we weren't wanted at all. That we shouldn't be allowed to play with other kids. There's a lot of discrimination within school system. They don't understand why you're missing school and get mad at you. They give you suspensions. They clean you out in front of the whole class and do all these things, when they don't realize there's a reason you're missing. I did not know what was going on in school. I didn't know what I was doing. I felt stupid and I wanted to leave, so I jut wouldn't go. When I went back to the school in the *Kids in The Hall* program, I got 80% and above. I needed the right guidance and the school had to know my disorders and my learning style to help me. I needed people to adjust to the way I learned best.

Fortunately, I am a strong advocate for myself and I'm also a strong advocate for my younger brother. I'm at every one of my brother's meetings with his workers and every one of his court dates. I was always his advocate. I want to take my brother into my custody; I want to adopt him, but not yet. Maybe when he is five. I'm just not able to right now. I want to start a career, but a career that I will be happy in. I'm going to take open studies at Grant MacEwan University and figure it out. I really want to use what I've been through to make a difference in the world. I want my story to be heard everywhere and the stories of all the other beautiful people who have been through the same things because there are so many of us.

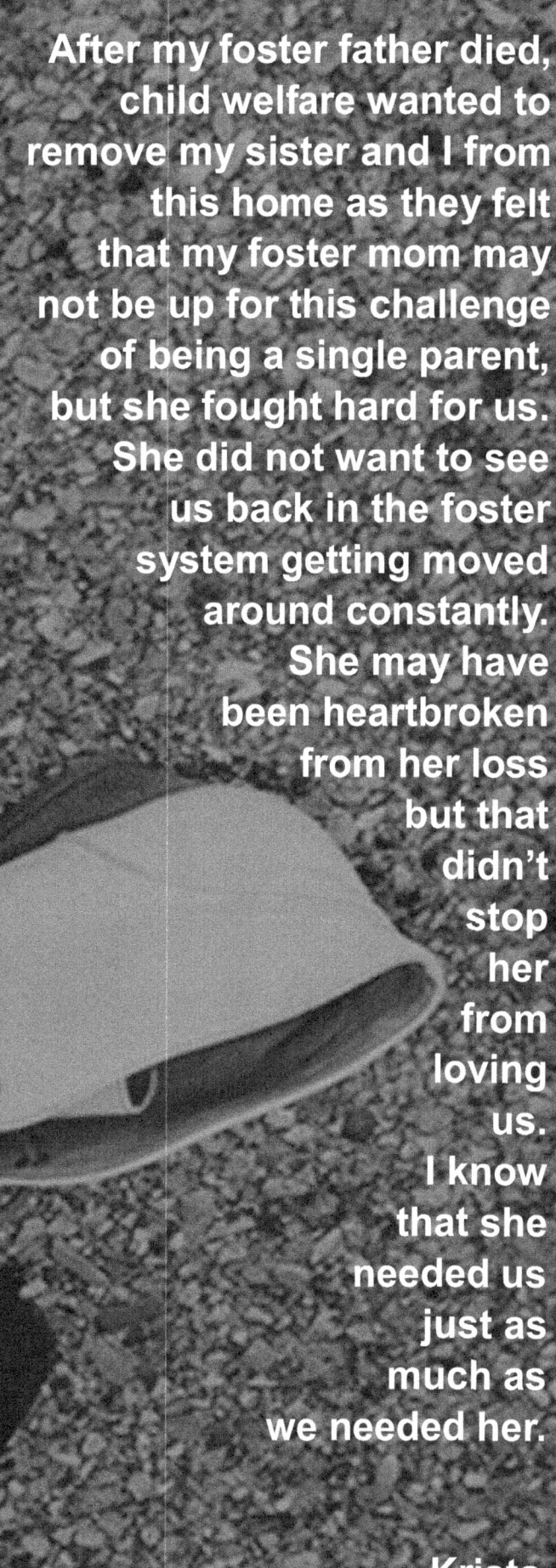

After my foster father died, child welfare wanted to remove my sister and I from this home as they felt that my foster mom may not be up for this challenge of being a single parent, but she fought hard for us. She did not want to see us back in the foster system getting moved around constantly. She may have been heartbroken from her loss but that didn't stop her from loving us. I know that she needed us just as much as we needed her.

Krista

Famous Former Foster/Adopted Kids

FOSTER FOCUS MAGAZINE   Chris Chmielewski, Founder/Editor

Athletes. Movie Stars. Movie Producers. DJs. Musicians. Writers. Comedians. Composers. Entrepreneurs. Entertainers. Philosophers. Inventors. Media Moguls. Activists. Politicians. Fashion Designers. Inspirational Speakers. Philanthropists. Leaders. Heroes.

To read the full article please click on headline or type headline into your search bar.

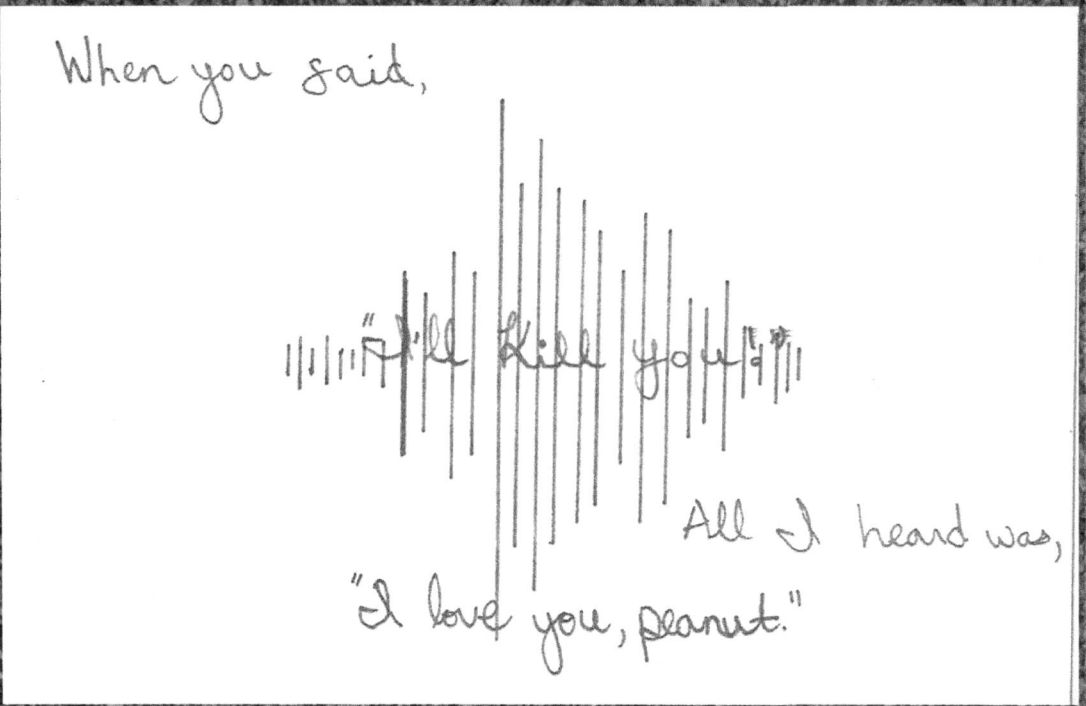

When you said, "I'll kill you!" All I heard was, "I love you, peanut."

Postcard courtesy of the Adoption Council of Canada—Youth Speak Out Edmonton

We must teach our generation and those who will come after us that it is okay to feel shame, guilt, depression, any of those terrible feelings that we try to avoid, but we must feel it and deal with it. We cannot let those awful things consume us. This only preserves the timeline of the intergenerational trauma we have all inherited. We must feel, accept, learn, and change, and we must do so with love and kindness for ourselves. Hurt people will hurt people; it is time to change.

Cassie

Damon

You have to stand for something ... says the guy in a wheelchair. But seriously,
if you stand for something, your influence and impact on others lives on.

I am 22 years old. I came into care when I was 11. Before I was apprehended, I was living with my mother, her boyfriend and my three older sisters. Life became very chaotic and unpredictable when I was around six years old, which coincided with when my father went to jail. When the support of my father was not there, things for my family spiraled out of control, and became very unsafe. I recognize now the impact my father's presence in the home and family had on my safety and stability. I remember really missing my father when he left.

While residing with my mom we were constantly moving due to noise complaints or being evicted due to unpaid bills or late night parties. I can recall times as a child where drinking and drug use was a frequent occurrence surrounding my siblings and I. There would be fighting and police coming to the home at all hours. My mom became more overwhelmed with the responsibilities of caring for my siblings and me, and lacked her own stability to navigate. It was tough for my sisters and me as we learned from a young age to survive as a unit, and we were all in this together. My sister's who are close to my age did their best to take care of me during periods of time when my mom would disappear. I can recall on several occasions we needed to steal food and groceries, as we had no food at home to eat. We all had our roles as kids in our family whether it was caring for me, or meeting our needs for survival.

Just prior to my apprehension, my home environment had really deteriorated. I had recently been released from the hospital from one of my eight surgeries related to my disability. My mom's boyfriend was living with us at the time and he was unpredictable as he was consumed by his addictions to drugs and alcohol; when he was under the influence, he would become physically abusive towards her. I can recall on one occasion that he threw a kitchen knife at my mother; this did not shock me as I had grown up with violence all around me. I can recognize now that my reality and what I thought was normal was very skewed. Following this incident, I tried to comfort my mom's boyfriend so that he would calm down and the fighting would stop. In retrospect, I can think of hundreds of times where I was the one who tried to calm and comfort the adults around me in order to re-balance the chaos and this was seen as my role in our family.

I remember one particularly bad incident of domestic violence where my mom's boyfriend had beaten her up in front of me which escalated to the point he threw her out of our home. Following this fight, my mom did not return for two days and I was left in the care of her boyfriend. This was a difficult few days as I was very angry with him for what he had done to my mom however, I needed to rely on him for my daily needs and survival. I cried when my mom finally returned and although I could see the injuries to her face, I was glad she was safe and alive.

The day I was apprehended the police knocked down the door (forced entry to our home), put me in the police car, and brought me to a group home. The scariest part about coming into care was that no one explained to me what was happening and why I was apprehended from my mother. I remember only having one meal that day, which was a peanut butter and jam sandwich all the while I kept wondering, 'Who are these people and where are my mom, dad, and sisters? Did they leave me again?'

I have lived in about eight different placements; six foster/group care placements were short term and temporary in nature. I resided in one foster home for almost a year and a group home where I resided for 5 years. I have been with my current family for almost three years. The lack of stability has affected me in many ways and my education has suffered greatly as I attended seven or eight schools. Through moving to new placements, schools, and communities, I lost my attachment to everyone because I was never able to settle. I know the frequent moves and people in and out of my life has caused me struggles in knowing how to connect and how to build and maintaining relationships. I am trying to learn these skills as an adult because unfortunately I did not learn this as a child in the care of my parents or in foster/group care. Over time I got used to everyone leaving and the struggles I had in making emotional connections impacted my self-esteem. It was hard to come to terms with the reality that my mother left me, and there were times in my life that everyone has left me, these experiences left me feeling emotionally numb. If I ever felt sad about losing connections with someone or someone hurt me, emotionally I would remind myself "my mother left me and I survived, I can survive this too".

While I was in care, I was separated from my sisters. I think we were separated due to the level of care I needed for my disability. I know this was further compounded by the high-level responsibility my sister's had grown up with, as they had been my primary caregivers. I know the responsibility of caring for me was a lot for them because we are all close in age. I had supervised access with my mom and siblings for the first few years I was in care however as I became older and under permanent care, contact with my family decreased. I had very limited interactions with my extended family for the five years I was in the last group home.

As a child and young adult, I lacked the natural supports of friends and family. This left me reliant on paid staff and left me feeling alone and isolated. However, this was a feeling I had grown used to and it actually felt familiar. I have realized that the hardest part for me in relationships with others is to be vulnerable in an emotional state. I recognize this is hard for me because of my childhood experiences and due to the fact that I am already so vulnerable in a physical manner. My inability to trust people has been part of the reason that I built up a wall, turned my feelings off and became numb to what was happening around me. This is how I survived my experiences. In my current family, it was hard for me to trust and believe in my auntie, Theresa, whom I live with now. It has taken time to open up and I know that even three years later I am still learning how to be part of a family as this has not been natural for me.

I used to live in a group home for five years with other residents who were both physically and cognitively impacted by their disabilities and unable to talk. Due to the dynamics of this group home, I was isolated in my room a lot, just playing video games, watching TV, and reading comic books. One positive of this time in my life was it allowed for a lot of time for me to focus on my love of writing poetry, drawing and researching comedy to improve my techniques. The group home staff did a good job at caring for my physical needs however my emotional needs were lacking. I know I was shameful about living in a group home so I never had friends over and my family was not eager to see me in this state either so I began keeping people away. I think my family struggled to see me in a group home as this made them feel like they had failed me and there was a lack of activities to do there.

Unfortunately, while in care I was not taken out of my wheelchair very much, so I lost some of the mobility I had while residing with my mom. Prior to coming into care, I would crawl and roll around the house and was able to bear weight with support for short periods. After coming into care, I spent increased periods of time in my wheelchair and was not taken out of my chair to be allowed to have time on the floor. As I reflect on this time, I know my physical decline was compounded because I was struggling emotionally and I lacked the motivation and the desire to retain these skills.

While residing in the group home I was called a 'product' twice in seven years by staff who cared for me. This comment left me thinking, 'What if I am just a product?' As in, I'm being passed around through the child welfare system and I'm just a means of making a paycheque, where staff clock in and out of my life, and they don't want me to be damaged or else they're in trouble. When you are residing in a group home, there will always be another staff member; there will always be another person for the staff to look after. I believe the group home model is like a circle, which will continue forever.

I had four or five caseworkers, but I did not really get to know them because they always seemed to be on vacation or have other files needing their attention as opposed to mine. Including all the group home staff, caseworkers, aides at school, in home support workers and foster parents, I think I have had around 70 workers and people who cared for me, a lot of them coming and going, quitting and starting up. Because of that, I never felt the need to stay in an emotional connection or relationship with caregivers and staff because they're either going to quit, or not stick around because my disability care needs were too high and the staff are underpaid for the care they have to provide. I would tell myself not to let them get close as they're going to go away, so why should I get attached, right? Why should I invest emotional connection with them if they are going leave at the end?

My first foster home placement was with a Christian woman. For my 12th birthday, she took me to Red Robin and got everyone to sing. She tried her best to care for me. The demands of caring for me due to my disability caused her to get overwhelmed and I had to move. I have heard many times in my life from people I have met or know: I would take care of you if you did not have your disability. This is really tough to hear as my disability is part of who I am and is something I was born with and have no control over. Part of the adversity I have faced with my disability has shaped me into the funny and spirited person I am today, which is what people are drawn to.

I can remember a female group home staff, who stood out to me as she showed me kindness and compassion when my wheelchair was broken. Situations when my equipment would break would be stressful times for me as I lost my independence, mobility, and worried about how I would pay for the repairs. Equipment repairs at times would take several weeks. On this particular occasion, I had to stay home and primarily in my room for about two weeks. During this time, I begged the staff to take me out to go for a walk, to take me to the corner store, and she was the only one that took me out to do those things. She was willing to help me in a time when I felt very isolated and alone. I remember she was a good baker and baked wicked brownies and cookies! I appreciated that she liked to read books to me and she supported the idea that I wanted to be a stand-up comedian. She would read the chapters of a comedian's book to me so I could be a better 'sit-down' stand-up comedian.

There was another female staff member who previously worked in the group home where I resided, she always took the time to talk with me and check in to see how I was doing. During these conversations, she would show me compassion and reiterate to me that she believed in me and knew I could do well. Although my time in the group home was a difficult period of my life, there were good workers who I crossed paths. The qualities I enjoyed in workers was their willingness to do extras, or things they did not have to like baking, reading, or doing things with me. It is through the unplanned times where you start to feel caring and compassion and get to know who someone really is.

The most helpful part about child welfare involvement was that they protected me from the unsafe situation I was living in. Although my in care placements were not ideal, I do not know if I would have survived living the life I was at home. Through my involvement in Youth Speak Out, I was able to meet people with similar stories and we began supporting each other. With the additional peer support I started feeling less alone. Through meeting other youth in care, it helped me to know I was not the only one with trauma or a messed up family and finally, I was not alone. It was nice to be surrounded by other youth in the same room who got my experiences and me. I guess we got each other. I also know that if I would not have been in care, Theresa and her family would not have met me and I wouldn't be where I am today. I recognize that for some people it might be important to go through their child welfare file but I do not like to focus on the past and I have been able to work on healing myself without revisiting my past volumes. I believe it is not healthy to dwell on the past. I have seen many adults who dwell in the past and they remain stuck. Where does it get you? If it does not get you anywhere except angrier then what is the point in dwelling, as you can't change the past.

MY DISABILITY

I was born with cerebral palsy. My disability has affected my life and ability to complete milestones in my life, which range from walking, going to the bathroom, and being independent. I have struggles with being in a dating relationship, because of my daily care and lack of independence however, this is further complicated by all the emotional hardships I had to go through. When I was little my mom believed I could walk so she always pushed me to the absolute limit, to the point where my hips were falling out of place and I had to get surgery. I would do an hour of standing every day and she would always push me further and further and one time I took four steps by myself, but it was terrifying. All that pain was not worth it. The way I look at it is if my mom would have accepted me for who I was and the fact I was born with cerebral palsy she wouldn't have been so hard on me for my physical limitations which I had no control over. From this experience, I believe that you do not push a baby that hard but you support them where they are at and teach them. They will learn to walk on their own if they are meant to walk.

The worst part about my disability and being in a power wheelchair is that a lot of people, who do not know me, automatically assume I am mentally disabled because I am physically disabled. Especially in schools, people will get down on one knee beside you to talk to you as if you won't understand them if they don't. I have had to battle with being judged for being in a wheelchair, being poor, being in foster care and for being Indigenous. It is not my fault who I am culturally, physically, or the fact my parents were unable to keep me safe. I was born this way. I was born into this family. Unfortunately, it is not just kids who would pass judgment, it happens with adults too. I have had to learn to just wear that shit. It shows a positive mental attitude to know that it is their ignorance and lack of understanding not mine. I know the prouder I became of who I was, the more strength I felt and the less I was impacted by other's thoughts. I choose to persevere and not let the negative thoughts of others define who I am.

FAMILY & LIFELONG CONNECTIONS

Family and lifelong connections mean love, help, and support. They are the people who are there when I cry or break down, because I am only human. Sometimes, I am angry and I break down; however, I work hard not to let the anger consume me. As a child I wished my parents would find a way to get their lives on track so I could be with them, but I have stopped hoping. If lifelong family connections are healthy, then I think they should be supported. If they are causing too much stress or are a burden, then no. Get to know the family and the kid, what and who are important to them, and what do they want. Regardless of your age, you may need to consider if the relationship is worth the hardship. I have resumed the relationship with my step mom, dad, five sisters, and one brother. We have visits, phone calls, and occasional sleepovers. It is important to me because they know me, they have my back, they know what I went through, but family does not have to be blood. It could be your best friend, your teacher, or whoever is closest; like Theresa and me. There has to be a bond, an emotional connection, that love, that trust, and that loyalty that makes family.

When I was a child I wanted to be close to my dad however, he was often gone from the home, seemed secretive when he was around, and did not seem able to handle the responsibilities of us four children. I never really hated him for leaving us, I just missed him and hoped he would come back. I knew even as a child that he had his own problems, which affected his ability to be present. I never doubted that he loved all of his children. My dad was like a very caring and protecting kind of person and I looked up him. He is sensitive but he is also very rough and very manly. He is kind of both. He knows how to cook on the barbecue but he has no problem changing diapers so he can flip roles easily – he just needs somebody to guide his vision. When I first reconnected with him, for some reason I never resented him, which was very odd for me. I just knew that everyone has their own struggles. My dad and his partner have three little ones now and ever since I saw them, I wanted to protect all of them so they might not have to feel the pain that I have felt in my life. I want to make sure of that, and this has remained very important to me. I believe this is something to fight for; it is all about breaking the cycle. When I first met my youngest sister, I felt somewhat scared but not for the reasons you might think. It was the fear of opening up and the fear of feeling love. To allow myself to feel joy was scary. The first time I kissed her on the cheek, I instantly dipped out and went home on the bus crying like a baby.

My mom never raised us to have feelings. She said if you feel pain that is how you know you are living and feel alive. I was 17 or 18 at the time when I met my sister, so I was just disconnected from life, and I had been emotionally shut down for a long time. Now I am learning how to feel and this is the most difficult challenge out of everything that I have faced. I have faced every kind of pain and over time, physical scars heal but it is the feeling of love that really takes me off edge because of its unfamiliarity. As humans, we always fear what we do not understand. I never remember experiencing love until I was almost 19. That's a long time to go without emotional connection and it took a long time to get here and that can be complicated by having two families (my dad's and Theresa's). I have had to learn to navigate struggles with loyalty and worries about, "If you go with them then you do not love us anymore". I felt pressure from my older sister's and they would primarily make me feel like I had to chose but over time things got easier and I have learned to have both families. The Universe always balances stuff out. I think you must be open to take any opportunity, like I did agreeing to move in with Theresa and her family, but now I have a family and I have kids that I love surrounding me and people I can connect with. This is the closest I have felt emotionally in my whole life.

MY THOUGHTS ON STEREOTYPES

As for stereotypes of youth in care, you just have to wear it; you just have to wear that shit and power through. I have chosen to accept the adversity, and transform it to something beautiful. Use that anger, that frustration, and power through all the stereotypes but do not exhaust yourself or you will be in mental limbo. I have found that proving people and stereotypes wrong helps me to move forward. I use the mistakes of my mother to motivate me to get through tough times because if I do not move through issues, I am one foot away from being my mom. Therefore, I have to persevere and do this for me.

As youth in care, I believe it is important to find something and hold on to it – fight for it with everything you have. In addition, for the people who are taking care of youth: believe in them, know that they are human, and know that we do not have families to support us. If we are acting up, it means we are hurting inside. We all need at least one person to rely on in the foster care system and a lot of kids in care probably have not found theirs yet.

Unfortunately, my mother was not able to teach me the skills mothers usually do which provides the knowledge of how to parent, nurture and give children a solid base. Without the care and guidance, I did not have the foundation I needed. Through this awareness, I want to support my three younger siblings to ensure they have a better outcome, role model, and love and care so they can have a normal childhood. I want to motivate them to strive to be all they can be and this will help me to know the struggles I have endured were worth it. It is all about spreading hope.

MY CULTURE & MY GRANDFATHER

I think my Indigenous culture has died out through the generations. I believe culture can be a good and a very important foundation for people. I am learning about my Ojibway culture as I recognize I was missing a piece of my identity, which is something I can honour as part of me. I think culture is something familiar, to hold onto, something that no one can take away and that can provide me strength. I had limited exposure to my culture during my upbringing with my family and while in care. I want to learn about my culture so that I can share this knowledge, keep the teachings alive, and share them with others to preserve and maintain culture.

I would ultimately like to do what my grandfather did because he made a difference in the community and was proud of his culture. He was a famous artist, musician and crafts person. He was a theatre prop designer in Los Angeles and at one point he ran a shop there that employed and trained Indigenous people who left their reserves and wanted to make a living in the city. I am proud of the accomplishments he made and the fact he was able to produce music albums that showcased his skills as a fiddle player. He was a really interesting and amazing person who accomplished many things in his life. He is a big inspiration to me and I aspire be like him in the way that he did a lot of good and meaningful things.

MY THERAPY & MY THERAPY CAT, SCARLET

I have gone to a lot of therapy with psychologists and psychiatrists during my time in care. It took time for me to find a therapist, who fit for me or with whom I felt like I could open up to. I learned that therapy can be helpful; I was able to learn to feel emotions, understand myself better, and work through triggers, which were causing me to be depressed and helped me to find my way out of the dark times. I also like to meditate because it is a powerful way to heal the mind and soul and I find meditating helps me a lot to keep my emotions under control.

I have a cat named Scarlet, now. I did not even like cats before I came to live with Theresa three years ago. Over the first few weeks with my new family, I began to become more comfortable around the cat. On one occasion, I was fast asleep and Scarlet jumped on my chest to cuddle. I did not know what to do but then Scarlet started licking my neck and my face and I remember thinking, she was okay and I can deal with having a cat in my life. Now, I love her to pieces. She sleeps on my bed and it always seems when I am feeling down she just climbs up and comforts me. She is very intuitive and now, I just love her to bits. She is my therapy cat.

MY DREAM JOB

My dream job is to become a stand-up comedian and hopefully people do not think I am ripping them off because I have to sit down. I have wanted to be a comedian since I was approximately seven years old. I want to make people feel better. Imagine if you were having a terrible day and you went to a comedy show and you felt a little bit better after. I like to help people and if sharing my sense of humor can brighten their day then that would be a good thing. I am also considering attending Norquest College to become an addiction counselor, as this is another area I am quite interested in.

THOUGHTS ON PERMANENCY

I think workers should try to find permanent or adoptive homes for older children because we are all people and we need a family regardless of our age. Finding families for youth helps them to heal their childhood hurts and helps remind kids in care that there are good people out there. In a family, there are opportunities to be human and have the support to weather the good and bad times, and know that someone has your back. Once you find yourself belonging, you find a sense of your humanity and learn what you could have had earlier. Through this awareness I have learned who I could have been, who I am, and this helps you to become who you were meant to be. Through healthy and loving relationships, it replaces some of the bad parts/memories with good parts and happy memories. I think I have a lot of Theresa's personality now, and I am starting to adopt some of her drive. It has given me a sense of identity and belonging since she welcomed me into her family. It is beautiful. Humanity and kindness has helped my healing journey.

Part of my journey is learning to come to terms with who my family was and who I choose to be going forward. With respect to my family, I know who they are and as I have gotten older, I have been better able to understand their struggles. I want to overcome the pain, trauma, and life struggle, to be a symbol of hope for other people. It can be hard to revisit tough times from the past, it is painful to remember difficult times again and again, be patient and do that a little bit at a time.

When I wrote my story a few years ago, it just seemed like a lot of hurt and a lot of aggression that I had which is no longer in my heart now that I love this family I have become a part of. I am very grateful to have them for so many reasons. It was not easy for them to welcome me into their home, as they had to apply for so many grants to have the modifications made to their home like putting an elevator in, mounting a ceiling lift to transfer me in and out of bed, and modifying the bathroom so my hygiene needs could be met. They had to do many things to accommodate my disabilities and it was hard to believe that anyone would do all that for me. I know now that joining their family was challenging for both of us. In the past, I would push people away or remain guarded, as I had learned most caregivers would give up around four months and drop me. When I saw all the work and advocating Theresa had to do in order for me to live with them, it was like wow, she just won't give up! Like, what is wrong with this lady? I was still distant but through time, I wanted to open up. Once I started knowing her own lived experiences, I felt more connected to her than I ever had with my own mother. There is people who are very nice but you are like "hmmmmmm…nice but not real." Theresa is real. You can feel it. Growing up in care you can feel who is genuine and who is not. Through my experiences, I have had to rely on my good intuition about people, and situations in order to survive. I just felt the instant warmth of Theresa ever since I met her. We attended the same meeting and she brought me pizza because I could not get through the crowd to the lunch table. I am not a very huggable person but I would always want hugs from her and I do not really know what drew me to her but something did and I am glad.

We live out in the country and I like it. The trees are so beautiful. It is nice because I grew up in the city in an environment where people were always breaking things and doing drugs. The police used to come over every Saturday when I was a kid. That kind of thing becomes like second nature and now I am still kind of waiting for something like that to happen even though I know it will not. In order to move to live with Theresa, I did have to give away some of my independence because of living in a rural setting, I am not able to catch a bus and go places on my own. Having that sense of belonging has been worth the trade-off and I have learned this is a good place to heal and I need to heal.

Darker Than Black

I knew I was built
to be lonely
my heart
and soul
are chilled
to the bone
maybe that's
why I drink
so often
the
constant
conflict
between
good
and
evil
I'm exhausted
maybe I'll just
close my eyes
to my surprise
I'm back in time
to deal with the
disastrous
aftermath
of my past
ain't no stopping
going to be this way
until the day I lay
down in my coffin
no options
had friends
drowning
their sins
and sorrows
with alcohol and
prescription bottles
those were my homies
and role models
eventually

fallen

into the stereotypes
stealing just to survive
most people don't get it
they're not empathetic
thinking that they're so intelligent
no reference for me or my relatives
thinking that were benevolent felons
people always fear
what they don't understand
for those who care it's OK
I don't expect you to be by my side ride or die
or want to know why mom lead me astray
I had no hope for you to stay anyway
pain and rage became commonplace
to my future lover
if the possibility were to arise
I would feel the need to apologize
if my disability became your responsibility
because it shouldn't be
I will try to keep chivalry alive
I would keep your wrist and fist icy
so it will match my heart
I'm wide awake wanting
to break these chains
that plague my race
gotta prevail
gotta be more ruthless
than the system
they set me in
no compromise
cannot fail for those people
who were in my corner
kept me in great shape
I just want to say thanks
for them I can't let my
relentless resilience
go to waste so I will let
my blood and sweat
shed before my

tears do

Damon

Smokie 1990

Theresa & Damon 2020

Scarlet 2019

Theresa

When I first began working in child welfare one of the trainers said to me,
"No matter what family you deal with in this role, you can be guaranteed one thing:
They never wanted it to turn out this way".

I arrived home from school on a fall day and when I entered the home I shared with my mother and sister, I immediately noticed this was not any typical day. There were two women standing in our kitchen who I vaguely remember directing me upstairs to my bedroom to pack a bag with a few of my belongings. This incident marked a change in my life, which at that moment, I could not have comprehended the magnitude. My memories of this day are fragmented and fraught with sadness, worry, and tears as I packed my bags and begged the two ladies to allow me to bring my one prized possession, my cat Smokey. I am not sure how I convinced the child welfare workers or even the foster parents I had not yet met, but with my cat, my favorite blankets, and a small bag of clothing, I finally agreed to get into their car.

The foster home I was placed in was on the other side of Edmonton; far away from everything familiar to me and the home I had shared with my family and to a youth in grade eight, it felt like I was being moved to another world. I recall being flooded with all the worries of school, my friends, my sister, and confusion about what had just transpired. My first few weeks in foster care were hard; my new room was in a primarily unfinished basement, which exasperated my fears of basements and the dark. Since I was a young child, I have had sleeping issues; from what I can remember, the change in environment further triggered challenges I had with sleep and managing feelings that flooded me, which had been a long-standing issue for me.

Over the next several months, my time with my foster parents was met with mixed emotions, as I longed to go home and be surrounded by people and places I had known. I missed my sister deeply and not being with her was really hard on me. I found myself worrying about her as I had always been her protector and advocate although she was 11 months older than me. I had conflicting feelings, which included feeling hurt, angry, and abandoned by my mom. This was complicated for me to understand as I wished my mom could find a way to create the new peace I felt at my foster home, which was free from drinking, fighting, tension, and unpredictability. I felt guilty for liking my foster parents and enjoying my time with them. My foster parents showed me caring and nurturing I had not experienced (at least not consistently). We ate dinner as a family, there was a stocked fridge and I never had to go hungry. They actually seemed to like me. I remember them taking me on a holiday with them to British Columbia to a wedding, they purchased me a new dress, and I actually felt like I belonged. My foster mother and I grew close and I recall on one occasion, as I neared being with them for a year, she shared with me their desire to adopt me if I was not able to go home. On one hand, I recall feeling worried that I would lose my sister, extended family, and would not be able to see my mom again. However, on the other hand in my heart, I felt comforted that they cared deeply enough about me to want me to be a permanent part of their family. I wish someone had told me then that I could have had both and that adoption would be an addition to my biological extended family connections, not a subtraction. I believe if I would have known I could have been safe, loved and belong while remaining connected to important people in my life, I know this would have made a world of difference and allowed me to accept the permanency and belonging I yearned for.

I was settling into my life with my foster family and my marks at school improved; I finally started to feel settled and less afraid and alone all the time. As I entered high school, the change was very hard for me. The transition triggered a lot of anxiety and feelings of being different from my peers and I once again began to feel like I did not belong. In retrospect, my teenage years were the hardest times of my life and I wish I could have known then that life would get better and I would be the master of my own destiny as it may have helped me through some dark days that lied ahead.

Unexpectedly, my foster mother had a stroke and my world started to implode at a rapid rate. I recall overwhelming worries of feeling alone and fear of what this meant for me. I felt I was a burden on my foster family while she was in the hospital as they had two of their own young children to care for. Due to my foster mother's health, my mom agreed to have me home on a temporary visit. I stayed in a room that resembled nothing as I had left it, and I felt like I had no one who could even understand one piece of the hurt I felt. In those very dark days, I had no hope left and attempted suicide. I remember the last conversation I had with my foster mother was following my suicide attempt and she said to me, "I am in the hospital fighting for my life right now and you are trying to throw yours away." That was the final blow to my fragile ego, I never spoke to my foster parents again, and my drift began.

Over the next several years, life was very difficult as my time with my mother was short lived and she asked me to leave so I began to couch surfing. I resided with a string of neighbours, and school friends and their families, often feeling like a burden and never feeling like I fully belonged. I envied the life my friends had in which their parents displayed genuine caring for their well-being and their ability to be carefree youth. I struggled to deal with the sadness and rejection, which clouded my thoughts, exasperated my sleep issues, and affected my ability to focus on my schoolwork. I began struggling to fit in with friends and began gravitating towards unhealthy peer choices and dealing with the flooding feelings in unhealthy ways. I was crying out for help and yearned to belong and to know that I was loved.

I had lost hope in the adults in my life and no longer believed everything would be okay. I know now that I did not have the skills or knowledge to help myself process the abandonment, I had experienced. I felt deep hurts, which had been caused by years of rejection, exposure to addictions, mental health, and abuse. I lacked the skills to navigate the trauma these experiences had caused and I built walls around myself, as I knew no other way to protect what little self I had left. Although I really tried to please the people around me, I always fell short as I couldn't explain the unpredictable mood swings caused by trauma triggers, reasons why I was shutting people out who were showing me caring, or my complete inability to trust. I recall wanting emotional closeness but I had not learned the skills to navigate these types of relationships, which caused me to push many good people away despite their good intentions.

When I was 16 years old, my sister and I got our own apartment. We attended high school and worked part-time jobs, as the government's assistance was minimal in the early 1990s. I recall a school counselor who would frequently check in with my sister and me. When we moved into our first apartment, he bought us a plant and took us for lunch. This small act of kindness meant so much to me then and it is still a heartfelt memory almost 30 years later. Somehow, my sister and I plugged on together as we had when we were small, depending on only each other and trusting in no one.

As a youth, I had never met anyone else who's life resembled anything like mine and when I would see the looks of shock in acquaintances' faces as I shared small excerpts from my childhood, this reaffirmed they didn't understand and I should not share my lived experiences. Although having my own place at a young age finally meant no one could tell me to leave, it did not heal the loneliness and hurt I felt. My struggles to relate to my peers continued as our journey thus far in life was so varied. I recall feelings of envy for peers at school who had parents to cheer them on at events or when they passed a test, envious that they had someone to take care of them and make them soup when they were sick, envious that they had meat and fruit to eat whenever they wanted, and most of all envious that they had parents who loved and wanted them. I remember other youth commenting about how they thought it was cool that I had my own place; however, it was not so cool when we were evicted a few months later due to noise complaints due to partying. Truthfully, I would have traded all the independence to have the safety and love of a family, which would have relieved me of the burdensome responsibilities I had and allowed me to feel safe, loved, and fostered feelings of belonging.

When I reflect on my experiences with caseworkers, my memories are limited to the time I came into care and a few lunchtime meetings. I remember being picked up from school by my caseworker whom I only agreed to meet with because she would take me out for lunch. I remember looking at her and making my own internal judgements about her and her lack of ability to understand or even comprehend what I had experienced in my life. I recall her telling me that school was the most important thing and all the while, I affirmed in my head that she had no idea how it felt to be me as love, food, safety, and survival were the most important things to me at this time in my life. She never asked the tough questions or built the foundation for me to open up and share the real hurts I felt in my heart. From these limited interactions, I always vowed as a worker that I would be approachable, authentic in my presentation, and I would never be afraid to ask the tough questions when working with children, youth, and families.

The fact that I was in care as a teenager is one part of my complicated story however, I chose for these experiences to not define me. I have learned that my past adversity has helped shape me into who I am today. The struggles I experienced as an infant being raised by teenage parents who were struggling with poverty, mental health, domestic violence, and alcoholism directly affected the quality of care I received. The neglect I experienced in the early years was later compounded when my family moved to central Alberta, away from our extended family, my stepfather, and other supports so my mom could attend college. The isolation experienced by my sister and I during this time was overwhelming as we no longer had the support and watchful eyes of our extended family. My mom quickly became overwhelmed, avoidant, and I stepped into the pseudo parenting role at seven years old. My sister and I would go to school and daycare by day and often have mean and unskilled babysitters by night. During this period, my memories of my mom were often during times of her rages, which would be followed by promises of a better life in the coming months, years. In retrospect, the unpredictability we experienced was likely linked to my mom's mental health however; I was too young to discern at the time. My sister and I had responsibilities beyond our years of cooking, cleaning, laundry, and ironing which left very little time for the childlike activities we yearned for. I recall during this time in my life (between the ages of seven and nine) often crying myself to sleep as I listed to the Air Supply song, Lost in Love, on my Walkman.

When I was nine years old, we moved to Edmonton, where there was the promise of a better life. My mom had reconnected with my stepfather who was now living in Edmonton. For the first few months, life was calm. We lived in a very poor neighbourhood but I liked my school and my new daycare. Shortly after we moved to Edmonton, I recall becoming more aware of my mother's drinking, mood swings, and the unpredictability that came along with it. On Easter day, she and my stepfather fought while my sister and I were at the park and when we came home, my mom was crying and a neighbour was present, telling us to get our favorite teddy. My mom, sister and I got into the car and on this rainy Easter night with no explanation, we checked into a shelter for abused women and their children. This experience was quite traumatic, as I had to leave my stepfather, school, friends, and home without warning or explanation. We stayed in the shelter for well over a month until my mom secured new housing on the other side of Edmonton. The hopes of a better life were shattering around me as I attempted to rebuild once again. It would be several years before I saw my stepfather again which was a loss for us that went unprocessed.

My trust and faith in my mother to care for my sister and I and provide for our basic needs had dwindled. Our basic needs for appropriate clothing and food went unmet more times than I can count while there was always money to ensure the fridge was stocked with a box of wine. The more my mother was avoidant, withdrawn, and combative (likely caused by her increased drinking and untreated mental health), the more I became parentified and independent. My home environment was tense and unpredictable, and I tried to adapt by becoming fiercely protective of my sister and developing over-functioning and pleasing behaviours to try to neutralize conflict with my mother.

I became angry with my mom and blamed her for not caring for my sister and I in a manner we needed and deserved. I felt disappointed in my mother for not meeting my emotional and physical needs, which caused me to resent her. My mom lacked the skills to nurture us the way a child needed to be. The unpredictability in her moods caused anxiety and fear, as we never knew how her mood would be or if and when it would shift. Although I felt upset when she was out partying or not home as I remember feeling scared, I also welcomed those times, as the house was peaceful. It was during those times that my mom was not there that allowed the opportunity for the supervisor of my newspaper route to sexually abuse me. I did not have trust in my mom to tell her what was happening, so I confided in my sister. Much like my apprehension, I came home from school one day to the police. Once again, there was no notice, no warning, and no control over the circumstance I had been put in by the adult who was supposed to protect and guide me.

As the years passed, there were periods of time where my mom tried to stop drinking and, to be honest, those were tough times as well. During her periods of sobriety, she would try to take over the parenting role she had vacated so many years before. I was no longer willing to relinquish this role because I did not trust in her ability to protect me or love me. It was also during those times that I realized she had other struggles and her moodiness, unpredictability, and hurtful ways were not all alcohol-related. In order to protect myself, I learned not to rely on my mother from a very young age. I began not expecting anything from her and, in many ways, that was easier to handle than the hurt, disappointment, and abandonment I repeatedly felt when I allowed her to be close.

The healing journey with my mother has not been linear. We have had many arguments, heart-to-hearts, and difficulties. I have come to realize that my mother lacked the skills to parent and nurture me in a manner that I needed. I recognize that her own childhood experiences did not equip her, and being a teenage parent compounded her deficits. I have awareness and understanding of both her addictions and her mental health, but I do not condone or excuse the way she treated my sister and I when we were small. I have found a way to forgive her and I continue to try to foster a relationship with healthy boundaries and roles. My mom has struggled with alcoholism, misusing prescription medication, and I believe overuse of Marijuana in the recent years has added to her mental health challenges. Over the years, I have learned to set strong boundaries with my mom, which can best be described as lovingly detaching during periods of unwellness when I need to. During periods of wellness, my mom is able to interact in a more authentic manner, which lays a foundation for us to have a relationship and lays the foundation for growth and heartfelt memories. When my mom is struggling, I am mindful of how this triggers feelings in me and I ensure I do not put myself in any position of relying or depending on her. I long to have a consistently close, stable, and loving relationship with my mom in which I can fully trust her; however, I have come to terms with the perimeters which are necessary for my emotional health.

The experiences I had growing up have profoundly impacted my life as an individual, woman, mother, wife, and worker. Through reflection, I have come to realize that the impact of certain experiences have played a more significant role in my life at some points than others. As a young adult and mother to my first child, I continued to be fiercely independent. I struggled with intimacy and lacked the ability to trust others. I felt in my heart that the only person I could count on was me and this was definitely affirmed throughout my childhood and early adult experiences. As I have grown over the years, I have learned to forgive my mother for her inability to provide the care and love for me that I so desperately needed, wanted, and through our rebuilding of a relationship, healing for those deep hurts has occurred. I have been fortunate to develop a few close friends over the years who have supported me to grow and learn healthy coping strategies that have benefited me both personally and professionally. It took me several failed relationships to find a partner who was able to support and nurture me and I finally learned what it is like to trust and love someone deeply. The security I am able to feel within this relationship was something foreign to me and initially scared me immensely; however it has allowed me to create a different destiny for both my children and I and for that, I am grateful. I recall a few years ago saying to my husband how thankful I was that his parents had loved and nurtured him in such a healthy way so that he could share these learnings and gifts with me and help my soul heal.

I always knew I wanted a different life and perhaps that is what drew me towards the helping profession at a young age. I can recall when I was approximately eight years old watching missionary type programs on the television and knowing that I wanted to be a missionary. In retrospect, I think it is ironic that I was a child suffering and in need but I still had the desire to help others who had even less than I did. Over the next few years I was able to redefine my goal and I knew at the age of 14, I wanted to someday work for child welfare. Of course, as a youth, I had some idealistic views of saving families but my core reason for wanting to work with families was because that even as a youth, I believe if my mother would have had additional supports as a teenage parent, she could have learned additional skills, learned to process her own childhood trauma, and that would have allowed her to be emotionally available to attach and parent my sister and I in a healthier way. I believe supports for my mother would have altered the course for our family, and our family's outcome would have been much better.

When I entered College at Grant MacEwan as a mature student, my dream was to work with youth in the addictions field. I remember speaking with my sister and I said, "If I complete the addictions program and Child and Youth Care program and this means neither of us become alcoholics and our children don't come into care, it will be money well spent." As I reflect on that comment, I realize that in that moment, I made a conscious choice at age 20 to change the trajectory of my life and my sisters life as both my mother and I had been in care, both my parents and our extended family have been significantly impacted with addictions and mental health for generations, and divorce has been common place.

From my lived experience as a child, I have a few key messages I would like to share. As a child, I was sad and hurt and I needed the adults around me to create the safety I needed. Through community supports, I believe my mother would have had the capacity to learn alternative strategies and strengthen her support system which would have allowed her to meet the needs of my sister and I on a physical and emotional level. When I first began working in child welfare one of the trainers said to me, "No matter what family you deal with in this role, you can be guaranteed one thing: They never wanted it to turn out this way. This phrase continues to resonate within me 20 years later as I reflect on my own experience and the experiences of many children and families I have had the privilege to support.

I recall early in my career that I was very shameful and secretive of my time in care and it took me several years to come to peace with the fact that I did not have control over what happened to me, my parents addictions, their mental health, or the fact I needed to be placed in foster care. I was a child who was hurt and sad and I needed to be nurtured and protected. There were behaviours, both outward and inward, that I displayed which was my way of showing the pain I felt in my heart because I did not have the words or skills to express how I felt. I could not verbalize this hurt so it came out in anger, misuse of substances, unhealthy relationships, and the creation of a protective fortress around me. I needed the adults around me to show they cared through their commitment, words of encouragement, and unconditional presence.

In my role as a child welfare worker, I think back to my time with my foster parents. I have often wished that I was supported to process through the adoption discussion more thoroughly as it weighed heavily on my mind. I needed to know that I could still have connections with my mom, sister, and my extended family. I needed to hear from my foster parents that they would honor my relationships and include me in theirs and that I did not have to lose anyone through the process of adoption. I have seen the evolution of child welfare from the inside looking out and have noticed the importance placed on connections and extended family. I recall as a young adult, I asked my grandparents why they didn't ask where I was; didn't they worry about me? My grandmother explained they did not think it was their business and she related that looking back, they have a lot of guilt that they did not play a larger role when they knew things were not okay for my sister and I Through family meetings and to us about who our natural/familial supports were and asking who we missed and who we spent Christmases with, the child welfare workers would have quickly learned to seek out my grandparents, or my favorite aunt, or even my stepfather who had been a stabilizing force in my life.

My own history and involvement with child welfare, couch surfing, and Independent living could have looked so much different. The feelings in my heart likely would have felt so much different as well. At the age of 19, I reconnected with my stepfather and he encouraged me to get my life on track and register for college, as he believed I was too smart to be working three dead-end jobs. I lived in Calgary and was accepted to MacEwan University in Edmonton, so I packed my few belongings and moved into my stepfather's home in Sherwood Park. This transition was a life-changing experience as he encouraged and supported me through my Child and Youth Care diploma. When I found out I was pregnant with my oldest daughter, he stood by me and encouraged me to finish the program, which I graduated from when my daughter was nine months old. He believed in me even when I did not and he showed me the kindness and compassion I craved. I remained living with him for almost four years. This was the first time I remember feeling like I had a real home and like I was truly welcome. His love and guidance changed the trajectory of my life. I know in my heart that I am who I am today because of the role he played when I so desperately needed it.

As an adult, I have been fortunate to work within the field that once guided me. I have worked with pregnant and parenting teens, which in many ways gave me insight into my own struggles being raised by a teen parent. I have had a wonderful career for the past 20 years within child welfare, which has allowed the opportunity to grow as a person and as a practitioner. I have witnessed many changes within the system, which aligns with supporting families and strengthening communities while attempting to leave the least footprints in a child's life. I have realized that the supports and agencies, which are now present, could have benefited the lives of my family. I have been fortunate to foster teens in the past with addictions and share my loving stable home with them to show them that their life could be different, and the youth I supported taught me that change is possible.

Healing comes in many ways. I have touched on the healing as a family and I also want to share a little about my own healing. I have learned to accept my past and it no longer defines me. It has made me who I am today and has been part of my journey. I believe my experiences have allowed me to have insight and compassion for the children and families my path crosses. Through the years, I have needed counselling supports to learn the skills to manage feelings of abandonment and not being good enough, process through the night terrors I had for years, and support me to manage crippling emotions. The journey has been worth it as I have learned to be a confident, driven, loving woman. I have achieved stability, love, and friendships in my life, which will last my lifetime even if they did not manifest until I was an adult.

I have created a wonderful life, which is full of hope and possibility.

THERESA

Self Portrait 198

Treasures from Theresa's teen years.

Things did get better.

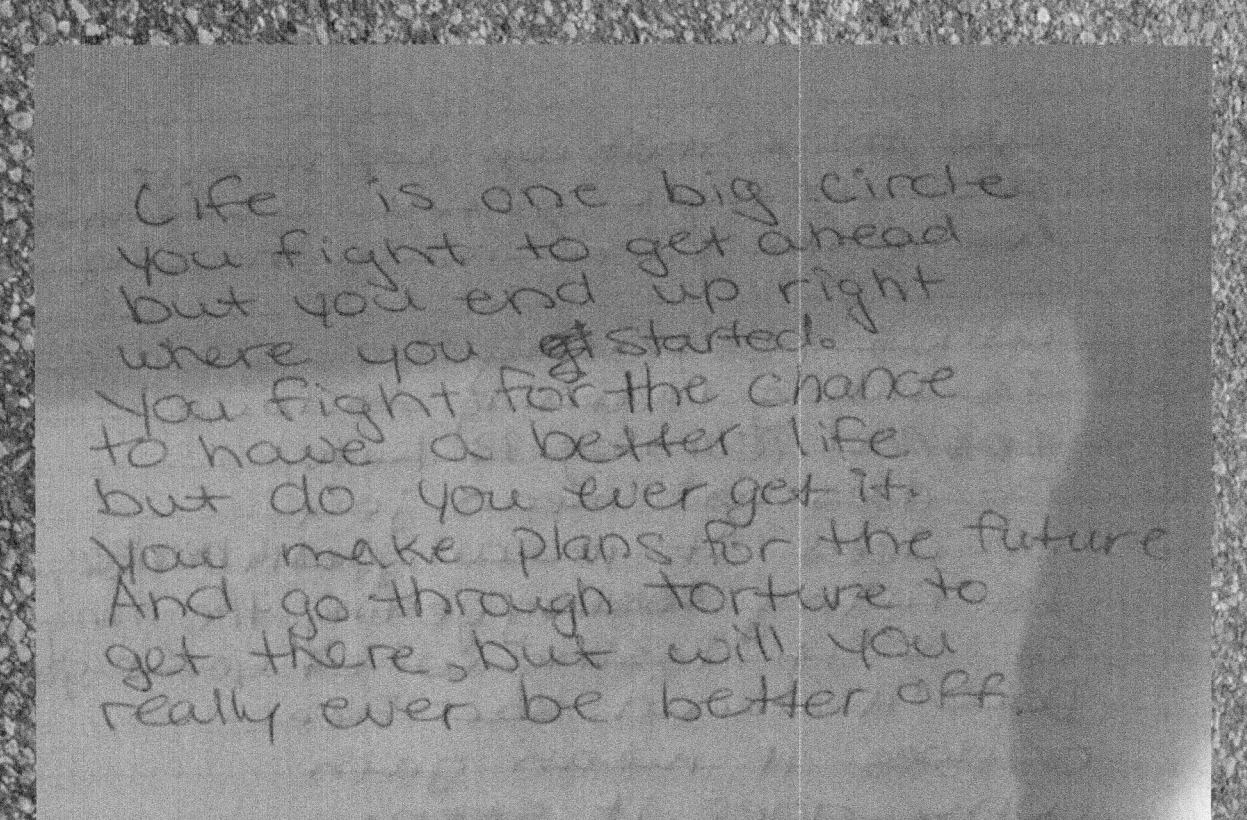

Life is one big circle
You fight to get ahead
but you end up right
where you started.
You fight for the chance
to have a better life
but do you ever get it.
You make plans for the future
And go through torture to
get there, but will you
really ever be better off.

Life is hard
but your friends are there
to help you through
to show ~~you just how much~~ they care
It's just the little
things you do
That makes them
glad that they know you.

by Theresa
Jan 19/89

I want people to know that we are people.
We have been through a lot more in life
than the average person.
We shouldn't be treated
like any less of a person
or be given up on.

Everyone has potential
but people sticking around
to help us out a little more
makes a huge difference.

Everyone that came into my life
whether it was my caseworker
or youth worker or staff -
a lot of them stuck around and they became
big parts of my life. And that's part of the reason
I am the way I am today.

The continuity of relationships is really important.
Somebody to stick with us long term like a family should.
Kids in care have already had everything taken away from them.
Everything is gone.

Then they move around from home to home with
a backpack full of whatever is most important to them,
so people need the opportunity to stay connected.

                                        Tyler

NEWS | INDIGENOUS | RIGHTS & JUSTICE

Youth Take The Lead In Tackling Colonialism, Injustice In Vancouver

Indigenous and non-Indigenous youth are working together to bring changes based on consultations with 2,000 young people.

Katie Hyslop SEPTEMBER 22, 2020   TheTyee.ca

On a smoky evening last week, 10 Indigenous and 10 non-Indigenous youth sat in the wooden pews of the Longhouse Church in East Vancouver talking about their plans for decolonizing and Indigenizing Canada. Starting with Vancouver's inner city neighbourhoods.

(To read the full article please click on headline or type headline into your search bar.)

> **GIVE US A CHANCE**
> **And**
> **Hear What We Have To Say**

Postcard courtesy of the Adoption Council of Canada—Youth Speak Out Edmonton

The folds of the system are deep and mysterious. So easily they can take a child and as the system folds over and over, eventually the child is lost, but the longing never goes away even if they do not know what it is they are longing for.

                                                                            Jade

Kaylen

I can't see myself doing anything else but working with animals because that is what I love to do. There's so many animals that need care. So many that need to be rescued and need to be loved and lot of them are misunderstood
— just like kids in care.

MY LIFE STORY

I talk about living in care, but I don't live my past.

I was apprehended in 1992, so I was four years old. I had an eight-year-old brother, a six-year-old brother, and my twin brother. When we were apprehended, my older brothers went to go live with their dad, but my twin and I went to live in foster care. I remember having my birthday there and then we went to a foster home until Grade 1 and then my grandpa came to pick us up. That was just before Christmas. I want to say October or November. I know there was snow. I guess my grandpa couldn't handle us so he put us back in foster care when we were six. I went to two different homes after that and then I went back to my mom for eight months. I don't remember my mom too much back then. I do remember lots of fighting and we were always in the middle of it. We got apprehended again, and then I went to six more homes. I spent time in two group homes, as well as a child psychiatric ward for a month. I also went to another place for a week-long assessment and then I was placed back home.

I attended 12 elementary schools. I went to three different schools for Grade 3. That is when my twin brother and I got separated. I went to two schools for junior high and then I moved to a group home for the summer and a couple months in the fall. I went to Ross Shepard High School and then I moved back home and then I finished high school at J. Percy Page. The impact of going to so many schools is that there is no stability. I had no friends. I was bullied a lot, especially when the teacher would tell the class that I was in foster care and then I'd be called an orphan. I'm sure it was an accident on her part, but you get a lot of dirty looks from other kids after that.

I started smoking pot and drinking in high school but managed to keep a level head and I graduated. I went to university but I decided halfway through that I didn't want to do it anymore, but I do want to keep working towards the animal sciences. I can't see myself doing anything else but working with animals because that is what I love to do. There are so many animals that need care. So many that need to be rescued and need to be loved and lot of dogs are misunderstood. I dog-sit sometimes, and people say their dogs never warmed up to anyone so quickly as they do me. When I got separated from my twin brother, the foster parent called and said I needed to be removed from the home but I didn't know why. Later on, I found out that she had stated that I was chasing my brother around the house with a knife, but I wasn't. We were chasing each other in the house, yes. We were being silly because we were eight years old. We had so much trauma happen to us that we took all our trauma out on each other. We were quite violent with each other, but we still loved each other and would unintentionally hurt each other. We were just rough. Much later, one of my youth workers said something about my blackouts and I was like: What blackouts? What are you talking about? She said that she read that I used to have blackouts when I would get angry but I remember everything that I've ever done. So, I realized that lots of lies were told about me. It's disturbing.

They tried to let us see each other but it was hard and then he got into other things and I was still like a square. We still talk to each other. We will message each other and talk on the phone. He recently called me a few weeks ago and needed to borrow money for his car insurance. I gave him the money right away. So, we're good. We still have arguments, but we're good.

I am not sure how many workers I had from the age of 8 to 22. I remember workers coming to the house when I was with my mom even before we went into foster care. I think that there was always abuse. I remember four workers really well from when I was older. I think I had five or six youth workers all together but I'm not sure. Not a lot of stability with people in and out of your life all the time but the ones I had the longest made the most difference. I had the same caseworker from the age of 15 all the way until I was 20 and I had the same youth worker from 15 to 22 as well. That continuity of care is so important.

I had a hard time with trust. They were always trying to get me to be more communicative. I became extremely withdrawn especially around the ages of 16 to 18. I didn't want to talk to anybody. I felt I wasn't listened to and I wasn't validated. For instance, one time I got really sick. I think I had the flu. I was 16, it was spring break, and I almost died. I couldn't eat because every time I would eat I would throw up and I was scared that my foster mom would go to my caseworkers say: She's throwing up again. I told them multiple times that I was sick but they weren't listening to me. I was scared that if I ate and I had taken my medications and then threw up that my foster mother would tell my caseworker it was my eating disorder but that time it wasn't. I was actually very sick.

The scariest part of being in care is never knowing what is going on. Never being sat down and told why you're moving because you just think you're just a bad kid. I think just the sense of longing is always there; just not really belonging anywhere isn't a good feeling growing up. I have an adopted family, now. I found them very late in foster care and I'm really glad but in ways, I still don't feel like I belong. It's kind of a lifelong struggle.

They don't work with you to transition you out of care unless you're one of the lucky ones who gets to go into an independent living program that helps you, but not everybody gets that. I was in a good one eventually. I lived on my own but I still had a worker and people to help me when I needed help. I was independent, but I had someone I could turn to for support. I stayed in that program until I was 22 and people said I'd never be able to drive. I'd never be able to take a bus. I'd never be able to hold a job. But, I can hold a job. I can drive and I do. I took the bus all the time as a teenager and young adult. It's all because of that program. They helped me to transition before I aged out. We need more of those programs.

The most beneficial part of child welfare is that I got to see places. I got to travel to the United States, I've been all over British Columbia (BC), I've been to Saskatchewan. I would like to do more travelling someday. The place I would most like to visit is Switzerland. It looks so beautiful and I have heard that the people are nice. I'm saving my Air Miles to go there. It sounds like utopia. I've been told they still have alarms and they still have these emergency drills and people tell me that every house has a bomb shelter in the basement. I think you have to spend two years in the military and they are a neutral country which is pretty cool.

MY MENTAL HEALTH

Last year, after my divorce, I went to go see a new doctor. He did an hour assessment and we talked about everything. He explained to me why I was diagnosed with bipolar disorder (BD) at the age of 11. I was told that a lot of illnesses look the same. My correct diagnosis, which I have now, is a panic anxiety disorder with bouts of depression and a mood instability disorder due to my anxiety. I started to take medication because I don't want to be that person I was, ever again. The medication works for me. I've been on it for a year and I don't have suicidal thoughts anymore. Once a month I get really depressed and my boyfriend is working on it with me. He's trying to do his best. He's never dealt with somebody with depression so it's a learning curve for sure and he's trying to be understanding.

I was 11 the first time I was put in a psychiatric ward. I was diagnosed with Opposition Defiance Disorder (ODD) and Attention Deficit Hyperactive Disorder (ADHD) and Bipolar Disorder. I was put on so many medications by the time I was 15. I have been told by another medical professional that there's a possibility that I can't pinpoint an emotion and deal with it properly because I was so over medicated that my brain couldn't do it for me naturally.

There was an 11-year span that I wasn't on any medication and I remember talking to my ex-husband after our first son was born. I told him I felt there was something wrong with me and that I needed help but he said there's was nothing wrong with me and that I didn't need help. He told me I just need to eat better and exercise more.

Unfortunately, last year I was struggling with my mental health and I called the police on myself when I was having a mental breakdown. They brought child welfare in and the caseworker told my ex-husband to take my kids from me or she would apprehend them. I told her my circumstances and she said that was not her fault and that I was an adult so to go to the Alberta Works office. I was very angry because I wanted help but all she just said was maybe I should get my mental health in check, so this won't happen again. I checked into the hospital and was kept under a Form 10. The psychiatrist there basically told me that my issues seem to be out of anger so to just stay away from the person that was making me angry which waseasier said than done considering that my husband was always at the house. It was so terrible because as a mom I had decided I was not going to be like my mom, but I had an unchecked mental illness. I wanted to get it checked out but I didn't have the support from my husband so after 10 years I just couldn't handle it anymore and I left. My kids are aged 8, 5 and 3 now but I don't get to see them as often as I would like because they moved to Calgary with their father.

I also have some physical pain. I have a really bad back. I might become paralyzed. I might need spinal surgery. I have a degenerating disc in my lower back. I go for massage therapy and I do yoga which is good. Yoga is good for a lot of things – physically and mentally.

THOUGHTS ON DIAGNOSIS

I'd say that my twin brother got most of the Fetal Alcohol Spectrum Disorder (FASD) but I don't really talk about that because it has not been diagnosed. I don't acknowledge it because I don't like the stereotypes that come with FASD. It makes me feel gross. I was diagnosed on the autism spectrum and my son is waiting to be assessed. He has behavioral issues. I did not drink or abuse any substances during any of my pregnancies. I never got into alcohol or drugs much in my life. If I drink now, it's just a bottle of wine once in a while. Or, if I splurge on rum or whiskey it takes me about a month or two to finish the bottle. I don't smoke cigarettes. If I do smoke pot, which is extremely rare, it's because I have insomnia and I need to sleep. Not having that lifestyle eliminates a lot of problems. It's hard to have an addict in your life.

My son is super smart. He was talking at six months and then when he was one, he just stopped talking. Then a week later he was talking in sentences. He didn't even crawl – he just kind of rolled everywhere and then he walked a week after his first birthday. Hopefully when he goes through his diagnosis they'll do a good diagnosis and then he'll get whatever help he needs in school. I read that Denmark doesn't let their children go to school until age seven. I agreed with that and so I just held him back a year. So he just went to preschool for another year. When he was in Grade 3, I did message his teacher saying, you know, he brought home these flashcards went through them in five minutes. He told me that he was the only one in his class doing double-digit times tables. He can add three-digit sums in his head. So he needs to get the right diagnosis and the right help.

MY THOUGHTS ON THE SYSTEM

I think that they really need to just stop allowing anybody to be a foster parent. They need to do like more serious background checks, and they also need to stop pulling Indigenous children from their families. Now saying that, I did live with an Indigenous family and they were not nice to me or my brother. But, just stop letting just anybody be a foster parent. Kids need to be placed in loving, kind, patient foster homes and if an Indigenous child does get placed with the non-Indigenous family, that family needs to ensure that that child has the opportunity to learn about their culture and stay rooted.

We need to have more attentive caseworkers. They need less cases on their caseload. My caseworker was supposed to see me once a month, but there is no way that she could. If she has 60 kids on her caseload that is two or three kids every day, she is supposed to see on top of all the other things she has to do. It's so much paperwork and they have to go to so many meetings all the time. It is not fair to them or the kids they work with.

MY THOUGHTS ON STEREOTYPES

The stereotypes of youth in care are statistics. There's not a very high success rate for foster kids. A lot of people just think that we're worthless. That we're garbage. That we'll never amount to anything. That's literally what I got being in foster care. You're going to be on the street, anyway. I have one really good friend I got in grade 11 and we're still good friends and when she first told her mom I was a foster kid, her mom had questions. It's kind of the assumption - you're in foster care so you're going to be trouble. I was able to get past those stereotypes because I'm a really strong-willed, pig-headed and stubborn person and sometimes that can be a good quality.

MY PLANS FOR FURTHER EDUCATION

I went to university but I didn't like it. I had a bad experience with my teacher. She was not nice. It seemed like nothing I did was ever good enough for her. Someone else I knew had her and we agreed that she probably shouldn't be teaching. I want to work with animals, and I think I might just take the plunge and try out for veterinary school. I am going to upgrade my math and then attend the Animal Health Technology Diploma

Program at Olds College. I have always loved medicine and biology so I thought maybe I should become a nurse and then I was like, "No, I want to work with animals". They can't talk. I guess my dream job would be to become a medical examiner. It is such an interesting field and like I said, I am curious so I think I would be good at it. Corpses can't speak either so I could just get to work without anyone bothering me. I've been trying to get a job at a vet clinic but I just don't have enough experience. It's the vicious circle, you know. I can't get experience if I can't get a job and I can't get a job unless I have experience.

FAMILY & LIFELONG CONNECTIONS

Lifelong connections mean a great deal to me. I think it's because I never really had a family growing up. My adopted parents are my family and my children are my family. My biological dad is my family. My twin brother is my family. I might not talk to my two older brothers a lot, but I still consider them my family. I also classify my dad's daughter as my family and now my boyfriend and his daughters. I found my biological dad when I was 19. I stopped talking to my mom when I was about 17 or 18 years old and have never looked back. I still wonder about her. I keep up with her because my brothers talk to her. She's in Quebec right now. She says she got kicked out of Alberta and I know that's not true – that's just how unstable she is.

MY ADOPTION

As a child I didn't want to be adopted because I thought it would mean I lose my twin and then when I was 18, I found a family and they just adopted me. I just changed my last name. They wanted to adopt me but the lawyer was like why don't you just change her name? She's 18. So I finally found a home. I found people that will always be there. Of course, there are struggles but every family has them.

THOUGHTS ON CULTURE

I think that if you are a person of colour or you immigrated here from somewhere or you are Indigenous or you have say, even really strong Ukrainian roots and you do the dancing and practice the customs of your culture – that's great. I don't really have a culture. I have some Scottish background, but my kids are mixed race. I put my youngest in Highland dance one year and it was cute. She was the only kid of colour and her teacher was always so amazed that I could get all that hair in a bun. Her hair is very different than her sister's hair and actually, they all have very different hair and different personalities.

WHAT PEOPLE WHO WORK WITH KIDS SHOULD KNOW

Youth in care are hurting. They act out. They're not acting out because they want to disturb you or your peace or your environment. Neurologically, they have a war going on in their head. They might feel like they are betraying their family if they get close to you. For children in my circumstances, you just give up eventually because you just feel unwanted because nobody sat down with you and told you why you were moving. So you just assume it's you. So, I don't know. I think that we need to be more understanding of the foster kid. I'm not saying let them abuse you, but don't get mad at them because they're angry. Remember that there's a reason they're angry. I just wanted to be listened to because feeling like you're not believed is very defeating and discouraging and it makes you really angry.

MY MESSAGE TO OTHER YOUTH

Don't give up hope. Just keep trucking and stay out of trouble. Put your head down and power through just doing the best you can. It might seem like it will never get better but it can.

If I hadn't gone into care,
I think my life could have
been far worse.
I come from a long line
of intergenerational trauma.
My mother was taken into
care as an older teen
because her mother had
serious mental illnesses
and her father was a very
abusive alcoholic who
beat my grandmother all
the time. Her younger
siblings went into foster
care and she was placed
with someone in the
community because at that
time she was too old to be
under government care,
So we have a three generation
history of trauma, family
violence, family dysfunction
and child welfare.

Linda

Canada's children have high rates of suicide, abuse, infant mortality: report

Health markers paint troubling picture of child welfare

The Canadian Press September 4, 2018

Canada's global reputation as a healthy place to raise children is belied by statistics showing strikingly high rates of suicide, child abuse and struggles with mental health, a new report suggested Tuesday

Health markers covering everything from infant mortality to obesity and poverty rates paint a troubling picture of child welfare in Canada, according to the report compiled by Children First Canada and the O'Brien Institute for Public Health.

(To read the full article please click on headline or type headline into your search bar.)

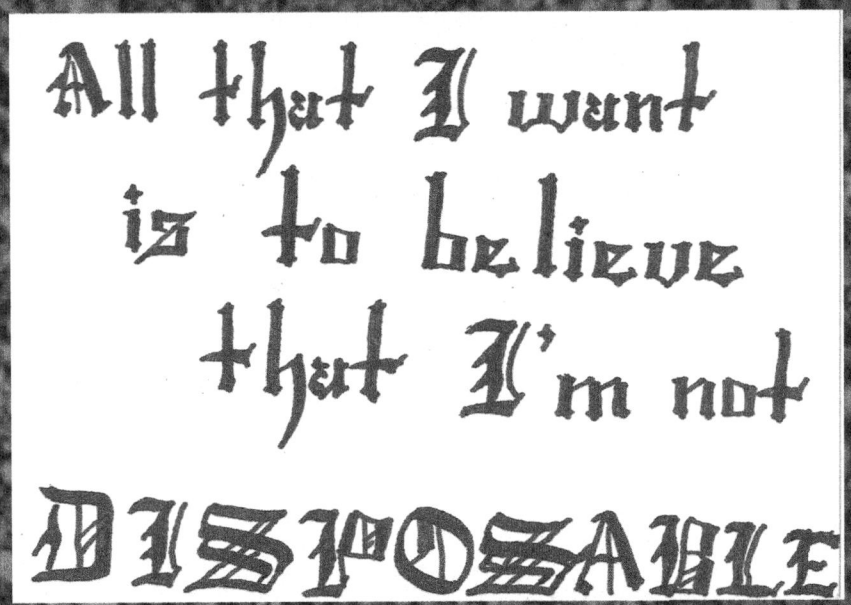

> All that I want is to believe that I'm not DISPOSABLE

Postcard courtesy of the Adoption Council of Canada—Youth Speak Out—Edmonton

Shortly after that event, I had started spiralling out of control and got put in my first group home, where I entered into the darkest chapter of my life and complete hopelessness consumed me. During my stay there, I often ran away, broke things, threatened others, and tried to hurt others. I felt that there was no way out and that life would not get any better. I had often dreamed of dying and not having to feel the pain and hurt that I had. On several occasions, I tried taking my life, but thankfully staff intervened and stopped me from making this irreversible mistake. Ironically, while I was living in the group home, I began to discover that I had the potential to succeed academically, which was previously unthinkable, as I believed I was stupid. A teacher worked on setting some academic goals with me and, although I struggled greatly, I began to make significant progress.

Cody

Krista

My "family" are a group of people whom I care very
strongly for and whom I know will always be there
— my foster family. They've seen me at my worst
and pushed me to be my best.

I am 22 years old and live in Edmonton. I graduated from the Social Work Diploma program at MacEwan University in June 2018. I was only a year old when I was removed from my family and placed in care. My years of experience growing up in care have led me to be in the social work profession. I am excited for my journey on the other side of care in my role as a social worker, where I hope to support children and families who are facing struggles and challenges. In addition to social work, I am also enrolled in the Dental Assistant Program, which will facilitate greater employment opportunities.

SUMMARY OF LIFE

I was just a year old when my older sister and I entered into foster care, as we were born into a very unhealthy home – a place where violence and drinking were a big issue. We were placed with our grandparents for a short time of three months, then apprehended from them because they left us alone with our biological parents when they went to work. We were then placed with a foster family, who were very loving and welcomed us very quickly when we first arrived. Our new family treated us like their own children. My new foster family consisted of a mother and father and a 20-year-old sister. I grew fairly close to my new parents in the years I was with them.

For the first eight years, my sister and I would have supervised visits with our biological mother, as well as visits with our older brothers who were in foster care and, eventually, my little sister, after she got placed in care at age six. After several years, we stopped seeing our biological mother because we could tell she was not very eager to really get to know us, so we didn't want to keep trying with a mother who did not show much interest in getting us back. Soon after, we slowly lost contact with our brothers, after they went back to live with our biological mother when they turned 16. From that point on, my sister and I grew up together with our foster family and had frequent visits with our little sister. When my older sister turned 17, she wanted less rules and more freedom and so she left our home to live with our biological mother. After two years, she decided to come back to our foster home, which was great as her and I are very close. I have not taken the initiative to directly contact or interact with my biological parents as I've grown older. I was approximately eight years old when I attended my last supervised visit. I am not comfortable pursuing a relationship with them, especially since they told me I was no longer part of their family.

When I first entered my foster home, I had court-ordered scheduled visits with my biological mother. That didn't last for long, as my mother continued to struggle with drugs and alcohol. I haven't seen my birth father since I was six years old. I've seen my birth mother in social settings several times since I was about 15 (my sister's high school graduation, baby shower, etc.) but honestly, it's really hard. I have never identified with my biological mother as my real mother and being around her has been awkward and uncomfortable. It has been extremely difficult to keep up or want a relationship with someone only because you share DNA. I do not have anything in common with my birth family and my life aspirations and values are vastly different from theirs. My birth mother, to this day, still can't admit that she made poor choices. Instead, she views it as people having "taken her children" from her. I am often reminded of what my foster mom would always say to us: Blood doesn't define family.

I'm so lucky that my foster mom was able to give me the emotional support I needed to be successful in school, life, and now my career. Not only has my foster family been the key to me succeeding in my goals, I have also had the emotional support from my caseworkers and financial support from child welfare. Growing up as a "foster child", I didn't feel different or negative because it was an aspect of my life that I chose not to share with classmates and friends. I wanted to ensure that nobody judged me or treated me differently. There were some difficult aspects of being a normal kid in care, which consisted of other kids wondering if my mom was my grandma (she appeared too old to have a child my age). I feel that being a foster kid also had a negative impact on my social development. I hid the truth from friends and, although that was simple, I missed out on bonding and fun experiences like sleepovers because the parents would have needed to have criminal checks, etc., so it was easier to decline. Not being included in those types of activities made me feel left out and, eventually, classmates stopped asking. For the first time, I felt isolated and a loss of self-esteem and confidence. I still struggle as an adult to make close friends and not feel left out.

IMPACTFUL STORY

For any kid, it would be hard to be apprehended from your home. I was very young when it happened, but I still knew, to a point, what was going on. Ages one to four were the years I had to adapt and figure out this loss and get used to this new environment. Through the first couple of years, I was connecting and starting to gain that love with my foster dad – the dad I needed in my life. I was a happy little girl who loved her new dad, but then at the age of four, my foster dad – the only father figure I knew – passed away suddenly from cancer. As I was very young, and the only father in my life was taken, this situation was very hard. Seeing my foster mom and family grieving and trying to cope with the issue myself was indeed difficult. It was very hard because, in this little span of time, I had gone through yet another loss and having to adapt to all these new changes. Child welfare wanted to remove my sister and I from this home, as they felt that my foster mom may not be up for this challenge of being a single parent, but she fought hard for us. She didn't want to see us back in the foster system, getting moved around constantly. She may have been heartbroken from her loss, but that didn't stop her from loving us. I know that she needed us just as much as we needed her.

FOSTER CARE HAS IMPACTS

Being in foster care can be a negative experience that could emotionally affect any child but being in this scenario helped me in a good way, by directing me to be the person I am today. If it wasn't for foster care, my caseworkers, and foster parents, I couldn't even think of where I would possibly be now. My experiences with the foster system will allow me to be a social worker that really does understand the child's perspective and be able to have an honest connection with others who are going through a tough time.

As a previous child of foster care, I can relate to others who are and were in care. I am able to understand being part of a biological family and part of a foster family. It can be hard not really knowing where you came from and being curious of what your life would have been like if you weren't in care. Having been in foster care will enhance my development as a professional social worker because I'm able to help out kids just as I was helped out. I grew up with grief, so I truly get what most kids in care feel, never knowing what is going to happen next.

Internally, from being in foster care, I think on some level I felt I had to manage my emotions. Although I can express emotions genuinely and wholeheartedly, I am selective regarding whom I share these emotions with openly. Although it was never expressed to me by any of my family members, I sometimes chose what emotion was OK to show at certain times and what was not. In my mind, from a very young age, I felt if I wasn't happy with a decision or a rule, then it might affect my future in regard to whether or not I would be switched to a new home. Because I often had to judge what emotion was appropriate and would make others feel comfortable, it directed me to my method of how I assess and show my emotions today. For example, in most cases when something traumatic happens, I try to focus on something else that will bring me a happy feeling. It's not because I lack empathy, it's because I try to handle situations in a positive manner. I learned that my way of expressing emotion is different from others and there's no wrong or right way; I just have to be aware of how my external display of emotions may affect others. My response is often calm and discrete and may not be typical of responses highly emotional people may display in the same scenario.

THE IMPORTANCE OF KNOWING

Understanding one's own personal history is very important in young people's learning and development. For me particularly, it is so important to know my story, the steps that led to my siblings and I ending up in care, along with the reasons why my biological mother never wanted us, or whether she tried to get us back. All these things are questions I've had growing up, hearing a different story from multiple people, and not knowing who to believe. Knowing about genetically inheritable diseases is very important information that would have been very helpful to know. My older sister had to go through rigorous tests and months of pain to find out she had ulcerative colitis, which runs in the family on my dad's side. If we had known ahead of time, she could have avoided lots of troubles. Stories about how relatives coped with a particular disease or condition can provide hope to those who have it too.

WHAT DEFINES FAMILY

When people say 'family,' they usually think of their biological family – those who they share common blood with. But for me, that's not true. Family is not who you share blood with, it's the people who have your back when you can't have your own. Throughout my life, being put into foster care meant growing up with my foster family and opening myself up to new people. My 'family' is a group of people who I care very strongly for and who I know will always be there - my foster family. They've seen me at my worst and pushed me to be my best. I consider them closer to my heart then my biological family could ever be. Some people may look at this and not understand that, but that's fine. Biological family does not always come first. Family comes first, but the family that comes first for me isn't my biological family. The quote, "blood is thicker than water," doesn't resonate with me. My foster family is not blood related, but they are my family and always will be. So in my case, blood is not thicker than water. Without them I wouldn't be the person I am today, because they have impacted me in such a positive way.

SIBLING CONNECTIONS

Currently I only interact with and remain close to my older sister. We grew up together and she is my best friend. We are in contact every day and see each other as often as we can. I can't imagine growing up or going through this experience without her. She has grown a lot over the years – building a relationship with her fiancé, purchasing a home, and she is now a mother to my beautiful niece and nephew.

As for my other siblings, we do not have close relationships. I had consistent visits with my younger sister through the years when she was removed from our biological mother's home and placed with her father's mother. During that time, her grandmother worked closely with my foster mom to ensure arrangements for my younger sister to visit every second weekend; however, those visits stopped when my sister moved back in with our biological mother when I was 16 and my sister was 13. Although I see my younger sister sporadically, it has been difficult to strengthen our relationship, as she doesn't have much interest and seems to be heading down an unproductive path. My birth mother has had two more sons within the last few years, and I met them for the first time two years ago. I only see them as often as I see my younger sister, as they live in the same household with my biological mother. Although I do want to get to know my youngest siblings, it is a challenge. My two older brothers have not been present in my life whatsoever with the exception of a Facebook friendship with one of them.

KEY MESSAGES

I hope that people do realize the label of 'foster child' doesn't define who we are or make us deviant; everyone has the power to make a better life and find success from this experience. I have grasped my life purpose and direction and, if I had not gone through this, I wouldn't be who I am today. After all that has happened with foster care, I feel like it has made me a better person. I can't imagine what my life would be like if child welfare had not interfered and brought me 'home'.

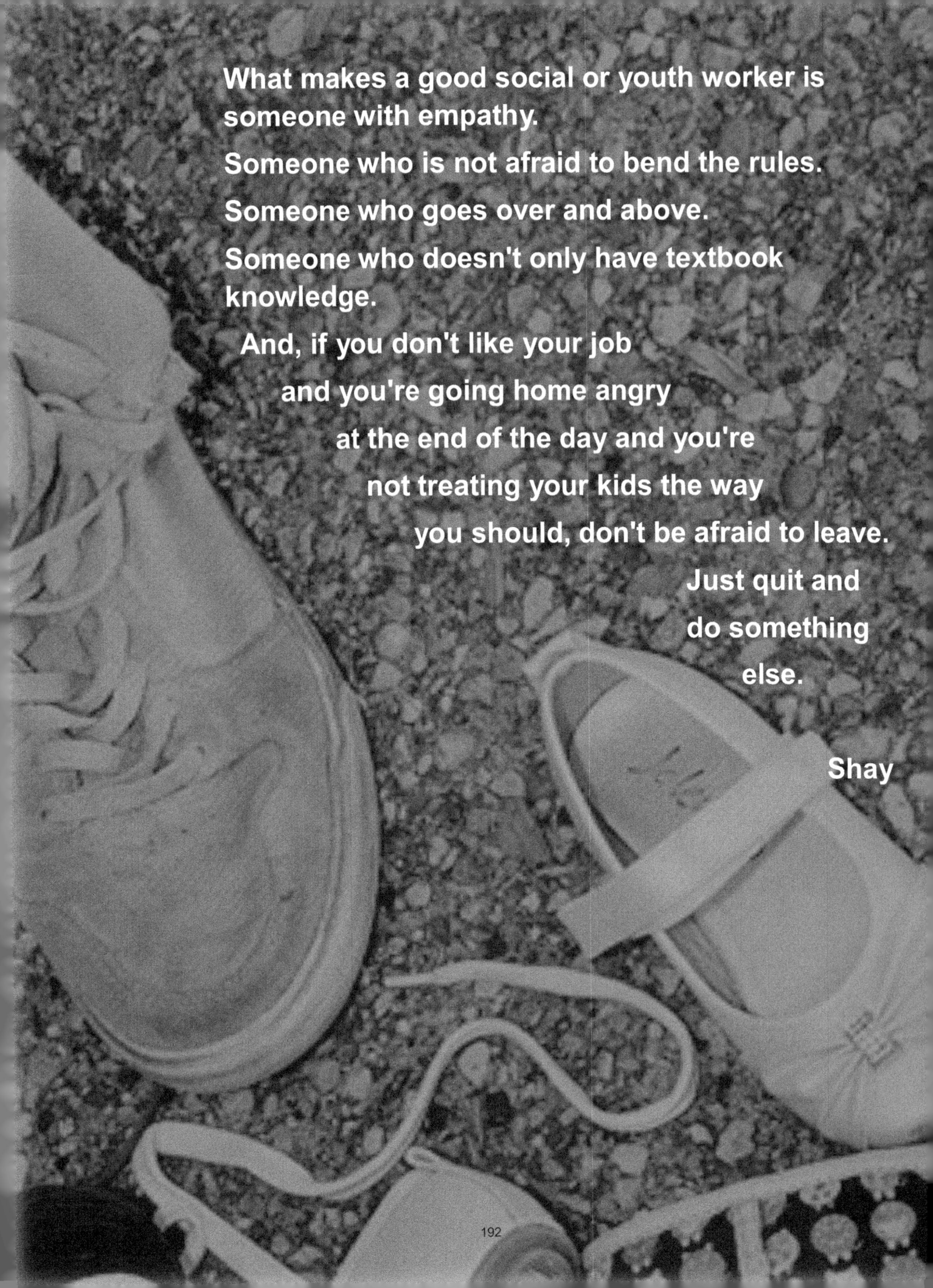

What makes a good social or youth worker is someone with empathy.

Someone who is not afraid to bend the rules.

Someone who goes over and above.

Someone who doesn't only have textbook knowledge.

And, if you don't like your job and you're going home angry at the end of the day and you're not treating your kids the way you should, don't be afraid to leave. Just quit and do something else.

Shay

Telus Mobility for Good & the Children's Aid Foundation of Canada help youth aging out of care

For youth leaving foster care, their phone can be their lifeline, helping them build credit, search for somewhere to live, find education and job opportunities, and stay in touch with friends and vital support networks.

A collaboration between TELUS and Children's Aid Foundation of Canada (CAFC) and select Centre de Jeunesse Foundations, Mobility for Good® helps these kids across Canada achieve independence by providing them with a free phone and a $0 plan, including 3 GB of data for two years.

(To read the full article please click on the headline or type the headline into your search bar.)

Postcard courtesy of The Adoption Council of Canada— Youth Speak Out Edmonton

My mother has a mental illness called Schizophrenia and my biological father was not present at my birth or throughout my life. My sister and brother's dad adopted me at a young age and taught me all about the sacred Aboriginal ways of life and practices. I remember him as funny – full of life, lessons, and love. Unfortunately, when I was around 14, my father became a homeless person after his father passed away and he was beaten by two teenagers who thought it would be fun to harm homeless people. He died from a slow brain bleed. I often think if only those teenagers had known the wonderful person he was, or the fact that he had a family that cared for him and needed him, that I needed him, maybe things would be different.

Patricia

Kenneth

I don't use the word faith, but I have a deep connection to my spirit and to my culture and to the Creator. I pray a lot, and I just try to make sure that my spirit is strong and I keep pushing forward and, eventually, I will get to where I need to be. It always seems to work out.

I am 27 years old and first went into care when I was six months old. I transitioned out of care when I was 24. I had been apprehended on an emergency basis five times between the ages of 6 months old and six years old. I think there were about four or five different placements. On the very last apprehension, which was on an emergency basis, child welfare applied for a Permanent Guardianship Order (PGO,) and I was put into a foster home. I was in the foster home for a year and a half and then I was brought back into my family's care and I stayed with them even though I was still PGO. My auntie was applying for adoption for us, so I stayed with my auntie between the ages of 7 to 17. When she passed away, I went into care again just before my 18th birthday and I was in care until I was 24.

I attended an ABC Head Start Program here in Edmonton and then I started kindergarten, but I was apprehended and brought to the foster home where I attended kindergarten and Grade One. I was brought back into my family's care and went to two other schools. I was lucky to have a little bit of stability there. I stayed at the second school until I was in Grade 6, and then I transferred over to another school or Grade 7, 8 and 9. I went to the same high school for Grade 10, 11 and 12. I was really lucky I didn't move around as much as a lot of others do.

In terms of the negative experiences that I had in care, a lot of them are just the same old story for most kids who are in care but, because I am an Indigenous person, I experienced a large disconnect from my culture. I missed opportunities to be with family and to learn the language and the culture that I'll never ever get back, and those were very pivotal moments when I was younger and my brain was at its best plasticity for picking things up and forming connections. My home life and being moved around a lot was disruptive and convoluted.

We had a very abusive stepfather. He knocked my mom out one day and she didn't wake up for three days. My brother and I were crying and screaming and kicking doors and trying to get somebody to help us and, finally, the upstairs neighbor called child welfare. The apprehension was really violent and scary. I was literally thrown over a fireman's shoulder while I watched my mom on the floor, not moving. My oldest brother was of age at the time - I think he was 15. He was able to be on his own, so he jumped out the window and after that he stayed on the streets and with my grandma. We didn't see him for a long time after that because he went to jail for four years, so I just watched my whole family kind of disperse. That was the last time that all of us were together. Being forcefully removed, put into a cop car, and brought to a police station to then be surrounded by a bunch of old white men in uniforms who gave me toys to try and calm me down, was really traumatic.

That very same day, we met our foster family in a parking lot. We were told to go with them, so jumping into the back of a white van and going out of the city with complete strangers the same day, literally didn't give us a chance to process anything. It was really reminiscent of the residential school system and was so surreal. What really sticks out for me is that we were expected to feel safe with these strangers. I was just a baby, only six or seven years old, and I had just lost my mom and I never had a father because he left before I was even born. So, to just hand two kids who were so young and defenseless and traumatized to a strange family who had no connection to any part of who we were, was also surreal.

I tried hard to form a connection with my foster mom because I'm such a mother's boy and as a Two-Spirit person, I really resonate with feminine energy. I really needed that in my life after losing my mother because she was my best friend and the biggest person in my life and my biggest source of love, and I just didn't get that from my foster mother. She was abusive. She would drink during the day. I remember her always having a beer in her hand doing her gardening and whatever else she did – just always drinking. They had a lot of money and they were getting quite a bit for us too. I remember they had four vehicles. They had a boat. They had horses. It was about a 35-acre yard. The house was gorgeous. It had seven bedrooms and was four stories, but my brother and I shared a small room in the basement. We really didn't feel like part of the family and I remember whenever our foster mom would get mad at me, she would grab my ear and she would twist it really hard. She would twist it so much that it would start clicking and making weird noises, and my ear would ring for hours and hours. That's one vivid memory that I have. Another one I have is that she would get really mad and she would force us to take showers, but they would be freezing-cold showers.

She would push me into the shower and I remember screaming because it was so cold, and I remember going up against the wall of the shower so the water couldn't touch me but she would demand that I went under the water. At the time, I thought she was bathing me, but I realize now how twisted that was, and I have a lot of trauma and a lot of fear from those situations.

My foster father sexually abused me. I don't know if he was like that with my brother, who was two years older than me, but he was like that with me. I'm not going to get into that, but he was a very bad man, and I didn't actually bring it up to anybody until I was 18 or 19 and I started going to counseling. I had an opportunity to file with a class action lawsuit that was happening. I got the papers from a friend who said, "Look, you can file for any damages or any physical or emotional abuse that you went through in care. They're doing this big class action lawsuit, and everyone needs to get their files in before X date, and you can receive up to such and such amount of money." I had the papers for two months and I kept ruminating over it and thinking should I, should I not? I even started to doubt my experience and I started to think if I write this down and make these allegations, it's going to go to court and it's going to be in writing and it's going to make it real and I'm going to have to see them again and I hadn't seen them in 15 years and just the thought of that gave me so much anxiety. I remember thinking that I had already done so much work to get past those events, no amount of money was going to make it okay for me to dig up a past that had died with my mom. I didn't want to go through all of that for the possibility of getting $10,000 or something. It was just not worth it for me.

The other thing that has stuck with me is that all the clothing we had, and our bikes and other things that were purchased with our recreation allowance didn't come with us when we moved. We weren't allowed to take it with us to my auntie's place in the city when we were finally adopted. So, we just showed up with two garbage bags full of whatever we had.

My mom passed away while we were in foster care. She passed away when I was seven. I went and visited her at the hospital during her last moments. She had developed HIV through intravenous drug use complications, and because of her HIV, she developed a cancerous tumor in her left eye and it was already Stage 4. My brother and I got a driver that took us to the hospital in Edmonton to see her, but we were only with her for 15 minutes. I spent that time holding her hand and remembering how beautiful she was before, when she had long hair down to her knees that used to always sway. I remember her hair would bounce when she'd walk, and it was so beautiful, and I would always play with it. Then, to see her with her head shaved and to see all that power lost. Her skin was gray, and her face was gone. To see that and to be so young, a baby really. To see my mom like that when I hadn't seen her for over a year and to be there for her last breath knowing that she was waiting to see us so she could pass away, that was the hardest moment of my entire life. After, we were driven directly back to the foster home.

I would have loved to have my mom visit me at the foster home even once every two weeks or even once a month, because we were there for a year and a half. It would have been nice to see her once in that entire time. I think someone, maybe an Indigenous liaison or someone, should have been aware of what was going on, because it didn't seem like anybody was really focused on my brother and I. We should have had visitations the whole time we were in that foster home, but we had nothing, and it would have made such a difference for all of us.

I have so many beautiful memories of my mother. I was always a dancer and my mom would always clear a space in the kitchen and put all the chairs to the side and make this little space and she would play these songs that I still listen to. She had this one song called "You're a Superstar," by the band Love Inc. She would put it on and she would say, "Dance my baby, dance!" I would grab her pashmina (her little scarf) and I would put her shoes on with these clunky little heels and I remember just dancing and sweating and she would just clap and clap. She would invite her friends over and I remember I used to call them my aunties even though they were just my mom's best friends. They would sit there and have a beer and just watch me dance and I would just dance for hours – huffing and puffing and spinning and twirling and jumping. I remember being so exhausted, but I was so happy doing it because I was so excited, and she was so proud of me. I just wanted to dance for her all the time.

I grew up really close to her and I remember never being scared of her. She always fed us, and we always had a safe place to sleep. My brother used to walk me to school every morning and hold my hand. He was my best friend and I was always so in awe of my older brother. I remember he would hold my hand and he would walk me to the end of the last block where the school field started and he would say, "Okay go to school now", and he would point to that little square in the fence where you could crawl through, and I remember thinking no, I don't want to go to school, and I would cry. He would tell me to go, and he would push me and say you have to go to school now, and I would go through that little square hole in the fence and I remember I would feel a little piece of me sink in my stomach because I wanted to spend time with my brother and I couldn't. He would start walking back to the house and I would get really scared when he wasn't around, so I had to run as fast as I could to the school. I was so in love with my mother and my brother. They were my home and my biggest everything and I never ever had issues with them when I was growing up. The only issues that arrived were with my stepdad, who was really abusive to us. He would do terrible things and beat us up and he broke my wrist one time. He would knock my mom out all the time and he always smelled like alcohol. He was actually the one who named me the name I used to have, so I changed my name because I had so much trauma attached to my old name – the one he used to yell. Every time I hear that name now, it makes me shiver and I feel like it's not me they are talking about.

So, I had a lot of negative experiences in care. If I had to choose any good experience it would be that my brother and I went to Catholic school with a bunch of white kids and we got a good education while we were there. The curriculum was quite high, we were expected to perform at that level and I did but unfortunately, my brother had learning disabilities and, instead of getting him help, they put him on medication and made a big disgrace of him at the school. They used to call him down to take his pills over the PA system and everyone would laugh at him. We were the only native kids in the entire school, and it was a big school. We were totally fish out of water, but I remember learning a lot. I remember learning sign language. I remember I was always very big into my studies and in my academics, and that's where I excelled. My brother was into horses and animals and bugs. He was also good in sports, but they didn't really facilitate any of that for him so he acted out in school. He was expected to be this academic superstar, which he wasn't, but nobody really tried to help him. They medicated him instead.

I don't think that anything I got from being in care was any better than what my own family could have given me. I could have gotten way more with my own family with less resources and I'm not going to pretend that I had a good experience in care because I really didn't and it's difficult. I feel almost guilty for trying to find good things about my experience there because of how bad it really was. Had I been with my mom and my family, things would have been a lot better and I would have been in a much better place. I think that's fair because that's the truth. The truth is what's important.

We finally left the foster home when I was seven and lived with my auntie. She was very poor and we lived in the inner city of Edmonton in this really disgusting place that should have been condemned. There were mice everywhere. There were around 15 people living at that house, but it was only a two-bedroom bungalow. I remember everyone used to scatter and jump out the windows every time the child welfare workers would come by because they weren't allowed to be there. I was really lucky that I was able to reconnect with my culture there. My family is quite traditional, so when I moved in with my auntie and other family, they, like my mom, spoke Stoney. We are Nakota Sioux. That was my grandmother's and my mom's first language, so they always spoke Stoney in the house and they practiced smudging all the time. They had medicines and would take me to see medicine people all the time. I helped with the building of sweat lodges with my family on the reserve, and we would go hunting. Sometimes I would come home from school and there'd be a big moose with a tarp over it and the whole family would be helping and making dry meat. I was really lucky to have a family that made culture a priority because it is really important. I got to attend so many different ceremonies including sun dances.

All cultural teachings are important. They contribute to a healthy, holistic outlook and they contribute to good mental health. We need to be doing that work for the Indigenous people that are in care, for all our young people and not only for Two-Spirit people. Remember the percentage of Indigenous youth that are in care. It's like if you have a restaurant where 70% of all people who go to that restaurant are vegetarian, why would you still have meat as the main offerings every single day? That doesn't make sense to me. We need to shift so that we cater to 70% of the children who are in care. My culture saved my life. And the reason that I'm here today is because I have such a deep connection to who I am within my community and I have that love for every single thing that I do in my life. I wake up and I smudge in the morning, and even the shawl I'm wearing and the beaded earrings that my sister made for me keep me strong. The ceremonies that I go to speak to who I am intrinsically as a Two-Spirit Nakota Sioux person from Treaty 6 territory. I can't disconnect myself from that. But when I was in care, I was no longer a Nakota Sioux Indigenous youth. I was a case number, so none of that mattered anymore.

When I turned 17, my auntie passed away suddenly one day. She actually passed away in her bed. I found her on a Sunday morning. She didn't come out for lunch and so I went to see her, and she was not alive anymore. I remember that being a really shocking and heartbreaking time for my whole family. We had a ceremony for her and buried her on the reserve. When we got back to the house, we found out that my mom was the one who had signed up for low-income housing and so her name was on the account and none of us could take that on. There was a really long wait list to get a place, so we couldn't afford to stay at that place anymore. Everyone had to figure out what they were going to do and everyone just kind of went into survival mode and did what they needed to do. Everyone just dispersed and I moved in with one of my classmates because I went to quite a revered school and I had some really good friends. I was one of only 12 self-identifying Indigenous people out of the 600 kids that were at that school. I went to Junior High and High School with the friend I moved in with. I got close to this family because I would go over and visit and we would always have food together and so, after my auntie passed away, no one really checked in on me. None of my teachers or the school called me. Nothing like that. I stopped going to school because I didn't see the point. I was really depressed. I really only went to school because it made my auntie happy and it made me happy to see her proud of me. So, after she passed away, I kind of lost all hope. I slept for two days. Then my friend's mom called me and said I was coming to live with them. I wasn't in any position to turn away any help because I had nothing, and I really liked my friend and his family. So I went and lived with them and, to make a long story short, my friend became jealous of me because I was close to his mom and I had to leave, but I didn't have anywhere to go, so I became homeless at age 17.

My auntie's daughter took me in, but she was having her second baby and she didn't really have any room at her place. She was also living in low-income housing and I slept on her couch for the majority of my Grade 12 year. I was really depressed, and I remember self-harming a lot. I was just not in a good place. Eventually, it got to the point after months and months and months of me just kind of freeloading there, she just couldn't afford to have me there anymore. I wasn't bringing any money in and I was an extra mouth to feed. She kind of told me that I had to do something, and so I pulled up my bootstraps and walked to the central regional office for child welfare and got a worker to take a look at my story and talk to me. We talked for hours and the worker worked really hard to get me into a placement. I didn't have anywhere to go, so I stayed in a youth emergency shelter in Edmonton. My caseworker was able to put me into their skills for youth program at the shelter society. I stayed there for two months until they told me I was overqualified because I already knew how to cook for myself, knew how to clean, knew how to do my laundry, and knew how to budget my time. I was also still in school and I had worked part-time before, so I just didn't meet the requirements. They decided that I wasn't right for the program, so they kicked me out of there.

Next, I went to a TSIL (Transitional Semi-Independent Living) building right in the rough part of Edmonton. I stayed in this really terrible apartment building. It had locks on everything and was like a jail. Basically, it was a big group home. We were all given our own units and I had keys to my unit, but I didn't have keys to the front door so I couldn't even get into the building. I had to be buzzed in and I had to tell them who I was every single time. I couldn't have people over. I wasn't allowed to furnish the place. I was only allowed to use what they had provided. They did checks on me four times a day and they would barge into my unit at 2:00 in the morning while I was sleeping and shine a flashlight on my face to make sure that I was there. It was invasive and terrifying. One of the kids stabbed one of the workers with a screwdriver and put their head through the front window. It was crazy living at that place, and I lived there for two months. I remember they made us walk to the grocery store every Thursday at 5:00 p.m. They would give us each $75 to buy groceries for ourselves. It was, like, a 40-minute walk and they had a huge van, but they wouldn't drive us there. They would make us walk beside the van and they would drive really slow next to us while we walked with all our groceries because they wanted to teach us a lesson. It just felt dehumanizing and it didn't serve me any purpose other than to make me resentful and to feel like an animal.

I told my caseworker that I hated it there and that I was scared for my life. I didn't belong there and it wasn't a good area of the city. I'm a Two-Spirit person and I'm quite feminine and quite small. It wasn't the best area of town for me to be walking around at night, so I just didn't want to be there. I kept getting turned down for other programs because I was overqualified until, finally, I got referred to an agency that had a program for me where I could live on my own. I was very thankful that I was approved. That was one of the best things that ever happened to me. They set me up with an amazing key worker who I'm still friends with to this day. She was a bisexual woman and she understood me. She was a little quirky, a little artsy, a little out of the box, which was totally what I needed. I got a living allowance and then she helped me apply for my first apartment on Whyte Avenue next to the university, because that's where I was going to be going to school. It was this shitty, little, 400 square foot bachelor suite that should have been condemned and it was $980 a month. After rent, I had about $120.00 to live on. It was terrible and I hated it.

I went right from high school into my first year of university and I didn't really want to go to university because nobody in my family had even graduated high school. I didn't know anyone in there and I didn't even know what university was really. I was more focused on trying to eat and not to get stabbed and trying to survive. At the time, I was also ignoring my sexual identity, which I was coming into at the age of 17. I also developed an anxiety disorder and was having terrible panic attacks and fainting. I didn't know what was wrong, and I was so depressed because I had just lost my auntie. So, I had a lot going on at that time, but I applied for university because people were pushing me to and I got accepted. I thought that this would be a way to make everything better.

If my caseworker wanted me to go to university and my key worker wanted me to go to university and the liaison at my high school wanted me to go to university, I just thought I might as well do it. So, I got that first shitty, little apartment and I was like, all right, I'm going to university and, boy, was that ever a terrible idea. I had no support and I was severely depressed to the point of being suicidal. I was poor, so I didn't have enough money to eat and I had to pay for a cell phone because my SFAA (Supports and Financial Assistance Agreement) required me to have a phone. So I had to spend $30 a month to have a phone. I do want to say that it was really good that I had a SFAA because, at the time, I knew that not a lot of youth were receiving supports after their 18th birthday. A lot of them weren't being signed for help so I felt very blessed to get an agreement signed with a caseworker one week before my 18th birthday. At that time, youth in care aged out at age 22 and now it's age 24. So, I was really lucky.

My first year of university didn't work out and after three months of trying really hard, I remember just breaking down and telling my caseworker, "I don't want to be here anymore. I can't do it." I really felt like one of a million kids at that school. I was just a little drop in the bucket, and I had no support and I was in over my head at the time. I knew I had bigger fish to fry than going to school so I withdrew from that term and got a counselor who was a really nice lady. I talked to her regularly for three years and, between that time when I turned 18 the next year, I met a boy and started a relationship with him and we were together for eight years. We just broke up seven months ago.

I worked for a youth advocate and I worked in a disability services position and eventually went back to school for a year. I then took time off to go to South America, where I lived in Columbia for six months. I just got back two years ago and got my dream job as a mental health worker but, due to Covid-19, I got laid off. I went through my breakup at the same time and on top of all that, I got really sick. Since then, I've packed up my life and moved to Toronto, which is where I am now. I'm doing what I like to call a "one month or one year" trial. At the end of this year, if it's amazing, I'll stay. And if it's the worst experience I've ever had, I will just go back home.

I did my first year of university at the University of Alberta, and their Indigenous program is so amazing. I met a lot of great people. I still have supports in that office to this day, and friends that I'll have forever. Then, I transferred to MacEwan University to do their Bachelor of Arts in Psychology with a minor in English, and I will continue at MacEwan online from where I am now. I just thought that now is the perfect time for me to transition to a new chapter of my life and start new projects, meet new people, and just kind of reset myself. Creator really has a way of looking out for me and making sure that the right things happen to me, and I meet the right people, and the right things teach me, and I'm really looked after. So many things in my life have clicked by complete chance – absolute coincidences, like never in a million years would that happen, but they happen. So, I'm just putting my trust in that, and I know that I have a lot of people up there watching over me, like my mom and my auntie and my grandma and my late brother and so I have a lot. I don't use the word faith, but I have a deep connection to my spirit and to my culture and to the Creator. I pray a lot, and I just try to make sure that my spirit is strong and I keep pushing forward and, eventually, I will get to where I need to be. It always seems to work out.

I was always told when I was younger that I'm just like my Mom – so free-spirited. She would travel a lot and not tell anybody where she was going. She's the only one in my family who traveled overseas. She went to Europe and nobody knew where she was, and she came back with all these gifts and a new language and everyone was so jealous of her. So, that's kind of how I've lived my life. When I took off to do the internship in Colombia, I did it on a whim with three weeks notice and I just left. I learned a new language there. I'm almost fluent in Spanish now, and I have new family down there and I grew a lot. In those six months, I learned that I love to travel and I love to learn new languages. I currently speak four languages (English, Cree, Chinese and Spanish) and that's something that's always kept me going. I'm a big believer in chosen family. So, family to me is a lot more than just blood. I had to realize that at quite a young age because of the amount of loss that I had experienced. My immediate family was just my mom and my two brothers, so just us four. After my mom passed, my oldest brother went into jail for four years so we had to get to know him all over again later in life. So, it was just me and my other brother that went through the foster system and I had to kind of choose people from my life. Unfortunately, I chose wrong sometimes. For example, I put my foster family quite close to my heart and tried to create that idea of what a family looks like, even though it wasn't healthy.

To me, family are the people that make me feel like home and that make me feel safe – my brother, my nieces and my nephews, the friends that I've chosen because after I came out and I came into my Two-Spirit identity, I really met a lot of amazing people in the Two-Spirit community who became my friends. I work for a non-profit called Edmonton Two-Spirit Society. I was the Director of Education and Outreach for two years, so I was able to do a lot of amazing workshops, panels, and discussions. I realized that the people I chose to spend my day to day life with, the ones I was in ceremony with, and those with whom I shared a lot of my personal struggles, they were also my family. My partner was also my family at the time. He was my family for a long time. My in-laws were family, too. So family is a lot more than blood. It's a connection that I have to people and their spirits and how they make me feel.

I went through my file when I was 18. I think it's important because I had a lot of repressed memories before the age of seven. And so my recollection and my vision of what had happened was completely shattered when I saw the file and knew what actually happened. I realized that I had blocked out a lot of those emergency apprehensions, so for them to sit me down and say, "Look, on April so-and-so of this year and this time, two policemen came to your house…" and blah-blah-blah. I didn't recall that happening, and then I'm able to read these files and see my name and see these details about what happened to me. It's like reading about a different person. I realized my mind and my spirit really tried to protect me by making them forget all of those things. To see it was quite sobering and quite shocking. I remember my caseworker at the time was not a good worker. He didn't really care. He was just like, "Yeah, I'll grab it for you," and he just kind of gave it to me. He didn't prepare me for what I was about to get into and so it was hard and could have been handled a lot differently. I would have preferred to sit down with someone, maybe an Elder or some type of counselor or someone who really loved me –just have a sounding board. Or maybe sit down with somebody who understood the system, the terminology and the jargon that was being used. It's really difficult as a young, Indigenous person to read all of these big fancy words with all these titles that had happened to me. I would have preferred to have somebody come and facilitate that.

I have had some good workers. The first one that comes to mind was my key worker from the independent living program. That agency has this unique rule where every youth has to meet with their key worker face to face at least once a week. So our once-a-week meetings turned into her taking me for coffee, meeting me at a park, taking me to go shopping, dropping off job applications with me, and she would just come and pick me up anywhere. Sometimes I would just call her if I needed a ride, and she would be working so she would pick me up and we would just talk and listen to music. I remember her introducing me to reggae music and how big of a deal that was for me because I'd never heard it before. She was just really amazing and talked to me about everything except my case file. She didn't talk to me about any of that. She talked to me about what kind of music I liked, what I was looking for in terms of hobbies or recreation, or she would want to know what I learned at school that day. She would remember things that I would tell her like small details that she'd bring up next time and say, "Oh, I remember you told me about your friend Brittany. How is she doing?" This was very new because no other worker had done that before. I had never really connected with professionals in that manner. So, to treat me like a human and to remember little things about my life was very different. I'm putting her on a pedestal and I need to, because I feel she went above and beyond at times. I was otherwise surrounded by egotistical, self-centered, overworked, stressed out non-Indigenous caseworkers every single day who didn't care about me. I was just one of their many files that they have on their caseload and to be around that all day is very dehumanizing.

That key worker was also the first person I really started to talk about my sexual identity with because she was the only person that I was able to feel comfortable enough with to talk. If I had not had her, I don't know who I would have told, but it would have been a long time coming. I feel like I have an obligation to speak about my experience with being a sexual minority and my gender identity, as well as my sexual orientation, and how that was really never something that was ever brought up by any of my caseworkers or any of my workers until I brought it up with my last youth worker. Not once in my life-long history of being in of care was anyone ever really equipped and ready to have that conversation with me about my identity, and I presented quite feminine for my entire life. Even though I'm not transgender, and I don't take that identity on, not once was somebody like, "Hey, I noticed you are wearing makeup and you painted your nails." No one wanted to ask me about that. In hindsight, I'm 27 now and I'm old enough to be a caseworker, so if I had a child or a youth on my caseload and I saw them wearing a skirt and eyeliner, I'd be like, "What's up? Let's talk. I love your look. Tell me about it." You know, I would have that conversation with them because, clearly, I'm dated enough to know about gender and sexual diversity. I give workshops on that subject. I know that it's important to have that conversation in a very healthy and facilitating way, rather than just completely ignoring it and focussing instead on where the kid is going to live in the future, what are they going to do for school, where are they going to get a job, and so on. That's what they focus on because they're not comfortable or educated, or they are straight-up homophobic.

I identify as Two-Spirit, and that's something that has been around since time immemorial. However, I think if you were to ask a lot of child welfare workers who are non-Indigenous, they would see it as a new-age term that is like a new movement of identity, which is not true. The term Two-Spirit is quite new because it's been adapted into contemporary English language so other people can understand it. It's not that we just started being Two-Spirit in 1990. Two-Spirit people predate the colonial structure of what LGBTQ is now. I facilitated the very first panel discussion on Two-Spirit identity with child welfare services in Alberta. I facilitated that in February of 2019 and I did the Indigenous Speaker Series as one of their key notes. It was the first time that we had ever discussed Two-Spirit identity here, so it made me realize that I was like the little guy who didn't even have a chance. They hadn't even heard of someone like me.

I don't believe in the child welfare system, personally. I think it is a death machine and needs to be dismantled completely. It needs to be completely given over to Indigenous communities to govern their own children because 70% of all kids in my province who are in care are Indigenous. That's disgusting and scary. And, as one of them who's just a statistic, I'm lucky to be where I am having gone through that horrible system. The amount of racism and the amount of just blatant abuse and neglect is totally unacceptable. To have worked with it through an advocate service, myself, and seeing them implement their special investigations team year after year after year is discouraging. They do investigations of suspicious deaths and care, and the majority are Indigenous kids who are dying. It is terrifying and horrible, and I don't want to advocate for anyone to work for child welfare, because I've seen firsthand the amount of workers who come fresh out of university, who are child welfare workers and who have studied the textbooks and they want so badly to jump into this field where they can make changes because they really want to help those youth, and they go into the situation and … BAM! They have a hundred plus case caseloads. Half of the kids are suicidal. The other half are mentally ill, addicted to drugs and/or homeless and they're expected to form a relationship with all of these people and to be that amazing person fresh out of school with no training. All they've read are textbooks and they're expected to have cultural competency and to deal with the complexities of being an Indigenous person on stolen land. That to me, is absolutely mind-boggling.

The burnout rate for most child welfare workers is less than five years because they're so overworked and stressed out and, even if you do have that good intention, there are procedures, there are protocols, there is approval required. It's pretty hard for anyone to make changes. What I would like to recommend to people in the field is to try to meet these youth where they are. Try to remind them that they are so much more than this process and what they're going through. Try to find ways to bring back humanization to their life. Try to remember that, while all of these things are happening and all these wheels are turning and all these processes are happening, that life is also still happening. These young people can't just sit around waiting for things to happen because all of their peers are growing up without them. They're missing out on essential life skills and love and connection and education. So, try your hardest to remember they aren't just case files.

I was a case file for so long that, when I went to university, I had the worst imposter syndrome I've ever felt in my entire life. I felt physically sick. I remember I would get nauseous and my anxiety would get so bad. My joints would lock up and my lips would get purple and quiver because I just felt so out of place and not welcome and like the entire system had been not made for me. To see all the blond-haired, blue-eyed kids smiling and having such a great time during their first year of university, I just remember feeling so disconnected from that and so ashamed.

I am pretty articulate now, and I have had a lot of opportunity for self-reflection. I have a lot of expression and I'm not scared to express myself. I have experience doing public speaking, so I don't get nervous when I go into situations where I have to explain myself or my history to large groups of professionals. I get asked to speak on panels a lot and to be a part of advisory committees and to be on this, and this, and this, and this, and this. It's become so many it's to the point that I'm starting to forget the acronyms and the names they come up with for all these programs. It's like they get all this funding and then they have to fill this quota, so they all need Indigenous youth. They come and ask me all the same questions. They've asked me year after year after year and the wheels keep turning, but no real change is being made. No one follows up with saying, "Hey, look at all of that trauma that we've got from you." This is what I feel it's turned into and this is where it's going – I'm a part of this box they check off so they get their money, but I don't get paid anything because nobody pays Indigenous youth, and they just keep going.   So, my word of advice to anybody who's trying to get into child welfare work and really wants to make a difference in, and improve the lives of kids in care is: You need to invite them into spaces that are theirs, that they're comfortable in, and you need to use their language. You need to make yourself accessible. You need to be transparent. A lot of the time, we know what's going on. We're not stupid. This is our life. The amount of times I've been put into situations where people are trying to disguise their language and they don't expect me to understand what's going on would surprise you. Don't speak over me. Don't speak above me. Don't invite me to have meetings in dingy, scary offices to sign papers. I had a caseworker who would make me write my own support agreement - every single time we had to redo it. She would just buy me lunch, slide over the paper, give me the pen and say, "Well, you're good at this so you can do it." So, I'm sitting there having to write this entire thing and it was long.

When I was in my first year of university, I was seeing a counselor and was starting to feel a little bit of security when my caseworker said we want to move you down to one-month terms for supports. I had actually never heard of a one-month term and it felt like a slap in the face. I said, "So, if I don't meet whatever, you're going to cut me off, I'm going to lose my key worker, I'm going to lose my funding, I'm going to lose my apartment, I'm going to lose my counselor that I just started seeing and I'm going to lose my phone." I'm just thinking of all these things that I am going to be losing and that added even more pressure to me wanting to succeed in university. I saw it as child welfare essentially being my parent, so they needed to be supporting me, not setting me up to fail. Indigenous youth, especially, are going to slip up; they're going to make mistakes. I'm surprised I didn't make as many mistakes as I could have. We can't cut these kids off. The alternative is that they die a lot of the time. I don't say that lightly because I've seen it. I have family members who went through it, and friends, too.

So, I got myself an advocate, and I said this was not okay - this is really bad. They came back and they said they would give me a six-month agreement instead, and I said, "Okay, but in six months, I'm still going to be in school. What's going to happen? Every single time I get a renewal, I write it myself – my case worker doesn't even help me. So how are you guys telling me that you have all these expectations for me, and I need to meet all these goals, when I'm the one writing the goal. I'm the one keeping myself accountable." I said, "This is not fair", and I pushed it back on them. Then, the manager came back and said they would sign a one-year agreement with me. I remember my caseworker at the time saying that this had never happened, so it was a big deal. So, the year went by and they moved it to a six-month agreement, and then three-months, and by that time I had aged out. There is so much that people don't know or understand about youth in care. Some of the stereotypes are that we're abandoned and aren't loved, and that's not the case. A lot of times, youth in care have families that love them that are fighting tooth and nail to get these kids back. I was not abandoned. I was not unloved. I had a home and I had a family that cared about me. Yes, there were problems, but those could have been worked on. Another stereotype is that we're all uneducated when that's always not the case. A lot of people think I get everything for free. This is one that really, really, really hurts and really bothers me, as I've even had close friends of mine that throw that idea in my face and say it's so easy for me because child welfare pays for everything. These are friends of mine who go to university, who don't have to take out a loan, and whose parents are paying for it. They're staying with their parents in a beautiful house. They don't have to pay $800 a month to live in a shitty, crummy apartment by themselves. Everything is handed to them and they have a family, and then they come at me and they want my independence. They say they wish they could live in an apartment, and that's also a slap in the face because I would give my left arm to have my mother still alive and take care of me in her house. It would mean the absolute world to me. So people have these ideas of what it means to be in care, like I'm being pampered and child welfare is doing everything for me when they don't realize it took it took two and a half months of grueling meetings and advocating for myself to even have my graduation cap and gown paid for. I almost didn't graduate because I couldn't afford to. I also get the misconception that because I am Indigenous, everything is handed to me. Meanwhile, I have applied for student loans because my reserve won't fund me and I don't qualify for child welfare funding anymore. So here I am. Everyone's telling me that all this stuff is paid for and I'm like okay, show me the money because I'd love to have it.

One of my favorite things to read is romance. I'm an old soul and a very hopeless romantic. I like reading the mushy-gushy relationships and falling in love stories, and all that kind of stuff. But I realized growing up, it was Hunger Games and Twilight. I just couldn't connect with most young adult stories because, most of the time, it's a heterosexual, cisgender, white couple. The girl's always nerdy and the guy's a bad boy and then they fall in love and all that cliché stuff. I just really couldn't connect with it and I never ever remember once seeing myself in a book. So, I've written about 25 stories and I write short novels about young, Two-Spirit people and young, Indigenous, queer people. I write about people who identify as male because that's who I am. And that's what I know. So, I write that and I write romance novels for young Indigenous career people, who are young adults, because I want to normalize same-sex love, especially in the Indigenous community. I want to really write about how it can be beautiful, and I really don't try to use the same amount of recycled tropes that keep happening in Western media when they involve Indigenous people. I don't want my characters as struggling addicts and I don't want to write my characters as residential school survivors. I think that representation needs to happen because it's true – it's our reality – but I want to take a break from that because I think that fiction can be whatever I want it to be. It makes me happy to read about an Indigenous young person who didn't have to go through care, and who wasn't sexually abused, and wasn't in the residential school system, and who wasn't suicidal and, you know, whose family wasn't homophobic because I would love to see that it's possible. I really want to be published. I hope that this book is going to be published to educate and inform and make a difference in the field, but more importantly, make a difference to any youth that are reading it, who are in care right now or former youth in care that are still struggling.

Being on drugs seemed fun when I started – having freedom and friends, living like hippies and always having a party.

But soon I found myself in a different crowd that was shady and involved in a lot more criminal activities than just using drugs. I realized that if I carried on with the life I was living – struggling, starving, dirty, and frequently scared – I would be raped or caught in a violent crossfire. That was all I would ever have to look forward to. Being a drug addict means living a really hard life. I had been doing that my whole life already, I didn't want to do it forever.

Ashley

Study shows 'empirical' link between residential schools and Indigenous youth in care: researcher

UBC study found descendants of residential school survivors at higher risk of ending up in care

Michelle Ghoussoub   CBC   July 4, 2019

"The crux of the argument is that the family exposure to the residential school system is driving the overrepresentation of Indigenous kids in care," she said.

Barker, who had previously investigated the child welfare system, said the findings are "probably the most powerful, important study I've ever done."

(To read the full article click the headline or type the headline into your search bar.)

> Do you know what it's like to have everything swept away?
>
> ...Again?

Postcard courtesy of The Adoption Council of Canada—Youth Speak Out Edmonton

I think anybody who meets any kid in care needs to understand that they need to have an open mind and a high level of understanding. Every kid is different.

Mike

Megan

I didn't want anyone to know I was in care, because I didn't want to be treated any differently than those kids around me who were not. I still wanted to be nurtured, and I wanted to be challenged in the same ways that everyone else was. I did not want to be defined by the fact that I was a kid in care, but rather defined by who I was as a person.

I went into care the day after my 15th birthday and was in care for almost exactly three years. I had three placements altogether, but only one official placement with my aunt and uncle in kinship care. Prior to that, I had been with my mom and dad until I was 12, and then just with my dad from ages 12 to 15. My mom wasn't around anymore, due to the fact that her sister had died in a hit-and-run accident around that time, and she was unable to cope with it, so she became more heavily involved in alcohol and started using.

My home environment was relatively normal, up until age 12 when I was first diagnosed with Type 1 Diabetes, and then my mom started getting into drugs and alcohol again. My parents had just separated and that was unfortunate, but I never really felt unsafe in my home, although my dad always had a nasty temper. He was never violent, but I did sometimes worry that he would be. He also had some other really messed up stuff going on behind the scenes that I wasn't aware of until my sister and I were apprehended and he was later incarcerated for sexually abusing my underage cousin for eight years.

I remember the day we were apprehended very clearly. Two police officers showed up at our house with a caseworker and they said we had 15 minutes to pack up everything we would need for the foreseeable future. We had been told the day before that something was happening, so I was expecting to be taken away from my father, but I didn't know what to expect beyond that. That 15-minute time limit to totally change my life really sticks in my mind to this day. It all happened very fast. We were put into the car and not told where we were going, but I was just happy that my sister and I didn't get split up. I have always been grateful that we were able to stay together for most of our time in care. Being placed with my aunt and uncle had its challenges. Being with family was good in some ways, but they weren't exactly the most stable people to be taking care of us. I remember my uncle using black nail polish to number all our dishes and assigning us each a number so we wouldn't use too many. He said the dishwasher was "too expensive", but I also know it was so we would eat less food for the same reason. I remember having to sneak food when we were living with them, and I never went to school with a lunch. I used the money I made at my part-time job to buy food or I relied on my friends to feed me. More often than not, I ended up eating a Twix chocolate bar as a meal – not exactly an ideal situation for anyone, let alone a diabetic child.

My aunt was heavily into gambling, so we were not very well off financially, and my uncle was constantly drunk and verbally abusive. Once, he screamed and yelled at me so loudly for no good reason that the next day he bought me flowers and a card apologizing for his behaviour. That stuck with me, because I thought it was very odd. They were both really hard on my younger sister, which had a big impact on her. They were unkind to her and said some horrible things. I think it affected her for a long time after, but I was always afraid to say anything that would jeopardize our placement with them because at least with them I was able to stay with my sister. I was terrified that she and I would be separated; it was a daily thought for me and made me very anxious.

I don't remember having more than one worker and I don't remember seeing her much, which probably would have been helpful. There were no home visits at my aunt and uncle's that I recall, other than once in the very beginning when she came because she found out my dad had been contacting me and she needed to confiscate the cell phone that he had continued to pay for after we were apprehended. I never got to know her that well, but I do remember she nominated me for The Great Kids Award for youth in care in Alberta and we went to a lunch together.

The worst part of all of this for me, and what was really scary, was having no one to help me look after my diabetes. I had to look after myself from the age of 15 on, with little training myself, and so I didn't know how to monitor it properly. I ate without taking my insulin, I didn't know all the factors that could affect my diabetes, such as anxiety, and my aunt never came to any of my doctor appointments with me. Consequently, I have had a really hard time getting it under control ever since. I just started an insulin pump in January of this year, and that's been helpful, but it took a long time for me to get to that point. I have had anxiety most of my life and anxiety increases cortisol levels, which increases blood glucose levels. My anxiety is much more under control now, as I have a counsellor and I take medication to help manage it. I am able to advocate for myself to address my needs, which I consider a positive outcome of being in care. I only went to one high school while I was in care, which was an hour and a half bus ride each way, but I used that time for schoolwork so, in some ways, it was a blessing. The most memorable story from my time in high school was in grade 12. We were meant to go on a tour of Germany for ten days with my band and choir classes. Of course, my aunt and uncle couldn't afford a trip that extravagant for both me and my sister, so I thought we wouldn't be able to go together; however, a well-timed anonymous donation meant that my sister and I were both able to go on this life-changing trip with all our friends! I never found out who made the donation but will be eternally grateful to whomever it was. When I graduated high school, my aunt and uncle came to the ceremony, which was nice, but after the ceremony they left without taking me home. It is kind of funny to look back on that now, but at the time it really upset me because I felt they'd abandoned me at this huge moment in my life, and I still to this day have no idea why.

I went on to attend university with a bursary for former youth in care to pursue further education, which I will always be grateful for, as it paid for both my degrees. I went to the University of Lethbridge, which has a really good Faculty of Education. I had started off with a biology degree but when my mom passed away in my first year, I decided I needed to do something more "fun," so I switched to a drama degree. I had never done drama, other than once in junior high, but I like to think it was meant to be because it became a passion. Three years into that, I applied to the Faculty of Education to do a combined degree. I was accepted and completed both degrees in five and a half years.

I have wanted to be a teacher since I was five years old. My mom wanted to keep me home for an extra year before I started Kindergarten, but I simply would not allow that, so she eventually gave in and I started in October. There was a time in high school when I contemplated becoming a nurse, but I always loved school and kids and the field of education, so it was really the only way to go for me. After I got my degrees, I taught for a couple of months in Alberta and then moved to England for two years where I taught Drama, Science, and English. Now I work in Calgary in a Grade 5 classroom for children with learning disabilities and other co-morbidities and I love it! This July, I am going to start my Master of Education degree. I think it's important to mention that there were a lot of teachers that had a positive influence in my life, particularly my band teachers, and I think that had a big impact on my decision to pursue education as a career is incredibly important to me.

Family is really important to me. Obviously, my sister is the person who has always been with me and so my relationship with her is extremely important. I do have a relationship with my dad now, which is a very confusing and strange relationship. It's a huge source of anxiety for me, my husband, and my sister. It's very toxic and I am glad I have a support system in place to help me deal with it. I think that because I lost my mom and he is my only living parent, I feel like I have an obligation to maintain that relationship, even though I really struggle with it. We have lost touch with some of the extended family on my mom's side, as they are not happy that I have continued a relationship with my father. My aunt who we lived with was my mom's sister and we don't really have a relationship anymore, either. So, while family is important, I also feel that some family relationships are not healthy, and I don't try to maintain those. Just because someone is blood, does not mean they should be in your life.

I think there is often a misconception about youth in care and, because of this, I was embarrassed about being in care myself. They are not bad kids, but they can often make bad choices and people hear those stories more often than they do the success stories. People need to understand that every case is different – every child is different – and to never treat a kid like they are just a kid in care. I didn't want anyone to know I was in care, because I didn't want to be treated any differently than those kids around me who were not. I still wanted to be nurtured, and I wanted to be challenged in the same ways that everyone else was. I did not want to be defined by the fact that I was a kid in care, but rather defined by who I was as a person.

It is important for kids in care to know their rights. I didn't know mine and I would have appreciated someone sitting down with me and saying, "Let's talk." I also think it is important to have access to our case files following our time in care. I don't have mine yet, but I do intend to get them when I'm ready. I feel like there are a lot of events and details that I may be blocking out, or that I didn't even necessarily know, and it's my right to know. It may be difficult going through my file, but knowledge is power. I am 30 years old now, and my life is really good. I am happily married and my husband and I just bought our first home together last year. We have a dog named Mocha and a cat named Odie, and they bring us so much joy every day. I have a strong relationship with my sister, and she is doing amazing things with her life. It has been a long road filled with many struggles, but I am extremely proud of the person that I have become, despite those challenges. If I were to leave you with one thought as you go through life, it would be that everyone is fighting a battle that you know nothing about, so always be kind.

One of the most significant and positive impacts of having grown up in care was that it helped give me a second chance in life – one that I did not think I would have. Although my experience of growing up in care is best described as chaotic, it also gave me many opportunities, like the opportunity to go to post secondary school, to get mental health support, to live in a stable environment, and to develop some positive role models.

Some of these opportunities afforded to me, having grown up in care, were beneficial in many aspects, but alone, they would have still left me stranded and incomplete. It was really the relationships I had with those outside the system that made the most significant difference in my life. These relationships extended far past my involvement with the child welfare system and are still critical to my success today. Without these outside relationships and the opportunities afforded to me by the child welfare system, I am ultimately unsure where I would be right now.

Cody

A Planned Adoption Delayed—By Nearly Three Decades

CBC Radio—Out In The Open—Updated August 16, 2018

"Having her lower herself down to my level, having her call me by my name ... it was indelible for me. I knew, instinctively, that she was different.... I could trust her. Regina Louise is describing the first time she met Jeanne Kerr, the woman she would eventually call Mom.

It was the 70s; Regina was just 13 at the time. She'd escaped a violent foster family two years earlier and had been checked in to a centre for abandoned and abused children, where Jeanne worked as a group counsellor. The two made an instant impression on each other, and, soon, they made a plan for Jeanne to adopt Regina. And then, the unthinkable happened.

(To read the rest of the article please click on the headline or type the headline into your search bar.)

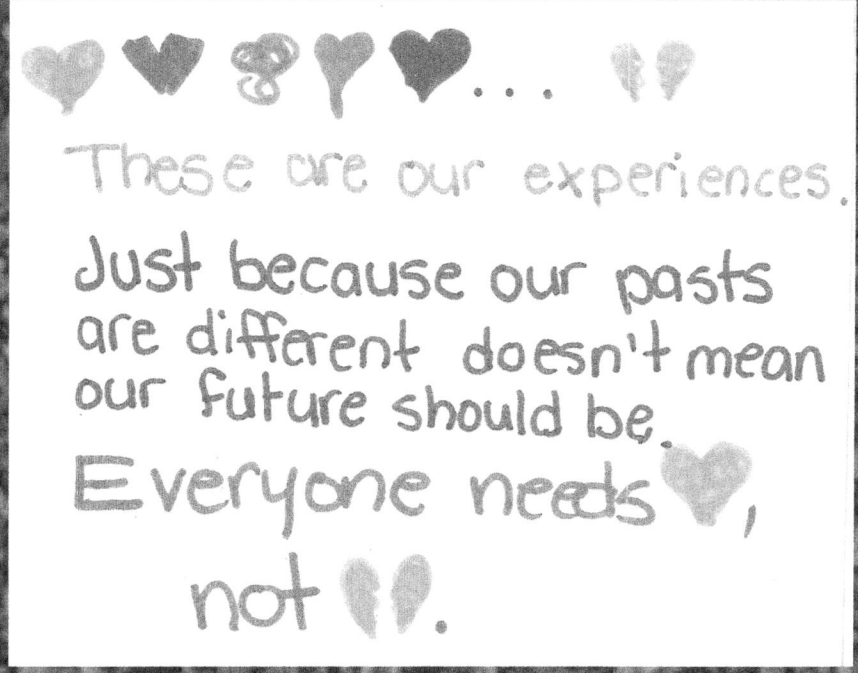

> ♥ ♥ ✿ ❥ ♥ ... 💔
>
> These are our experiences.
>
> Just because our pasts are different doesn't mean our future should be. Everyone needs ♥, not 💔.

Postcard courtesy of the Adoption Council of Canada—Youth Speak Out Edmonton

It has been extremely difficult to keep up or want a relationship with someone only because you share DNA. I do not have anything in common with my birth family and my life aspirations and values are vastly different from theirs. My birth mother, to this day, still can't admit that she made poor choices. Instead, she views it as people having "taken her children" from her. I am often reminded of what my foster mom would always say to us: Blood doesn't define family.

                                                Krista

Ashley

I always comforted myself with the belief that everything happens for a reason,
and I still believe everything a person endures has a reason behind it,
even when that reason is not obvious.

I am the youngest of three girls to whom my mother gave birth. My mother also bounced around foster care as a child, and she never had any real relationships with her biological family. Her family all live on the other side of the country, and all I really know about them is that there is a great deal of secrecy, trauma, and unhealthy dynamics among them, and a long history of serious mental health issues. She did maintain some relationship with her adoptive sister (the rest of the family she shared with her adopted sister perished in a house fire when they were little), but as far as any family I had growing up, my mom, her adoptive sister (who I call my aunt), and my two older sisters, were it. My sisters shared the same father, but I have a different father whom I never knew until my adulthood.

I still don't really know all the details about why child welfare got involved with us. What I do know is that my mother doesn't seem to have any maternal instincts and from my perspective, my mother has always been selfish and incapable of putting anyone else's needs before her own including her children. She would leave my four and six-year-old sisters to take care of me when I was just an infant so she could go out with friends. She would sneak out in the middle of the night to go party and leave us all alone at home. My aunt told me about a time she visited and there was no food in the house, the place was filthy, and I was a baby sleeping on the floor in a closet that stunk of dirty diapers.

We went hungry often and she parented using a lot of yelling and force (according to the memories of my sisters). She caused my sister lifelong, third degree burns over her face and body by asking my sister to light a cigarette for her on the stove when my sister was just five years old.

When child welfare became involved, despite their best efforts and offering support and guidance (having obtained and read my file as an adult, I could see they made some very strong efforts to support her), my mother was either unwilling or unable to make any changes. We were eventually apprehended from her care on the grounds of neglect and inability to provide the necessities of life.

So, my first move was with my sisters to their father's home, as he was separated from her at the time. Their father had a mean temper and was very ill-equipped to parent three girls, which resulted in a lot of emotional trauma for my sisters and me. Physical abuse was the most common punishment for any misbehaviour, and I had nightmares about him for years. My sisters have some vague recollections of inappropriate sexual activities that occurred in that house as well, which are buried deep and not talked about, so it isn't clear what happened in that regard except that some sexual abuse definitely did occur. He was reluctant to engage with child welfare workers and did not follow the agreements made with regard to not allowing unsupervised contact with our mother.

When it was determined that it wasn't safe for us to continue living with him, and we couldn't return to our mother's care, my sisters and I were placed in foster care for the first time. My sisters were placed together because they were full sisters and closer together in age and I was placed separately as the youngest and only technically a half sibling to them. As I was only two years old, my mother was told that if she couldn't produce a family member that could take me in, I would be put up for adoption and may never know them as family. I've wondered how my life would have been different if that had happened and often wished that my mother had made a different choice, but I also always comforted myself with the belief that everything happens for a reason and I still believe everything a person endures has a reason behind it, even when that reason is not obvious.

My mother asked my aunt, who was living out of province at the time, to take me in. She was a single mom to a teenage boy and she always worked at least two, sometimes three jobs but she agreed to care for me. She brought me home with her to Horseshoe Bay, BC (British Columbia), just outside Vancouver, and she took legal guardianship of me shortly after that.

My earliest memories are of living with my auntie. Living with her was the first time in my life that I felt true love, care, and safety. She made efforts that nobody else had to show me love and affection, and to give me structure and guidance. I remember her in those days as being funny, loving, and sophisticated, but also firm. I thought she was the greatest person in the world.

Now that I had finally found somewhere stable and safe, the impacts of the trauma and abuse I had been through started to show. The food insecurity I had faced living with my mom led me to disordered eating where I would gorge myself eating until I threw up. I was easily triggered and had no idea how to manage my emotions. Having always witnessed rage, yelling, and meanness in my first three years of life, I expressed myself in those ways as well. I was stubborn and defiant at home, and at daycare I was rude, violent, and tempestuous. My aunt was constantly getting calls from the daycare to pick me up early because I was out of control and they couldn't manage my behaviour.

At this time, in the early 90s, supports were not provided to kinship caregivers. My aunt had contacted child welfare in BC and requested support including respite or financial aid (considering she often had to leave work to pick me up early when I had outbursts), but she received none. She was no longer able to keep working multiple jobs to keep us all taken care of while also being called in to the numerous times a week to pick me up. She had hired some babysitters to assist, but they were short lived due to my behaviours as well.

My aunt, feeling she had no choice, requested a foster home and therapy for me so she could have a break and I could get some help, with the plan that I would return to her care again in the future. It was around this time that I began to understand that I was 'a bad kid' and that adults (and other children) wanted to be rid of me. I was confused, hurt, and angry about my world, so I acted out.

I don't remember my second foster home, but I know it broke down before long and I returned to my aunt's care. Whenever I was with her, I felt so relieved to be back with the one person I knew who loved me. Unfortunately, little had changed, and I needed more therapy before my emotional state would improve, so things broke down again and she put me back into foster care. It hurts me to remember how much I loved her and how painful it was for me to be given up by her again. Already the multiple moves, multiple losses, multiple rejections, had begun to stack up against me, teaching me I was unlovable and expendable.

Although my aunt was unwilling or unable to care for me herself, she always remained involved and had visits with me, and she advocated for me whenever she was unhappy with the quality of the homes I was placed in. It used to enrage her that child welfare workers would talk about needing to find me 'a bed,' and she would remind them repeatedly that I needed a home, not just a bed. Shortly after the next placement, my aunt came to an arrangement with friends of hers, who had been unable to have children and were looking to adopt. She requested me to be placed back into her care, and once that happened and child welfare was out of the picture, she brought me to live with those friends in Surrey, BC as a private arrangement.

I have really happy memories of that home. I knew that they were supposed to adopt me, and I remember practicing writing their last name because it was going to be mine soon. I remember learning to ride a horse, getting my first bike, playing with Barbies on the grass with my new cousins, and having an amazing birthday party outside with lots of people. I began kindergarten there, which marked the beginning of a very rough road of constantly getting in trouble and struggling to make friends. It would take decades before I was ever able to let someone get close to me, so socially I always struggled. I was mean to other kids, but then I would get frustrated and not understand why they didn't want to play with me. I had no respect for authority and I enjoyed shocking adults with how rude, defiant, and arrogant I could be. I refused to share and expected to be able to just do what I wanted to do, when I wanted to do it.

So, although kindergarten was only a half day, I was frequently being sent home and even suspended. Whenever this happened I would have to go home and sit at the kitchen table, not allowed to talk, watch TV, or play with any toys until the dad (for ease of reference for the rest of my story, I'll use FD for the father figures in placements, and FM for the mother figures) came home to spank me. I got so used to this routine that it didn't even bother me. I made up little games in my head to pass the time and listened to FM watching her soap operas. At first FD would use his hand, but when that stopped having the desired effect, he began using a belt or kitchen utensils. I vividly remember one occasion where I was being spanked with a spatula and FM remarked, "she isn't even crying, you need to do it harder," at which point she went to get the belt. Although she never had the nerve to do it herself, she always stood and watched. I remember this being humiliating, scary, and painful, and it never led to any positive changes in my behaviour.

I feel like I tried really hard to make them happy so they would keep me. I remember once I was asking for some things when we were shopping, and I was snapped at and told that it wasn't nice to ask for things. From then on, there and in all my future placements, I never asked for things when shopping in a store, no matter how badly I wanted something. My understanding was that asking for things is bad, so I should never, ever do it (this became problematic in other contexts as I got older, as it led to thinking it was wrong to express my needs). I was (and still am) a perfectionist and I was seeking acceptance, which is likely why I was always an excellent student – the rules to follow for academic success are very clear. But if I ever sensed that acceptance was unattainable, I would revert to the complete opposite and put on the front that I didn't want or need anybody's acceptance and I would actively try to ensure rejection by acting out in ways I knew would make people angry with me. This way, I could try to avoid getting hurt again.

Regardless of the regular corporal punishment, this home was the happiest and most loving placement I ever had. Having two parents, extended family, and no siblings was wonderful for me. These things made it very different from living with my aunt, especially as I was told that this was going to be my permanent home. I think they tried the best they could and, in their defense, I don't believe they were made fully aware of my needs and behaviours prior to taking me in. I don't think they expected or were prepared to parent a child with high emotional and behavioural needs like mine. So within less than a year, they gave up on me. Even now when I think back, I feel a great sense of loss. I was devastated to leave that family.

I returned to my aunt's care and moved to a new school and a new house, in Vancouver this time. I still loved living with my aunt. She had been the only consistent person in my life. I held her on a pedestal and wanted so badly to please her, but things broke down again after just a few months. She couldn't handle my needs, my continual suspensions, and the stress of trying to hold it all together as a single parent (she still had her teenage son living with her at this time). She was told that she could not receive any supports and if she couldn't handle it, then a new plan would need to be made for me since the constant back and forth was having a devastating impact on me. Back to foster care I went.

I was told the next home was just going to be for the summer. It was a nice enough place with a big yard and I learned how to ride a bike without training wheels that summer. But I never bonded with that family, and I don't even remember their names. I remember telling FM at bedtime one night that I didn't want a goodnight kiss. I can't say for sure exactly why I didn't want it, but my gut told me that receiving kisses from these temporary people in my life was just too close for my comfort. I remember feeling that she was offended by this, and she never offered that affection again. Even after I once told her that a goodnight kiss might be OK sometimes (I think I was envious of the affection the other kids were getting and may have been regretting my earlier request in that moment), she refused to kiss me goodnight ever again after that, reminding me that that's what I told her I wanted.

I also remember having my first sensory processing issues around this time, which is something I still struggle with today. It's likely they emerged before this time, but this is when I remember them starting. I recall moments of feeling extremely frustrated or even angry about experiencing certain sounds, or textures, and usually getting in trouble for my inability to tolerate something as simple as an uncomfortable sweater, very loud music, or feeling crowded. They didn't know as much about trauma or sensory processing disorders back then, so people generally assumed that I was acting out intentionally.

At the end of that summer I moved on to the next placement. I don't recall having any emotions over leaving that place. By this time, I was becoming an expert at being able to detach from my emotions and compartmentalizing my feelings. I was in continuous therapy through these years, and I've read in the reports that even at the young age of seven I had very advanced defense mechanisms, according to a few psychologists. It never even bothered me in school when kids would ask me why I didn't have parents. I told them the truth. I would just say "my mom doesn't know how to be a mom, so I have to live in foster homes."

I had several siblings in the next placement, some who were also foster kids and some who were biological children. I still had a lot of trouble in school, and I attended regular therapy. I had weekly overnight visits with my aunt which I looked forward to. Despite the very harmful back and forth with my aunt, I loved her unconditionally; I looked up to her, even idolized her. I remember her advocating for me and being there for me if there was ever any doubt about the care I was receiving. She demanded that the caseworkers follow up to ensure that I was properly fed and clothed, and I admired her strength and persuasiveness.

My foster parents in this home must have been very patient and consistent, because I started to calm and settle a bit emotionally and I was finally able to make some friends in school. I relaxed enough that I began to call them mom and dad - that is, until their daughter cruelly reminded me one day that they were *her* parents, not mine, and I had no right to call them that. I decided that day that I would never call anyone mom and dad ever again, no matter what. This was just as well, as I never came across anyone ever in my life afterwards that made me want to. It was not the first or the last time the biological kids of foster parents I lived with were cruel and resentful towards me.

In all this time since leaving Alberta, I had never talked to or heard from my mother. I recall calling my aunt 'mom' occasionally when I lived with her the first time, and my two sisters, who lived in a foster home together in Alberta, came to visit us once. But there was no contact from my mother. A caseworker came to see me one day (I had so many caseworkers up until that point it felt like every time I had to see a caseworker it was someone different), and he asked me if I wanted to move to Alberta to get to know my mom and my sisters. My mother has a rare brain disease that typically has a grim prognosis, and there was concern that she would die without us ever having really known each other, which would be yet another loss in my life (she is still alive today, however). My sisters had been returned to my mother's care, so I believe they hoped that as we were older, she might now be capable of parenting. It didn't appear that my aunt was ever going to be willing and able to care for me and not knowing anything at all about my mother, I think I really hoped that I could have a normal mother - daughter relationship with her.

So, I agreed and my aunt signed over her full guardianship rights to the government. I packed up and left everything and everyone I had known. I remember feeling very scared and sad that I would no longer be living near my aunt, but despite that being very difficult, I really thought that I would find some more love and stability with my family from Alberta. It was a gamble, and I lost.

I was placed in a home on a farm outside of Edmonton with two older biological children (the BC caseworkers had recommended that I be placed in a home ideally with no other children, or at least no other foster children around my age). A couple weeks after moving, when the time came to arrange a first visit with my mother and siblings, I was informed that, although they knew I had moved to Alberta to be closer to them, there could be no visit because my mother and sisters had moved to Ontario. At this point, I was nine years old and really, truly alone. I was angry that my mother could be so selfish and must not have thought at all about how her actions would affect me. I no longer had my auntie to visit, to look out for me, or to remind me that at least one person in the world loved me. Nothing was familiar, and I felt very little attention or care from this new family. With nobody to talk to and no way to process all this change, I was reeling on the inside.

I lived with this family for over four years, but I never felt love from them. FD was firm and scary when he yelled, but he was the only person there that I did really like because he was also funny and playful at times. I have some fond memories of him, and I looked forward to the rare moments of one-on-one time that I got with him. His wife, on the other hand, was cold and uncaring. I was criticized by her at every opportunity and I cannot remember a single positive memory of her.

That first summer, they provided respite for a 16-year-old boy who sexually abused me. When I finally disclosed what had happened, the first thing FM said was "so did you like it?" I was sent to therapy and it was never talked about again. That fall, they took in three more foster kids all within two years of my age. I held up great grades at my new school, and I did make some friends, but I had a hard time keeping them and I still got suspended often for being disruptive and defiant toward my teachers.

I was miserable at home. I made the mistake of calling my foster sister fat during an argument one day. She turned it around and said the same to me. For the remaining four years that I lived there, from age 10 - 14, I was bullied and body-shamed daily. I was called names, excluded from activities, ridiculed, and humiliated regularly. I had a very average body type for my age. And even if I had been overweight, it wouldn't have been my fault considering my age, my history of food insecurity, and disordered eating. I was their emotional punching bag and their scapegoat for what seemed like everything.

My foster parents allowed the hateful behaviour and teasing to go on, and only very rarely intervened in the most extreme circumstances. I was the butt of jokes made by my foster parents quite often. When I tried to stand up for myself or get the tormenting to stop, When I tried to stand up for myself or get the tormenting to stop, I was told that I was too sensitive. That I needed to just ignore them and they would stop (they didn't). That they did it because they liked me (wildly untrue). Even when I told the caseworkers of these events, it was always minimized.

School and summer camps became the places I looked forward to being because it was somewhere I felt normal. School became a refuge, somewhere I could feel happy and where I was successful. I wasn't reminded of how unloved I was with every interaction. It was the only place I didn't feel lonely and hated. It was the only place I was able to have positive social interactions and actually feel good about myself.

Case conferences were the worst. I would have to sit there at the kitchen table while we all read through FM's report, which read to me like a list of everything that was wrong with me and all the things I had done wrong in the previous three months. If I did have the courage to say that I wanted the bullying to stop, it was minimized and I was gaslighted and told to toughen up and ignore it.

I was also starting to really realize how messed up my life had been up to that point. One could argue that the preteen years might be the most challenging of all for kids in care. At that age, you are old enough to understand that your life is far from normal. You're old enough to really feel the injustice of it all in a way that younger kids just don't have the awareness to really see. And yet, you are young enough that you can't make sense of it and you certainly can't do anything about it but feel completely powerless because everyone still treats you like you're a child, even if you are mature beyond your years. I always knew that I was lucky to have been removed from my mother's care, and later removed from my sisters' father, because that saved me from years of abuse and neglect. But the life I had to live to replace that was just a different kind of neglect. I grew up without knowing what love and safety felt like. I don't know the details of what happened in my first few years of life, which contributed to my behavioural issues (once I began bouncing around homes I think that trauma became the main cause of my troubling behaviours), but I am grateful that I don't have to carry the burden of the memories that I would have had.

I cried a lot during these years and felt very alone. I got to have a couple great visits where they flew me back to Vancouver to visit with my aunt for a week. My mom and sisters did move back to Edmonton eventually and we had our visits, but I quickly learned that I wasn't going to get any gratification or comfort from those relationships either. My mother was still unable to meet any of my sisters' or my needs, emotional or otherwise, so my sisters were moved into group homes shortly after they returned to Edmonton. Going on visits to her apartment was agreeable to me only because it got me out of the worse situation I had going on in the foster home, and because we would sometimes get to do an activity like go to a movie. I think she tried in some small ways, but she was never nurturing. She never asked me about myself or my life, and she wasn't willing to talk about our past, answer any questions I had, or admit to any fault regarding it. I'm not sure why, but she started communicating with FM. It seemed as though they became friends (FM was a cat breeder and my mother even bought a cat from her). This enraged me because I thought she had no right at all to talk to FM. As far as I was concerned at this point, she was my mother by blood only and she didn't deserve to know about me, especially if she was going to learn about me from someone that hated me instead of showing an interest in me directly. I felt truly hated by FM and it made me furious to know that she had the power to tell other people about me when I felt that she didn't know me at all.

I also cried for the father I never knew. All my mother could tell me about him was his name and that he was in the Hells Angels in Edmonton in the 80s. Based on this, and the fact that their 'relationship' was so short lived, I assumed that she never even told him she was pregnant, that I would never find him, and that even if I could find him, he probably wasn't worth finding. I pegged him to be in the same category as my mother and figured he was probably dead or in jail.

I spent a lot of time alone in those days, internally working through the mess that was my life. Eventually, I was able to turn my defiance into a strength. I was very resentful of all the people in my life who led me to believe I could trust them and then had let me down repeatedly. I hated feeling helpless and at the mercy of something as fleeting as people's care for me. I had come to realize by this time that nobody else truly cared for me or was going to be there for me, so I would have to care about and look out for myself. I had always been terrible at caring about other people's feelings because I was too wrapped up in my own, so I became selfish in a way that made my self-preservation achievable. I knew that people thought I was just this terrible kid, and I was so defiant and adamantly resentful of people's assumptions about me that I made it my mission to ensure that nobody got the satisfaction of being right about those assumptions.

This shift in my thinking was also aided by a caseworker I had when I was about 12, who had a conversation with me about my future options for independent living. She told me the next transition they saw for me would be me getting help to be able to live in an apartment on my own. This was the first I had heard of supports for independent living and it was a light at the end of an awfully long, dark tunnel. Finally, I had something I could look forward to! Before that conversation, I hadn't given much thought to my future, but I had felt pretty sure that I was going to be stuck in this miserable home with these miserable people doing all their farm chores forever.

When I could start to see a different future for myself, one where I could finally have some control over my life, I felt empowered. I put my stubbornness and determination toward changing my ways and breaking the mold that I was stuck in. As I started my first year in junior high, I decided that I would stop acting out in school because I didn't want to be seen that way anymore and I wanted to prove I had matured. Just like that I went from being sent to the principal's office almost weekly to not at all. I still had a feisty and abrupt attitude (that, I'm sure, will be with me for life), but I was more careful and well-spoken.

I finally mustered up the courage to request a move from that foster home. As I began to grow and mature, it became apparent to me that nobody in that home wanted to see me succeed or thought I could. It occurred to me that nobody should have to live in circumstances like this, where they felt hated, ridiculed, and bullied at home where people are supposed to feel safe. My caseworker said I would need to express this wish openly with my foster parents, so at the next case conference meeting, I had to sit at the table in front of my foster parents of over three years and tell everyone that I was very unhappy and wanted to move. It was an incredibly difficult confrontation to go through. Although I was very unhappy, there had been happy times – not with FM, but with FD, who sat at the table and cried as I told them this. I felt terrible for having hurt his feelings, but I forced myself to stay strong in my resolve, knowing that this incredible discomfort and his hurt feelings now didn't come close to comparing to all the emotional abuse I had endured up to that point.

I was told that I should think long and hard about my request because if I moved, there was no coming back. This was still a really scary thought. The unknown is usually scarier than the known, but I truly believed that things couldn't get worse than how I felt daily in this home. I knew that it was the caseworker's job to ensure I was cared for and I didn't think they were doing a very good job. This also wasn't the first time I had asked about moving because of the way I was treated there. But every other time, immediately following the meetings, things would improve a bit and I would think to myself that maybe they did care about me and if things could just stay this way, I would be happy enough to stay. The caseworker would follow up and I would take my request back, but then everything would return to the way it was before.

I learned from this cycle and was resolute that I wasn't going to be manipulated that way anymore. Regardless of what minor changes occurred at home after that meeting, I continued to request to be moved whenever I saw a caseworker. Even still, it took over a year before a move finally happened. I thought at the time that it was my perseverance and staying true to myself that made them finally take me seriously and oblige to my request. I later learned, after reading through my file, that the decision was financially motivated, since my behaviour had improved enough that they no longer needed to be paying for specialized placement that receives greater financial compensation for providing care to children with above average behavioural needs. I'm glad I didn't learn that until much later, because I felt proud for standing up for myself. Feeling like I was able to exercise some control over my life really helped my confidence at the time.

Suddenly, a week before my 14th birthday, I returned home from school and was told that I would be moving to a new home the very next day. I would not get to go to school to say goodbye to my friends and I had to start packing right away. I was in shock. I was allowed 15 minutes to talk on the phone with friends that night, so I had to call and say a very brief and sudden goodbye to my friends. That was a really big deal to me considering that by that time, I had finally made some solid friendships (which took me years to learn how to do) and in an instant I was ripped away from them without warning.

I cried as I was bringing my things out to the caseworker's car the next morning. I had been given no time at all to process that this was finally happening, and I had no idea where I was going or what was going to be in store for me. I was terrified. And even though I had requested the move numerous times, I was still leaving the place that I had lived the longest in my whole life. And although I recall so many negative memories there, it was still difficult and sad to leave a place that I had called home for four years. I gave FD a teary hug as I was leaving, but I never touched FM as she stood there and told me, "This is what you wanted." She was every bit as cold as always.

So, I moved to the city. Leaving that placement behind was like finally taking a breath of air after being certain that you were about to drown. I was going to miss my friends, but I was thrilled to get a fresh start somewhere where they probably weren't going to make fun of me and criticize me all the time. Somewhere I could talk about things that interested me without being laughed at. Somewhere that wouldn't make me feel like I was always under the suffocating, thick fog of a huge, dark storm cloud.

In the next house, I was relieved to be the only foster child. I was given the only room in a cold, dark basement while everyone else slept upstairs. That probably would have bothered me more if I had paid much attention to it, but at the time I was just so happy to feel like I finally had some space to breathe. There is definitely something to be said, though, about where foster children are kept in relation to the rest of the family in a placement. That separation between myself and the rest of the family did not go unnoticed once the shock subsided, and it sure didn't make me feel welcome or like a part of the family.

I don't even remember the names of those people because I was there such a short time. I only went to that school for maybe a week. What I do remember is sitting at the table for supper one day, trying to chew on a piece of meat that was so chewy I couldn't help but gag. I never said anything or complained, but I couldn't help my reflexes! FD began to yell at me stating that old adage, "When I was your age, I ate what was put in front of me and I didn't make any faces!" Then he threw my plate at the wall, breaking it, and sent me downstairs.

I had such a mix of feelings that night. I was so relieved to not be at my last placement anymore, but this one seemed like it was going to be just as bad if things like this were happening within the first week! I couldn't believe this man lost his cool like that even when I was trying so hard to be polite and stomach the bad food. I laid low after that. A few days later, there was a 'family' outing with some extended family of theirs. We went and had a fine time – unremarkable in my memory. When we got home, I was sent downstairs, told that I was ungrateful, and that they would be calling my caseworker to come pick me up the next day.

This floored me. Ungrateful? I hadn't even said or done anything. Clearly, they had no concept of what it is like to have to move into a stranger's home and pretend like they're suddenly 'family'. Clearly, nobody had told them anything about me and what I had been through. Otherwise, they would have appreciated the fact that me being quiet and polite was a huge leap from my previous demeanour, signifying gratitude in itself as I had wanted that next placement to go well and I tried to get it off to a positive start. I had had no outbursts, attitude, or trouble in school. But, regardless of being on my best behaviour, these people cared so little about me as a human being with feelings that they were perfectly comfortable kicking me out of their house after less than two weeks.

So, on to the next one. The next place was a pretty good one. They were friendly, and FM was caring. I made friends in school who lived in my neighbourhood and I was able to visit their houses and have sleepovers, of which I had only ever had a couple before that. I finally started to feel a bit normal and happy, at least for the first six months.

My friends started smoking cigarettes and then smoking pot pretty soon after that. I had been curious about drugs since I was younger, so it isn't surprising that drug use became a chapter in my life. I've looked back and asked myself what it was that led me to start taking drugs and why I had that curiosity to begin with. I really think it was simply seeking some excitement and friendships in my life. I knew for a fact that nobody really cared enough about me to be bothered by me using drugs, so why not have fun and take some risks. I figured the absolutely worst-case scenario was that I could die and even if that happened, at least I was having fun, which I deserved after the life of misery I had led so far. By this time, I had plenty of experience with suicidal thoughts and even one attempt while in that current home. So at least with drugs, I could maybe get away from it all, forget my shitty life, and just have some fun. Interestingly, even though I was in a good home, doing well, and stable, the heaviness and despair I had felt in the past came back and I truly felt I had nothing to live for, so I made an unsuccessful attempt at taking my own life.

When my foster mom discovered I had been using drugs, which she had always told me she would never condone, things got very strict and I started to feel really stifled. I didn't like all the new rules and started to resent having to follow them just to have a bed to sleep in at night. I felt I had been at the mercy of the judgements and decisions of foster parents and caseworkers my whole life and it had brought me nothing but hurt, and I was tired of it.

I was sent to respite one weekend and I really liked the foster parents I stayed with. I was able to talk with them and they made me feel respected, so I requested to move to their home, since things really weren't working out in the current home anyway. My wish was granted. I left and never looked back, which I had become pretty good at doing by that point. I didn't care that they had me sleeping on a mattress on the floor in an unfinished basement (they were over capacity and in over their heads with their other foster kids, but nobody had bothered to investigate enough to notice this), because I was getting away with hanging out at the mall every day and getting high with my friends. Smoking pot turned into using Ecstasy and MDMA, and nobody even noticed.

One day, for the first time in a long time, I came home sober and I made myself a snack. A ridiculous argument started because, when I closed the fridge door, it didn't close all the way. I was snapped at and accused of being wasteful and lazy. I told them how ridiculous I thought that was, as I hadn't done it on purpose. They accused me of being high. I laughed in their faces and told them I was high every other day when I came home, but not that day. They were shocked at my attitude, since up to this point, we had been honeymooning. And just like that, I was told once again that my caseworker would be called to have me moved the next day.

I stayed up all night that night, waited for everyone to go to sleep, and then I left. I was too proud and indignant to stay somewhere when I was obviously not wanted and I was tired of having to live by a new set of rules everywhere I went. I walked for hours, crossing the city to get to the mall where I met up with my friends, one of whom I knew would be happy to offer me a place to stay. It was our usual hang out place anyway, and there it was no problem to have one more body on a couch.

Once there, I had no restraint. I was going to the after hours clubs every weekend (they never checked for ID at that time and I always had a friend willing to pay my cover), panhandling for change (all I needed was $20 to get a pill that would last the night), shoplifting, and staying wherever the party led me.

When my friends all started smoking crystal meth, I did too. That made things worse, of course, and my decisions got riskier. Only now do I look back and see just how risky my choices were at that time and I'm lucky I made it through relatively unharmed. We would hang out at the malls or downtown during the day and, every once in a while, a security guard would snag me (I was well known to them for often being listed as a missing person, or AWOL). They would take me to a 24-hour child welfare emergency centre where the workers would find me a bed for the night or send me to the shelter, from which I would usually leave the next day. Sometimes I would try to stick it out long enough to get an allowance and then I'd leave. My thought process at the time was that I was having way too much fun getting high and doing whatever I wanted to do with my friends to be bothered living in a depressing, boring group home with a bunch of other messed up kids.

My friends got evicted from our usual spot and I found a new place to stay. It was the basement of a house downtown in an area rife with shady activity, so the drug dealing and frequent traffic that went through there seemed to go unnoticed. In this arrangement, I was always the youngest person around and there were several occasions where older men invited themselves to try to sleep next to me to take advantage of a young girl who was probably too high and sleep deprived to notice what was happening or defend herself. Thankfully, I had some friends there looking out for me that always intervened just in time. My time with that group ended when a competing drug dealer and several gang members broke down the door and stormed the place with machetes, slashing every which way before forcing everyone to get naked to ensure nobody was hiding any drugs on them. I was lucky to get out of there needing only a few stitches in my hand.

You would think this would be enough to make me come to my senses, but it wasn't. I continued on, finding couches where I could, sleeping in broom closets or stairwells when I couldn't find somewhere else, and getting bites where I could at the youth drop-ins around the city. I began staying with a girl who was a sex trade worker and was sleeping around in exchange for money or drugs, and who was a crack user in addition to the drugs I was already using. Hanging around with her, of course, I found myself in even more dangerous situations. Only after some really scary incidents and a lot of peer pressure to use crack (which I successfully declined) did I finally start to think that maybe that wasn't the life I was meant to be leading.

Being on drugs seemed fun when I started – having freedom and friends, living like hippies and always having a party – but soon I found myself in a different crowd that was shady and involved in a lot more criminal activities than just using drugs. I realized that if I carried on with the life I was living – struggling, starving, dirty, and frequently scared – I would be raped or caught in a violent crossfire. That was all I would ever have to look forward to. Being a drug addict means living a really hard life. I had been doing that my whole life already, I just didn't want to do it forever.

I had also noticed that people's expectations of me had dropped significantly. I had become just another druggie kid in the system. Neither group home workers nor my caseworkers ever bothered trying to talk me out of the choices I was making. I stayed with my oldest sister for a brief period, but she kicked me out when I didn't follow through with trying to get a job. She had a child and no patience to deal with my coming and going. I had seen my mother a few times while living there, too, and she never thought to ask me what I was doing, or why, or to ask me to stop. So, I was still really, truly alone. If something didn't change, I knew it would stay that way forever.

Nobody had taken care of me or looked out for me for years, so I knew I had to do it myself. Nobody was going to be there to be a support or to encourage me, so I would need to find strength from within myself. Meth is a hard drug, but I was harder. I don't know anyone more stubborn, determined, and tenacious than myself, so I knew that if I set my mind to changing my life, I could succeed.

Hoping for sheer luck to be in my favour, I showed up on the doorstep of one of my old group homes, asking them to take me in. I told them I wanted to get off drugs and go to school, and their group home was closest to the school I planned to go to. I was told that isn't the way they do things and I remember the staff seeming quite irritated with the whole business, but eventually they allowed me to stay since they did have space available.

I quit that drugged up lifestyle cold turkey. I didn't communicate with any of my old friends or acquaintances, and I didn't hang out at any of the places where I used to spend time with them. It was the end of summer, so I registered myself in school a week after they agreed to let me stay at that placement. I put my focus and energy into school and spending some time with my sisters and my new little nieces. With that drastic shift in my environment and the people around me, I dare say it was easy to cut off my addictions.

Going through that process was a huge boost of confidence for me, because I knew that not many people could get off drugs and start doing things right in their life with little support. So that gave me something I could feel proud of. I still smoked pot and cigarettes, and I still did more than my share of partying and drinking with my friends from school once I got to know people. But I also kept an excellent attendance record and kept my grades up. I got a part time job and even got promoted to supervisor.

I still had an attitude, one which got me kicked out of that first group home and moved to another, but I always tried to make it hard to argue with me about my choices. Occasionally, I would get flack for showing up to school high or being a bad influence on my roommates at the group home. But once I retorted with facts about my excellent grades and attendance at school, my adherence to curfew 75% of the time, and having kept a steady job for several months, there was little anyone could do to argue that I was making bad choices. As long as I was still keeping up all those responsibilities, my weed habit became small fries.

Keeping that up for a while made me a good candidate for independent living, which had been my goal for years – ever since that caseworker way, way back had told me about it. I got set up with an apartment and help from my caseworker to pay my rent so I could continue going to school. Having that financial support enabled me to get my diploma, but the funds provided by child welfare to support youth living independently do not keep youth out of poverty, so I began working full time as soon as possible.

In some ways, life became so much easier once I was living on my own. I could finally just be myself and discover who I really was, without being constantly reminded that I was some lost, unwanted, unloved kid. I finally didn't have to feel like a charity case. I didn't have to cope with feeling pitied by the people I lived with and saw every day, which I think was the source of a lot of my anger in my younger years. I no longer felt like some rag doll thrown around from home to home as if I had no feelings.

I was proud of everything that I had overcome and I was thrilled to be able to face the world as I wanted to be seen, not as the file people had read about me. When I made good choices, I felt proud of them and I got stronger. When I made less than stellar choices, I learned from them. The good moments at this time in my life were really great.

But the low moments were really, really low. It is impossible to live through a life in the system without some lasting effects because, although our past does not define us, it certainly does influence and shape us. As a young adult, while the freedom and ability to define myself in new ways was amazing, it was also incredibly, deeply lonely.

The reality that in my 18 years of life, of all the many, many people I had come across, nobody - not one single person - valued me enough to stick with me, was a huge burden to bear. I was suicidal often and I thought if I killed myself, it would probably be months before anybody would find me because I really had nobody that would have noticed. But I did my best to focus on just putting one foot in front of the other, day by day, and not letting my past get the better of me. I still believe that I was meant to live this life for a reason, even if I still didn't know what it was.

I did have some contact with my mom and sisters during that time, but it was not very positive or supportive. My oldest sister is a cold and mean-spirited woman who was busy raising her kids. When I was about 20, she cut me out of her life forever after I made the mistake of missing one of her daughter's birthday parties. My other sister and I have a good relationship now, but it took years and years of slowly getting to know each other. As a young adult, we were not close, we didn't have much in common, and she was also busy raising her kids. So, I never wanted to bother her with anything I might have needed (she did provide me a place to stay a couple of times when I needed it several years later). My mother was the same as always. She never called unless she needed something, and she knew I didn't have anything to offer since I was poor. Any time I did spend with her just triggered me and made me feel frustrated and angry. Given that she had never tried to be a mother in any sense of the word, I eventually decided that it was best for my emotional and mental health to not have contact with her. She was never willing to be accountable for her actions and inactions that caused the life of pain my sisters and I had lived, nor show any remorse, and I got nothing out of my relationship with her aside from feeling completely drained and angry every time we interacted. Currently I have not had contact with her in many years and that is for the best.

It took a lot of strength to turn my life around and put in the work to succeed at school and stay employed so that I could pay my rent and feed myself. But I didn't do it just because I could, because I was strong enough. I did it because I had no other choice. If I hadn't, I would have lost my apartment and been living on the streets.

On the good days, I would go to work, maybe go to a nearby bar and meet some new people, spend time in an online chat room, or go for a walk or a rollerblade or bike ride. On the bad days, I would stay in my pajamas all day, get drunk alone and cry for hours, and stuff my face with so much food I could have thrown up. It's hard to even explain how defeating it feels to have nobody to call to hear some words of encouragement, no one to turn to for advice or to get a home cooked meal.

Over time I made new friends, most of whom I met through work. I had kept only a few 'friends' from high school and they made it clear that I was very low on their list of priorities. When I started waitressing in bars, I found that I was pushed to be social and that helped me immensely. Waitressing and bartending are very social jobs, and that helped pull me out of the cyclical depression I had fallen into.

Succeeding socially was huge for me, especially considering that as a child, I had struggled in that area so much. It helped me start to value myself. I saw that other people liked me and thought I was fun and worth hanging out with and life got better. I still struggled emotionally and often financially as well, but I had a confidence that I had never known before and that kept me afloat.

When I started to feel tired of the night life, I thought about going back to school. I was proud of how far I had come, and the fact that I did it on my own. I thought my life experience could be of value and, even though I had had several workers in the past tell me that it was a bad idea for me to become a caseworker because it would bring up too much trauma from my past, I decided I didn't believe that was true. I had always thought that many of my caseworkers had done a terrible job. I wanted to prove that I could do it better and actually help young people in a way I wish someone would have cared or been skilled enough to help me. I felt that I had overcome my trauma enough and matured enough to be able to be a good caseworker, someone that people would see really cared and really wanted to see them succeed.

I made it on the Dean's list for my social work diploma and I completed my last two years while also working full time. I was able to obtain a bursary that pays for tuition, books, and a modest stipend for living expenses for current or former youth in care, made it possible for me to start and finish my post-secondary education. Without that bursary I'm not sure where I would be today.

Ten years after my file with child welfare closed, I stepped into the role of a caseworker with child welfare. This was a huge accomplishment and symbolic to me of how far I had come to overcome the odds, build a professional career for myself, and to now have the privilege to help kids and families. I am in a rare and special position of having been on both sides of this work. I now understand the systemic issues faced by very well-meaning caseworkers, which undoubtedly impacted how my life was managed growing up. Growing up, I thought that all these caseworkers must hate kids, or at the very least hated their jobs, and I was happily surprised to meet so many kind and passionate people working the front line of child intervention who are consistently trying to be the voice for their clients and speak up against those systemic issues that impact the lives of children and families. And I also know how scary and confusing it can feel to be a child and feel unwanted, with no sense of control, feeling powerless and worthless. Every child is different though, and I've worked with plenty of young people who have had even more difficult lives than mine, and I am grateful for what I learn from those young people.

I am grateful for the role that child welfare played in my life in ensuring that I didn't grow up among physical abuse or the immature and erratic 'parenting' of my mother (my sisters have some stories). In this way, I know that my story is not as hard as many others who endured significant abuses before or even after being placed in care. However, it serves no good to compare grief, loss, or trauma. Whatever the worst is that someone has been through is the worst *for them,* and it is an injustice that does nobody any good to undermine their own or someone else's feelings towards their own hardships under the reasoning that it is simply not as bad as someone else's. I was saved from a life of abuse and neglect. But what I endured was neglect of a different kind. Neglect of love.

When I was 32, I was gifted an Ancestry DNA kit for Christmas. After I received the results, I spent a year trying to connect with anyone who I shared DNA with that could help me find out anything about my dad. Trying to piece together a family tree from data I found online, I could not have been more surprised when I succeeded in locating him and I met him for the first time at age 33. He and his extended family welcomed me and I now see and talk to them regularly. My dad and I are getting to know each other more and more, and I've loved being able to notice all the little 'family traits' and things we have in common. I am now 34, married to an amazing, kind, understanding, and supportive husband. We are an average middle-class family and we recently had our first child. I finally have everything I ever really wanted in life – love, security, family. Life has settled for me now so much that even writing this story was a bit surreal. All of this happened so long ago and my life has changed so much since then, that it's almost hard to believe this is the life I came from.

But I haven't come out of all of this completely unscarred and for all the things I am proud of in my story, there are just as many things that I am not proud of. There isn't a day that goes by that I don't stress and worry about being left alone, that my son and husband will be suddenly taken from me by some freak accident or who knows what else. I am still a perfectionist. I get anxiety that shows up in ways that are annoying and frustrating for myself and those around me, and I get stuck in black and white thinking. I still have a bit of a hard time making and keeping friends because I am honest and passionate, and my bluntness often offends people. But what I've learned is that everyone has their own set of baggage, and everyone is just trying to do the best that they can to get through life. This is my baggage, and I can own it and know that it isn't there because something is innately wrong with me. It's true that, as much as I wish I didn't, I still seek acceptance and I still struggle with low self esteem at times. But these traits are only a part of me, they do not define me. I am also strong, spirited, and intelligent. And often, our biggest weaknesses can also be our biggest strengths. Being detached can be a negative thing, but it is also what makes me excellent in managing things in times of crisis because I can act logically rather than emotionally. Being a perfectionist feels like it causes me never ending stress sometimes, but it is also what pushes me to get things done and do good quality work and meet deadlines. My direct attitude, that has so often gotten me into trouble, is also what is behind how I have learned to have open and honest conversations about difficult subjects when necessary, particularly in my career.

So, to whomever Is reading this, I hope my story will inspire you to be kind to yourself and find the meaning or purpose behind your own story. I hope that you, too, will persevere to see how far you can get, and that you will learn to own the scars of your past and figure out how you can turn them into your biggest strength. And thank you for taking the time to let my story be heard.

Permanency
is crucial to
youth in care,
but this requires
constant consultation
with every individual
to intentionally
accommodate
their wants
and needs.
Permanency is
different for
everybody,
and oftentimes,
family is the people
we meet along the way
who keep us in their hearts.
Blood does not mean family.
We must remember when dealing with everybody
that it is never a matter of category, but of degree.

                                        Cassie

Meet 5 Indigenous youth who are spreading hope in communities on World Suicide Prevention Day

Ka'nahehsi:io Deer CBC September 10, 2019

Suicide Prevention Day. It's an important day for Indigenous youth involved with We Matter, an Indigenous youth-led non-profit organization founded by Dene/Metis siblings, Kelvin and Tunchai Redver. The organization has over 30 First Nations, Métis, and Inuit youth who were trained in self-care, public speaking, mental health training and workshop facilitation so they can return to their regions to support their peers directly as Ambassadors for Hope.

(To read the full article please click on the headline or type headline into your search bar.)

Postcard courtesy of the Adoption Council of Canada—Youth Speak Out Edmonton

My foster mother and I grew close and I recall on one occasion, as I neared being with them for a year, she shared with me their desire to adopt me if I was not able to go home. On one hand, I recall feeling worried that I would lose my sister, extended family, and would not be able to see my mom again. However, on the other hand and in my heart, I felt comforted that they cared deeply enough about me to want me to be a permanent part of their family. I wish someone had told me then that I could have had both and that adoption would be an addition to my biological extended family connections, not a subtraction.

Theresa

Jesse

Learn about residential schools and intergenerational trauma. Learn about the
families of each child and where they came from because maybe they
came to Canada from a place that has been at war for a long time.
Residential schools, refugee camps, war zones, being in care.
It's all about trauma.

My life was pretty good until my grandma got sick when I was aged nine. My parents weren't able to parent me for a number of reasons and so my grandparents looked after me. It was a good life. We lived in Whitecourt and my Grandpa drove a school bus and my Grandma stayed home to look after me, so we were very close. I was always by her side or on her knee. She was a Cree woman from Frog Lake First Nations and was a very caring person. My grandfather is of German and Russian descent and he was a good provider who really cared about me. My birth mother is a member of Maskwacis First Nations but I have only seen her once since I was a baby. My Dad lives in Edmonton and I see him regularly. He struggles with addiction and homelessness, but we have a pretty good relationship. Sometimes he tries to treat me like I am still a little kid, but I think all parents do that. I talk to my Grandpa everyday and we are still close. He lives in Edmonton so I get to see him a lot. He has been a constant presence throughout my life.

Things changed forever when my Grandma died. It was a very sad time for all of us and I don't know if I fully understood that she was gone at first. I think I was in shock even though she had been sick for quite a long time. My Grandpa couldn't look after me so I was sent to live in kinship care with some relatives on the reserve and that's when everything started going downhill. It was a very dark and confusing experience that scarred me for life. I think that is where I developed Post Traumatic Stress Disorder (PTSD) as I was sexually, physically and mentally abused by multiple people from the beginning until I was put into foster care around the age of 11 - maybe 12.

As far as I can remember, I have had 46 placements since my grandmother passed away. Maybe there were more. I have lived in kinship care, foster care, group care, support homes, residential care, correctional facilities, psychiatric facilities, supported independent living, independent living, high risk housing and shelters. I was also homeless at one point. I have had my own apartment a couple of times. I have moved 18 times since I turned 18. I am 26 now and for the past 22 months I have lived in a housing development for Indigenous people who have a hard time finding and keeping housing for various reasons. They have a harm reduction model which is a great program for those who need it but it was hard for me to live among so many alcoholic and drug addicted individuals because I don't abuse substances. I just moved into their new housing development which is a different model and much more suited to my needs. I have my own apartment and receive the help that I need for the most part. I have a disability pension and some other supports for people with permanent developmental disabilities so that is a big help. I was lucky that I had a really good caseworker before I turned 18. She made sure all those things were in place before I

aged out because I have Fetal Alcohol Spectrum Disorder, Post Traumatic Stress Disorder, Major Depressive Disorder, Severe Conduct Disorder, Schizoid Personality Disorder, Authority Defiance Disorder, Generalized Anxiety Disorder, Schizophrenia and some other stuff. I don't even know how many scars I have from self harm and I used to have suicidal thoughts every day – at times I still do - so I am grateful she got me at least some of the help I will need for the rest of my life.

Living with Fetal Alcohol Spectrum Disorder has not been easy. Basically, you have brain damage and it affects your thinking. You can't process information as fast as other people. I have learning disabilities because of it. I also have an extremely low alcohol tolerance and I have to be careful because I could easily become an addict. I also have other disabilities - not just mental but physical like deformities. It's a hard thing to live with but I just take it day by day. I just learn to live with what I have and know that I can't repair it. There is no cure for it. What I want to tell other youth that have FASD is not to feel discouraged that you can't do certain things or learn as fast as you want to. Just take your time. There are many things you can be good at.

My other mental health issues aren't easy to deal with, either. I have so many that it really complicates my life and sometimes I don't know which one is causing the problem. Every day is different so I just take it day by day. I just learn to live with what I have. I try not to focus on it. I just let things go day by day and if something occurs, I just ride it out. I listen to music. I play video games. I play my guitar. Sometimes I have conversations with myself – not because of my schizophrenia but I talk to my self in the third person and say, "You're going to be OK". Then I respond to that and it helps me. It really helps to talk to other people who understand me, too. My schizophrenia only flares up when I am really stressed or really angry. I have been taken to the Emergency

Room (ER) by ambulance many, many times because of my mental health but over the past year I have only gone a few times.

I have no idea how many workers I have had including social workers, caseworkers, child welfare workers, youth workers, support workers, therapists, psychologists, psychiatrists, and everything in between, but I know it's in the hundreds. I have had a lot of people cross my path in over 46 placements. Some good. Some not so good. If I had more staff that actually listened to me and who tried to understand what I go through, maybe a lot of things would have worked out different for me. I felt like some were just in it for the money. The workers that I remember most are the really great ones that made the biggest difference in my life. I have three or four I could talk about including the one I mentioned earlier.

My first caseworker that I had was good because I felt like she understood me at a young age. The first time I met her the staff told her not to take me out in public because I was a risk to society but she took me out anyway and somehow she knew I was just an angry, messed up kid that needed help. She was also from the LGBTQ community so that was kind of cool.

Then there was this other woman that volunteered at an agency who showed a real interest in me and introduced me to a lot of the music I still listen to today. She looked really cool and she was really cool and even though she was just a volunteer – she had a big influence on me at that time. I looked forward to spending time with her.

I also had this one youth worker who took me to Galaxyland one time and he also took me to my first concert when I was 13 and it was the band, *Rancid*. I will never forget either of those events. He didn't have to take me to but I guess he wanted to and that meant a lot.

When I was in my early twenties, I also spent a lot of time at an inner-city agency that helps the highest-risk youth in Edmonton. They have a lot of arts and music programming and counselling services and the staff there are good at what they do. They really care about the youth that come there. I had some good relationships with some of the people who worked there and if I hadn't aged out at 24, I would still go. They have invited me back to work on a few projects which is pretty great.

The worker who has made the most difference in my life is the lady who looked after my old group home in 2012 and 2013. She was really cool even though she was pretty old. She was definitely different. I was still really angry at that time and didn't have any real hope for my future just like all the other youth there and she just kind of accepted all of us and all of our issues and I remember that we laughed a lot. She didn't have a lot of rules, everyone got treated with respect, and we did a lot of fun stuff. The coolest thing was when she started a punk band at our group home. She knew I wanted to learn to play guitar and so she brought in the coolest volunteers and we all started playing something and yeah, we had an actual band called *Gimme 5* and we played at the agency Christmas party. We played some *Ramones* and punked out Silent Night. Ha ha.

When we first started that band, I felt like I couldn't do it. I had no confidence in myself and I wanted to give up, but I started to get good at it and I found out I could sing too. It was just so much fun. I think that is part of what made it work is that everyone was just having fun. That lady and the volunteers were so calm and cool and supportive, too. They just kept believing in us and eventually we started to believe we could do it and we did. Having people stand up and clap and cheer for me at that Christmas party was like nothing I had ever experienced before. I knew I had found a purpose and was doing what I loved.

I left the group home in 2013, shortly after I turned 18, but the lady from the group home and I always stayed in touch and we formed a really strong bond. She also became my personal advocate because I went through a lot of dark times for several years and I really needed a lot of support and she was always there for me. In 2016 we started documenting my life on film. She told me I was a natural speaker and I felt comfortable in front of the camera with her so that was cool. We also got the band back together that year. Three of the people who volunteered with the original project and a couple of other people we knew wanted to play with me again and the main guy called the band, Jesse Jams & The Flams. A flam is like a drumming pattern. So, I was very happy to be playing with everyone and having fun again. We started playing and recording until Covid-19 hit and ended up having about 10 original "mumble-punk" songs – enough for an album but that hasn't happened yet.

In 2019, a cool film maker named Trevor Anderson became interested in the filming we had been doing and the band we had and wanted to make a documentary about my life. He already knew everyone in the band and I had met him a few times before and I liked him so I agreed to do it. Trevor and my advocate got funding from Telus Originals and we filmed it that summer and that was kind of life changing. Never in a million years did I think anyone would ever want to make a film about me. It is called *Jesse Jams* and has been shown in film festivals around the world and has won some awards. It seems unreal. Trevor did such a good job showing people what my life is like and the ongoing struggles I have with my mental health. I would really like you to watch it if you can. And, the music in it is great! Ha ha. Mostly, I like that my film can actually help people like me who struggle daily to feel a little better when they see what I have accomplished, or maybe it can teach people in the mental health field how to understand some of us better. Before Covid-19 hit, we played live a few times and were planning on maybe going to Calgary for a gig and when the pandemic is over, we probably will. I really miss not being able to jam with my band.

Music is a huge part of my life. It has been since I was around 13. I remember the first CD my grandpa bought me was *Green Day* – American Idiot and I still like them to this day. I listen to music all day and all night. I like all kinds of music from rock and punk to rap and hip hop to Johnny Cash. I also like listening to music from other countries and cultures. Music takes my mind off of a lot of things that might be bothering me and I can play the music that fits my mood.

As for my culture, I have opportunities to practice it and I do appreciate it – I just don't always follow it. I have so many friends from so many cultures, I feel lucky that I am not just familiar with one way of life. I find it interesting what other people believe in and I like to ask them where they came from. One of my support workers was from Rwanda and was there during the civil war and I felt bad that he had to experience that. Another one was from another part of Africa and another one was from South America.

Some of my support workers have been Indigenous and some have been white. No matter where anyone is from – they have interesting stories to share. One thing I learned in care is to not judge others based on where they came from or how they look. I am glad I did because there is way too much racism in the world. I have dealt with lots of discrimination based on my race and how I look. A lot of people think I am in a gang because of the way I look, but I'm not. I am also transgender which other people are not always comfortable with but I am comfortable with who I am, and I don't really care what others think. I am also kind of scary so people generally leave me alone.

What makes a good worker is to remember that every child and youth has their own way of trying to communicate and you really have to pay attention to them to get them. Listen to them - but I mean really listen. Find out what they like to do and do it with them whether that is music or football or drawing or video games. Like just show an interest in whatever it is that interests them. Have some laughs because there definitely isn't enough of those when you grow up in care. Not everything has to be about chores and life skills and routines and goal setting or whatever. Everyone who works with us needs to get proper training, so they understand how the child and youth mind really works and what trauma does to a person. Learn about residential schools and intergenerational trauma. Learn about the families of each child and where they came from because maybe they came to Canada from a place that has been at war for a long time. Residential schools, refugee camps, war zones, being in care. It's all about trauma.

Other than being in the punk band when I was in care, the most impactful moment I had was meeting my mother for the first and only time I remember. My old caseworker took me out to our reserve when I was around 12 and I spent the day with her. It was nice that I could put a face to the person who gave birth to me. I wanted to hear her side of the story and why she left. Her saying, "Sorry for your life and sorry for leaving you", was good but what was bad is that she still had active addictions at that time and I think she still does but I don't know because I haven't seen her since and I am 26 now. She has never shown any interest in seeing me again or getting to know me so at this point it doesn't really matter. I mean it still hurts a little, but I have to accept it. I am past it for the most part. I try not to blame anyone for my life in care. It is what it is.

I have never read my file but I would love to see what I was like throughout a lot of my younger years because I don't remember too much. I think it would answer some questions I have. Maybe it would have too many triggers, though. I would have to have someone I trust with me if I ever did. I think it is important for some kids to go through their history but not for others. Some people don't want to look back and that's OK. I guess my time in care was a mix of positive and negative. On the positive side, I learned how to raise myself and I learned how to deal with things myself because I didn't get the help that I needed in most cases. Over time, I have just accomplished what I accomplished on my own or with the help of people who cared.

I want to leave youth in care who are reading this with some hope. Keep your head up. You can do anything. Put your mind to it. Find something you love and go after it hard and make sure that it distracts you from the things that are bothering you. Don't give up. I used to think that nothing good would ever happen to me and my life would never change, but it did. I used to think that no one would ever like me, but they do. I never thought I would have some of the things I do today like a band and a film and good friends, but I do. Good things can happen.

I want to leave the government people who are reading this with some hope, too. Youth in care need easier access to arts and music programming. Edmonton needs a big arts and music center where any of us could go and find a forever community. It would make a big difference in so many lives. A lot of us struggle academically because we have learning disabilities, or we move around too much. Lots of us aren't good at athletics. We may not have a lot of family or friends. We have trouble fitting in most places we go but there is a place for everyone in the arts community. They don't care if you are a person of color or LGBTQ2S or have disabilities or are poor or look weird or whatever. You can heal because you are accepted and supported. I guess you kind of heal through whatever kind of creative expression you use. It not only changes lives—it can actually save them. I am living proof of that.

Thank you for taking the time to read my story and I hope you can watch my film. It is only 17 minutes long. You will find the link on the next page. You can find links to film reviews and articles about our band and a link to our documentary soundtrack on Bandcamp.

Watch JESSE JAMS & read reviews here

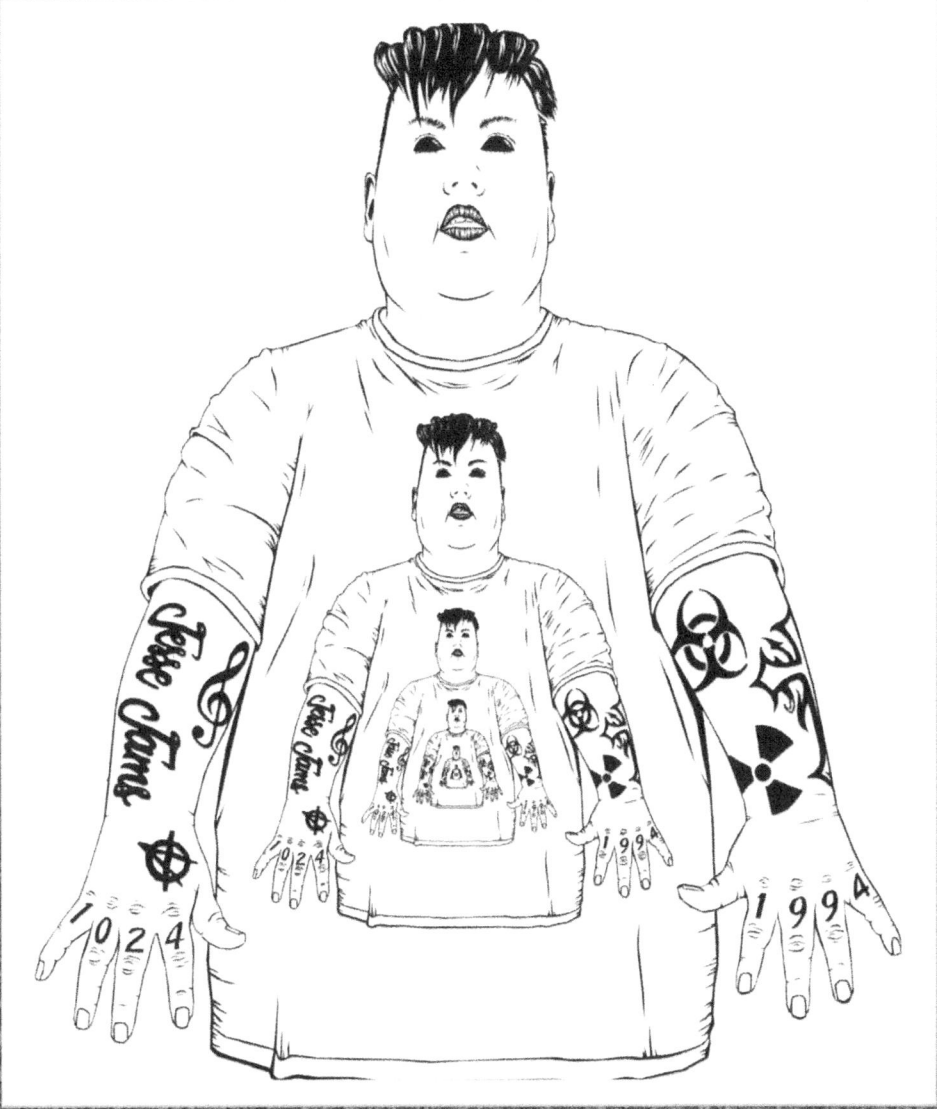

This is a drawing of me that our band leader, Lyle Bell, made to get printed on our Jesse Jams & The Flams band t-shirts. We also make cool hats & buttons that we sell at our shows.

Me and five of the Flams recording the gang vocals for our song "Hit The Hole!" Lyle was taking the picture.

Jesse Jams & The Flams — our last live show right before the pandemic. It was a fundraiser for iHuman Youth.

What Foster Care Feels Like Photo Gallery
FOSTER FOCUS MAGAZINE   Chris Chmielewski, Founder & Editor

During Social Worker Month I thought it might be beneficial to tell social what foster care felt like to help give them even more tools to do their jobs effectively. What followed was a flood of foster care alumni descriptions of what foster care felt like.

These are not descriptions that warrant sadness. These are descriptions from doctors, lawyers, advocates, parents, foster parents and social workers whose uniting quality is time spent in care.

These are success stories. These are not the people that need to be looked after or are in need of your sympathies. Those people are going to find their way out of the system soon enough. These are alerts. These descriptions are a call to action. A call to advocate. A call to protect.

(To read the full story please click on the headline or type the headline into your search bar.)

She watched her Father live in regret. She heard her Mother cry in an empty bed, and she swears this is the best life gets.

Postcard courtesy of the Adoption Council of Canada—Youth Speak Out Edmonton

I used to call that worker every day to tell her how much I hated her and then, about nine months in, I phoned her one day and told her how much I loved her. I wanted a different life and she was just so awesome. We planned for when I got out of jail and she supported me in every way.

Linda

Postcards courtesy of the Adoption Council of Canada—Youth Speak Out Edmonton

Postcards courtesy of the Adoption Council of Canada—Youth Speak Out Edmonton

> When I need someone to talk to, I have no one to call without feeling like I am bothering them...
>
> So I hold it in.

Postcards courtesy of the Adoption Council of Canada—Youth Speak Out Edmonton

> If you adopt a teenager you just might end up saving their life and future.

Postcards courtesy of the Adoption Council of Canada—Youth Speak Out Edmonton

> Family is the safety net that gives you the courage to take big risks!!!

Postcards courtesy of the Adoption Council of Canada—Youth Speak Out Edmonton

> It's Amazing How Much A Family Can Change One Child's Life. New Family Means New Memories. A New Future, & A New Beginning. ♡♡♡♡

Postcards courtesy of the Adoption Council of Canada—Youth Speak Out Edmonton

Youth in Care Chronicles Learning Guide
Reflections for Students and Professionals
Supporting Children and Youth in Care

The purpose of this learning guide is to further explore some of the themes and learnings incorporated in the stories shared in this book. The following five themes reoccurred often throughout the book: relationships, advocacy, connections, transitions and compassion.

This guide reflects three core areas: What Professionals Say? What Youth Say? And Practice Reflections. Core aspects of child protection work/youth work include direct support, building strong relationships with youth in casework, providing mentorship, engagement in casework supervision, and advocating for youth. Critical intersections for this work include engagement with the youth justice system, health care, policy, and research. This learning guide was created to inform 'best practice,' grounded in the collective wisdom gathered through the voices of adults who grew up in care. Reflecting on youth voice and the experiences of contributors provided an opportunity for the editorial team to ask critical questions in relation to the five themes and to engage in knowledge translation to inform practice for others engaged in this important work.

The editorial team has many years of experience working in the child welfare field and for three members, lived experience growing up in care. In sharing these perspectives, we offer fresh eyes to the field and share well-earned wisdom. We invite readers of this book, whether you are new to the field or are seasoned practitioners, to engage in reflection on your practice and perspectives through these guiding questions.

Theme #1: Relationships
Many stories in this book discussed important relationships. What does a healthy, helpful, and professional relationship look like between a youth and me? How does practice inform the development of this relationship?

What Professionals Say?	What Youth Say?	Practice Reflections

• Utilize strengths-based, trauma-informed, and harm reduction practice approaches.
• Stick through the "testing phase," such as testing boundaries, name-calling, or throwing things. This is a good opportunity to discuss, understand where they are coming from, and
	• Characteristics of a helpful worker:
	   ○ Intentional
	   ○ Compassionate
	   ○ Consistent
	   ○ Human-centered
	   ○ Attentive
	   ○ Available
	   ○ Caring
	   ○ Flexible
	   ○ Knowledgeable
	   ○ Real
		• Was there an example of a safe and supportive adult in your life?
		   ○ If yes, what characteristics did they have that made you feel safe?
		   ○ If no, what was missing that you needed from the adults in your life?

- reframe defiance as resilience.
- There is a difference between relationship-based and punitive-based practice. Be intentional to not reinforce that the world is a hostile, frightening and lonely place; don't reinforce shame, guilt, and a sense of failure.
- Given that there is often a history of rejection and abandonment, appreciate that youth can be taking a significant risk by letting you into their world and will likely initially be reluctant to.
- Workers need to know the importance of allowing youth the opportunity for a proper goodbye when ending their involvement. This may be getting coffee or lunch, going for a nature walk, having a sharing circle with important people in the youth's life, or a letter to the youth to reflect on your time together[1].
- Find opportunities to connect with youth on a personal level. This allows opportunities for a trusting relationship to form.
- Strong relationships are built on trust, authenticity and on reciprocity.
- Involve youth in making decisions and engage

  - Trustworthy
  - Reliable
  - Nonjudgmental
- It is important to develop relationships that value our autonomy and interests. Take an interest in our interests and find ways to show you care.
- Maintaining relationships even when work hours are over is important to me as my life and struggles don't end at the end of your workday.
- Treat us with compassion even if "we're not your problem," and go above and beyond. We take notice.
- Don't give up on us even if we initially push you away. We are testing you to see if you are worth investing in.
- Don't judge us, show us that you care and are worried about us.
- Know that when I lash out at you, it's not personal, even if I say it is. I am struggling and need you to hear me.
- When you're with me, be physically, emotionally, and mentally present.
- Ask me if it's okay to talk about what we are talking about. Empower me to tell you when something feels like a trigger and if I'm in a good space to talk about it.
- Avoid labelling me (delinquent, junkie,

  - What can you take away from your personal experiences and apply to your work with youth?
- What have been the most meaningful relationships in your life and why?
- Does the language I use enhance relationship or does it sound punitive? Will a youth in care be receptive to the language I am using?
- Is the challenging behaviour I am witnessing a personal attack or based in fear of the unknown, or in making a connection?
- What are my boundaries as a professional? When can I be flexible with them to show I care and when can I not?
- What can I do to help enhance my relationship with a specific youth in care?
- If I am worried about a youth in care and the harmful impact that their behaviours have on them, when should I show support/care and when do I challenge them to help with change?
- How can I let a youth know I care but still challenge harmful behaviours?
- What impact could I have in role modelling healthy relationships?

them in planning for themselves. • Work *with*, rather than *doing to* or *doing for*. • If you have a strong relationship with a youth you will be able to challenge them in ways that they will be more receptive to.	defiant, resistant, manipulative, etc.) I'm not a bad person, I've had bad things happen to me and this is how I have learned to survive.	• In which ways can I plan a proper goodbye for the youth when I am leaving my role in working with them? How can I make this intentional and significant? • Have I asked the youth how they would like to say goodbye to each other? How can I include them in this transition?

[1]Smyth, P. (2020, August 1). *The respectful goodbye*. A4YC. https://www.a4yc.ca/blog/2019/8/1/the-respectful-goodbye

Theme #2: Advocacy
Many stories in this book discussed the role of advocacy or advocates in their lives. What role does advocacy play in working with youth in care?

What Professionals Say?	What Youth Say?	Practice Reflections
• Advocacy comes in all forms and at times includes advocating for client centered and youth driven supports and resources within/outside of the agency you work in. • New and upcoming workers should know that they have control over their own practice and authenticity when they are one-on-one with their youth. This is the essence of practice and what makes each worker unique. • Workers should advocate for the youth's goals while balancing the need to meet practice and policies standards within their own agencies.	• Youth want to see their workers advocate for their interests, talents, goals, needs, life plans, and their desire for family. • Many of us have experienced emotional and/or traumatic apprehensions where caseworkers remained in passive roles instead of being our active ally. • Understand that we deserve to know what is going on, to give consent, to make decisions on what happens to us whenever possible. • We lack control in our lives. Providing me with options will help me have a sense of control over	• Thinking of many of the youth who shared their stories, there were some examples of workers who advocated for the youth outside of work hours, such as attending parent/teacher interviews with them. Imagine that you are working with a youth who has an interest in theatre and landed a role in a community production. They are very excited to have this opportunity to demonstrate their talent, explore a new skill, and express themselves creatively. How might you support this youth so that they know someone is proud of them, while also balancing paperwork, caseload

• Empower youth to advocate for themselves, if they lack the skills, embrace opportunities to support and empower them to do so. • Remember that your own advocacy work and efforts demonstrate that the youth is worth it and has value as a person. Youth learn through example and this will also allow opportunities for them to learn self advocacy. • "Help youth navigate and negotiate the resources they need for their well-being:"[2] This is not enabling, it is guiding, coaching, and teaching as parents do with their adolescent-aged kids. They will need these skills to be successful adults.	my life and the ability to impact my future. • I may be young, but I've been through more than most people in their lives. I need to have my voice heard and know that the adults around me trust my judgment and capacity to help guide decisions that will affect me. • Know that I may not have the best advocacy skills and when I lash out or my behaviours escalate, it means I am trying to tell you something and advocate for myself. • Ask me what is working well and what is not. • Help me gain some control in my life. Teach me how I can effectively advocate for myself as what I am doing is what I know.	demands, and so on? Where would you prioritize? Who would you encourage to get involved? • Where is the line between advocacy/empowerment and enabling? • Why is advocacy important and how could I help youth in care build this skill? • Think of a time when you advocated for your self or someone you were supporting. What advocacy skills did you use? What were you most proud of? What would you do differently? How can the learnings from this experience help increase your confidence in advocating for youth in the future?

[2] Ungar, M. (2020). *Working with children and youth with complex needs: 20 skills that build resilience (second edition).* New York, NY: Routledge.

Theme #3: Connections
All stories in this book shared the importance of meaningful connections. How can I support children and youth when it comes to connections, whether it be cultural, relational, legal, or otherwise? What are some of the challenges that I might face?

What Professionals Say?	What Youth Say?	Practice Reflections
• Learn, know, and understand the multidimensional impact and harm, which was caused by colonization for Indigenous communities and the role child welfare has had	• Ask me what I need to learn about my culture and to build connections with my community. Many of us wish that we grew up with this knowledge and we don't always know where to find it.	• What kinds of questions can I ask youth to learn about their connections, resources or relationships that they need in their lives? Examples may include: 　○ Is there anything about your culture

- both historically and presently.
- Cultural connections are essential for identity and should be the basis of connection and healing for children and youth in care.
- Family connections should be encouraged, supported and maintained, particularly when it comes to sibling relationships, as these relationships will last the young person's lifetime.
- Make sure youth have placement permanency and that active efforts are made to achieve legal permanency whenever possible. Every youth needs a sense of belonging and to know they are loved.
- Youth may form attachments to their workers or staff. As youth learn to have healthy and safe relationships, they are able to draw on these skills to navigate other safe relationships.
- Minimize the number of professionals involved in the life of a youth. The more temporary relationships they experience, the more it has a negative impact on them. Help them to develop natural connections and a strong social network.
- Youth generally reconnect with their

- Connect with me during times when I am doing well as much as when I am struggling. It is important to have someone to talk to even when I don't have a problem.
- I want to have people in my life who take an interest in the things that I enjoy.
- If I want to connect with a previous workers, caregiver or staff to check in and chat, find ways to support this.
- Chosen family is extremely important and family is not always blood related, honor all my connections.
- Ask me if I want supports in terms of counselling or seeing an Elder, and then follow through with connecting me.
- The desire to be adopted or part of a permanent home never goes away regardless of how old I get.
- I can often feel lonely with so many temporary connections in my life and separation from my family. Help me to feel not so alone.
- Know that because of my trauma, connections are hard for me to develop and maintain, but I desperately want them. Be patient with me and please don't give up.

you are curious about? How can I support you to be culturally connected?
- Can you tell me about the people who loved and cared about you before child welfare came into your life?
- What support would you need to have safe and healthy connections with your family or another significant person?
- What would you like the connections with your parent(s), sibling(s), extended family and significant community connections to look like?
- How will you know if the youth has placement permanency where they are living? Are the current caregivers meeting the youths needs for relational/cultural connections and able/willing to provide legal permanency for the youth? If not, whom else does the youth think you should explore in their circle who may be a permanency option?
- What other supports and resources can

parents and extended family with or without the help of workers. Familial connections are important and whenever possible support youth to navigate how they can be safely connected to their family. • It is imperative for children and youth to have relational connections, which are comprised of family, friends and community that enhance the paid services offered by the child welfare system. Once the young person is an adult consider who will care for them when they have surgery, help them move, celebrate their birthdays/weddings and be a part of their life 10, 20, or 30 years from now when workers are no longer involved.	• I have family, I did not hatch. Ask me who is important to me from my extended family, community, school, church etc. I need to be connected to these people in safe and supportive ways. • I need to have my siblings in my life, and I need to see the adults around me making this a priority. • I may not be able to live with my parent(s) and/or family because they were not able to keep me safe, but know that not all my experiences with them were unsafe. They are still very important to me. • Support me to know and understand my life journey, which may include how many placements I have had, why I moved and parts of my story I want to learn more about. • I need unpaid people in my life that care about me.	you access to assist in permanency planning? • What boundaries around contact would be necessary with a youth once the professional relationship has ended? • What do healthy connections look like and how can I help support these for the youth I work with? • If a youth has limited connections, what could I do to help build some of these? Where might they be able to build connections?

Theme #4: Transitions

Through their stories, many contributors highlighted their experience with transitions. As children and youth go through many changes while in government care, how can I, as a professional, support them best?

What Professionals Say?	What Youth Say?	Practice Reflections
• Support youth with seeking interdependence and not independence. Every single person requires a network of	• Be there for me when I need you and when it counts. • Don't assume I know how to do things such as	• Thinking back to a time when something big changed in your life – transition from high school, to adulthood, a

- people to support them in their lives.
- Active care and compassion should be demonstrated when bringing children into care as this moment remains with many youths for the rest of their lives.
- Any transition can be stressful, including turning 18. Children and youth need increased support during these times, whether they are 10, 16, 18, or 24.
- When children and youth move, they should not have to do this using garbage bags. Workers always need to maintain the dignity of the youth they support.
- Give space for youth transitioning out of care or into adulthood to make mistakes. They will certainly make them like every other youth, but will often have less supports to fall back on.
- Be purposeful with your support for youth during transitions. Give as much notice as possible about upcoming transitions and help prepare them for transitions. This will help reduce the stress for them caused by transitions.

applying for programs, registering for school and getting a driver's licence, if no one has taught me how to do these things.
- I need more of a worker's time when transitioning, not less time.
- I need you to stand with me when going through an apprehension. This time is scary, it is emotional, and I may not feel safe with all the professionals involved.
- I want to maintain connection with the people who are important to me and this needs to be honored through my transitions.
- Tell me why I am being moved and give me some notice so I can say goodbye.
- Change and transitions are scary, ask me if I have any questions and what I may be worried about.
- I need room to make mistakes. As I transition out of care or into adulthood, I am going to make mistakes. If I make a mistake, just lecturing me won't help. Know that I often have less support to fall back on having grown up in care, which means I need more support when I make mistakes so I can bounce back and learn from them. Don't teach me

death, a change in family dynamics, etc., what helped you to be brave during times of transition and uncertainty?
- Change is challenging and transitions are big changes. Recognizing transitions are stressful, what supports and strategies could you use to help mitigate the impact of the transition on a child or youth you support?
- How am I feeling about the relationship with the youth ending and how can I appropriately convey this to them?
- What would be a meaningful way to have closure and say goodbye to a youth?
- How might a youth's life experience, peer group or self esteem impact transitions and their perception of transitions?
- If a youth is feeling stuck in a transition, how could you explore what may be affecting them from moving forward? Could the youth be struggling with a fear of failure or success? How might this cause them further feelings of alienation and loneliness?
- What allowed you to successfully transition into adulthood and how could it be applied to your work with a youth

| | that making mistakes is a bad thing. | transitioning into adulthood? |

Theme #5: Compassion

Some stories shared examples of times in which workers appeared to lack an understanding of the young person's thoughts and emotions during their time in care. How can I best show compassion, kindness, and empathy to children and youth in care?

What Professionals Say?	**What Youth Say?**	**Practice Reflections**
• Be transparent in your practice and decision-making when it comes to the young person. • Be brave and model compassion and care to the children and youth that you work with. • Admit it and apologize if you make mistakes. • Don't be afraid to tell a youth you don't know what to do next, when you don't know what to do next. Tell the youth you need their help and want to support them. • If you have worries or fears for a youth then share them with the youth and let them know you want to support them. This will show that you care enough to worry about them and want to help. • Be intentional about sharing that you care about the youth, and that you have hopes and dreams for them. • Show that you want to understand them, that you are invested in them	• It is helpful when my worker is interested in my interests and in me as an individual person. • It is meaningful when a worker remembers the things that we like or are interested in. • We need people who care for us and love us. Honor the people who are important in my life and find ways to connect me to them. • Listen to me and try to understand where I am coming from. • Explain to me the decisions you make about my life; it helps me to understand what is happening and shows that you respect me. • Encourage me to be curious about my story, my interests, my family, and my culture. • Be patient with me. Through our interactions you are teaching me. • Understand that when care ends, we struggle. You will not always be there so I need you to	• Thinking about a time when the people in your life did not understand how you were trying to express yourself or felt, reflect on how this made you feel? How might a youth in care feel when they are in a similar situation? What could you do to help them feel heard and understood? • How do I honor the importance of relationships with a youth and balance the competing pressures such as high caseloads, paperwork, or updating electronic files? • What skills can I use to foster difficult conversations in a compassionate way? • Do I take the time to reflect on my practice, including how the youth I support impact me as a professional? • What have the youth I have worked with taught me? • What do you think the children and youth you support would say about

and that you are cheering them on. • Remember that when you are connecting with a child/youth that you are connecting with another person. Be sure that your words and actions always respect them as a person. • Building a strong connection or relationship requires some degree of vulnerability and openness. • Connect with experiences in your own life that have been challenging and try to put yourself in the shoes of a youth you are supporting. Having empathy for a youth and their experiences is key to better understanding them and being able to compassion towards them. • Children and youth in care need extra care/compassion as many have limited **experiences with compassion.**	connect me to natural unpaid supports. • Try to understand that my life has been really challenging, that I may not know how to make it better and that I need help to figure out ways to make it better. • We remember the small things. We remember when workers go out of their way to do something for or with us when they didn't have to. The smallest displays of kindness go a long way and can have a lifelong impact. • Treat my mistakes as mistakes. Show me that you understand that I made a mistake and that I am not just a failure or a delinquent. • Share or admit when you make mistakes. If you never do this, I will not trust you as I know I have made a lot of mistakes. • Know that your compassion may save my life as it will let me know that people care, especially when I may not have experienced this much growing up.	how you interact with them? Are their observations congruent with the value you place on connections and practice? Would they say you care about them and if not, what could you do to help them feel that you care about them? • If you asked a youth what they see you do that is most helpful for them, what do you think they would say? • Based on your own personal experiences, what are other ways you can show youth that you care and that you are compassionate? • How can you support a youth and show you care for them while still maintaining professional boundaries? When can I be flexible with them to show I care and when can I not?

Conclusion

In closing, this work requires ongoing critical reflection to examine the environmental, relational, and systemic influences, which impact the lives of the youth we support. This means that there are an endless number of questions that we can ask ourselves daily to make sure that we are viewing the whole picture when it comes to the youth's life. The contributors to this book demonstrate that each young person has their own important story to share. In our practice as professionals and advocates, it is crucial to recognize these youth are strong and resilient. We place high value on the lives of these young people and believe that they have a future, a life to live, and that we have a key role in supporting their hopes and dreams for the future.

The following questions are some final reflective/discussion prompts to take forward in your practice to help identify strengths in the youth you are working with. Whether you are a registered social worker or child and youth care worker or providing support from another human or social service background, we know that your work is important and has a meaningful impact on the lives of youth.

- How have the contributors done so well? What was it in their lives and in my own life that allowed me to be successful?
- Where do I hold power in my position and how do I navigate that power to best support the youth I work with?
- What learnings and insights can I take from the contributors' stories and incorporate into my own practice?
- Has reading this book changed my view as a practitioner? Has it reinforced what I do in my work?
- Why do so many of our youth want to "give back" when life has not given them much? Where does this resiliency come from?

Further Suggested Reading

Appelstein, C. D. (1998). *No such thing as a bad kid: Understanding and responding to the challenging behavior of troubled children and youth.* Weston, Massachusetts: The Gifford School

Batmanghelidjh, C. (2006). *Shattered lives: Children who live with courage and dignity.* London, U.K.: Jessica Kingsley Publishers.

Blaustein, M. E. & Kinniburgh, K. M. (2010). *Treating traumatic stress in children and adolescents: How to foster Resilience through attachment, self-regulation, and competency.* New York, NY: The Guilford press.

(Bell) Kennedy-Kish, B., Sinclair, R., Carniol, B., & Baines, D. (2017). *Case critical: Social services and social justice in Canada.* Between the Lines.

Brendtro, L., & du Toit, L. (2005). *Response Ability Pathways: Restoring bonds of respect.* Claremont, South Africa: Pretext Publishers.

Carrington, J. (2019). *Kids these days: A game plan for (re)connecting with those we teach, lead, & love.* Victoria, BC: Friesen Press.

Eigenbrod, R., & Hulan, R. (Eds.). (2008). *Aboriginal oral traditions: Theory, practice, ethics.* Brunswick Books.

Farmer, R. L. (2009). *Neuroscience and Social Work Practice: The Missing Link.* California, USA: Sage Publications, Inc.

Heller, L. & LaPierre, A. (2012). *Healing developmental trauma: How early trauma affects self-regulation, self-image, and the capacity for relationship (The NeuroAffective Relational Model for restoring connection).* Berkeley, California: North Atlantic Books.

Howe, D. (2008). *The emotionally intelligent social worker.* New York, N.Y.: Palgrave,

McMillan.

Kagan, R. (2004). *Rebuilding attachments with traumatized children: Healing from losses, violence, abuse, and neglect.* Binghamton, N.Y.: The Haworth Maltreatment & Trauma Press.

Levine, P. (1997). *Waking the tiger: Healing Trauma.* Berkeley, California: North Atlantic Books

Luckock, B., Lefevre, M., (eds.) (2008). *Direct work: Social work with children and young people in care.* London: British Association for Adopting & Fostering.

Maté, G. (1999). *Scattered minds: A new look at the origins and healing of attention deficit disorder.* Vintage Canada.

Maté, G. (2008). *In the realm of hungry ghosts: Close encounters with addiction.* Canada: Alfred K. Knopf.

Perry, B. D., & Szalavitz, M. (2010). *Born for love: Why empathy is essential--and endangered.* Harper Collins.

Perry, B., & Szalavitz, M. (2017). *The boy who was raised as a dog and other stories from a child psychiatrist's notebook: Revised and updated edition.* USA: Basic Books.

Purvis, K. B., Cross, D. R., & Sunshine, W. L. (2007). *The connected child: Bring hope and healing to your adoptive family.* New York, NY: McGraw-Hill.

Richardson, B. (2016). *Working with challenging youth: Seven guiding principles (second edition).* New York. NY: Routledge

Roszia, S., & Maxon, A. D. (2019). *Seven core issues in adoption and permanency: A comprehensive guide to promoting understanding and healing in adoption, foster care, kinship families and third-party reproduction.* Jessica Kingsley Publishers.

Ruch, G., Turney, D., & Ward, A. (Eds.) (2010). *Relationship-based social work; Getting to the heart of practice.* London, UK: Jessica Kingsley Publishers.

Saleebey, D. (ed.) (1997). *The strengths perspective in social work practice (second edition).* USA: Longman Publishers.

Smyth, P. (2017). *Working with high-risk youth: A relationship-based practice framework.* Oxford, UK: Routledge, Taylor & Francis Group.

Solomon, M. & Siegel, D. (2003). *Healing trauma: Attachment, mind, body, and brain.* New York, NY: W. W. Norton & Company, Inc.

Strega, S., & Sohki Aski Esquao (Carrière, J.) (Eds.) (2009). *Walking this path together: anti-racist and anti-oppressive child welfare practice.* Canada: Fernwood Publishing.

Ungar, M. (2006). *Strengths-based counselling with at-risk youth.* USA: Corwin Press.

Ungar, M. (2021). *Working with children and youth with complex needs: 20 skills that build resilience (second edition).* New York, NY: Routledge.

Glossary

Adolescent Residential Treatment Centre: Refers to a living arrangement where a child, who has been brought into government care by a child welfare authority, would reside in a specialized shared living facility with trained staff who have been approved and paid to care for children in care. An Adolescent Residential Treatment Centre is typically for children/youth that require a supervised living arrangement with a major therapeutic or treatment component. An Adolescent Residential Treatment Centre is typically only considered when less intensive treatment is insufficient.

Apprehension: In a child welfare context, apprehension typically refers to the process, undertaken by a child welfare authority, of removing a child/youth (legally and physically) from their guardian(s) or parent's care when there are reasonable grounds to believe that a child is at imminent and substantial risk of harm. After an apprehension a child welfare authority would have custody of a child until that child is returned to their guardian or parent's care.

AWOL (Absent Without Official Leave): In a child welfare context, AWOL refers to a child/youth being away from their approved placement.

Band (Indigenous Band): Refers to a form of municipal governance that was imposed on First Nations communities under the Indian Act. Bands are governed by an elected chief and council and band membership includes the right to live on reserve, to participate in voting in elections and share in assets[1].

Case Conference: In a child welfare context, a case conference is a regular meeting that occurs with a child/youth, their child welfare worker and other supports or workers involved in child's care and planning.

Caseworker: In a child welfare context, a caseworker is a child welfare worker who is assigned to a particular child, youth or family when there are substantiated child intervention concerns that exist. Caseworkers help to ensure that children/youth are safe from abuse/neglect and that families have the necessary supports to care for children successful. Caseworkers may act as legal guardians for children in care. Depending on the province, territory or state, Caseworkers can have a variety of educational backgrounds which include but are not limited to Social Work and Child and Youth Care.

Child and Youth Care (Worker): Child and Youth Care is a profession that specializes in using therapeutic relationships with children/youth who are experiencing difficulties in their lives and with promoting emotional, social and behavioural change and well-being through the use of daily life events. Child and Youth Care Worker is a title typically reserved for those who have completed post secondary schooling in a Child and Youth Care program, which includes the completion of mandatory practicum(s). Child and Youth Care Workers must abide by the profession's ethics and standards.

Child Welfare: Is a term that refers to the broader child welfare systems, where a variety of services are provided to children/youth/families, under the authority of each provinces, territories or states unique laws, which are designed to ensure that children/youth are safe from abuse/neglect and that families have the necessary supports to care for children successfully. Child welfare authorities investigate/respond to allegations of abuse and neglect, provide care to children/youth in their custody, supervise kinship/foster/group care placements and arrange adoptions. The names of child welfare authorities vary by each province, territory or state. Depending on the jurisdiction, child welfare authorities may be managed by governments or by private agencies (when they have been privatized). The name for the child welfare authority in Alberta is Children's Services. The Child, Youth and Family Enhancement Act, The Protection of Sexually Exploited Children Act, The Drug-Endangered Children Act and The Protection Against Family Violence Act are key legislation which guides Child Intervention in Alberta.

Family Support Worker: Refers to a worker who works with families to help develop their capacities through mentorship and a connection to community supports.

File: In a child welfare context, a file typically refers to a case (child and/or family) that is being managed by a child welfare worker or the entirety of what is recorded about an individual during their time in care.

Form 10: In Alberta, a Form 10 refers to a certificate issued under the Mental Health Act which authorizes a peace officer to involuntarily and temporarily detain and transport an individual who has been identified as (1) living with a mental health condition, (2) likely to cause harm to themselves or others, and (3) there is a foreseeable timeline in which waiting for a warrant would be dangerous to the individual or others. Individuals under a Form 10 are transported to a designated mental health facility for up to 24 hours. Rights held by individuals apprehended under a Form 10 include knowing why they have been apprehended, knowing when their certificate expires or is cancelled, and the right to refuse treatment, among others.

Foster Care/Home/Parent: Foster care is a living arrangement where a child, who has been brought into government care by a child welfare authority, would reside with a family that has been approved and paid to care for children in care. A foster home is typically for children who are able to reside in a family home living arrangement.

Group Care/Home/Staff: In a child welfare context, group care is a living arrangement where a child, who has been brought into government care by a child welfare authority, would reside in a shared living facility with trained staff who have been approved and paid to care for children in care. A group home is typically for children/youth that need a more supervised living arrangement with a therapeutic component. Group care is also often referred to as residential care.

Harm Reduction: Harm reduction is a philosophy and an approach that seeks to reduce the negative or harmful impacts of risky health behaviours, such as addiction, by meeting people where they are at. Harm reduction acknowledges that many individuals are coping the best that they can. Using addictions and substance use as an example, a harm reduction approach would promote the understanding that people who use substances may not be able, at all times, remain abstinent. Instead, this approach would seek to minimize the risk of using substances by using such strategies a supervised injection sites, where the individual may access education, counselling, and other services and relevant professionals.

In Care: In a child welfare context, in care refers to a child/youth who is in the care and custody of a child welfare authority.

Independent Living: Refers to a living arrangement where a youth or young adult resides in their own home with minimal supports.

Indigenous/Aboriginal: A term that typically describes a person or group that identifies as First Nations, Inuit, or Métis. In Canada, the term Aboriginal has recently been replaced by the term Indigenous.

Key Worker: In a child welfare context, a key worker refers to a worker or staff member at by a group or residential care facility who works directly with a certain child/youth as a support/caregiver and a point of contact for that child/youth.

Kinship Care/Home: In a child welfare context, kinship care is a living arrangement where a child, who has been brought into government care by a child welfare authority, would reside with an extended family member or someone who has a significant connection to a child that has been approved and paid to care for children in care.

PGO (Permanent Guardianship Order): In Alberta, a Permanent Guardianship Order refers to a court order where the government is given sole guardianship/custody of a child and the legal rights of all other guardian(s) or parent's care ended. A Permanent Guardianship Order is granted when it has been determined that a child cannot return to their guardian(s) or parent's care in a reasonable amount of time given concerns for a child's safety/well being. The name of such an order can vary between provinces, territories and states.

Placements: In a child welfare context, a placement refers to the living arrangement of a child who is in care. Typically, placements include kinship homes, foster homes, group homes and residential/treatment facilities.

Private Arrangement: Refers to an informal living arrangement for a child who is not in care and that is made by a guardian or parent of a child. An informal living arrangement may include a child residing with a family member or close friend.

Respite: In a child welfare context, this refers to child residing with another caregiver temporarily, giving the primary caregiver some time for themselves.

Social Work(er): Social Work is a profession that specializes with helping individuals, families, groups and communities to enhance their individual and collective well-being. It is a profession concerned with individual problems and broader social issues such as poverty, addictions, mental health and domestic violence. Social Workers is a legally protected tittle reserved for those who have completed post secondary schooling in a Social Work program, which includes the completion of mandatory practicum(s). Social Workers must abide by the profession's ethics and standards.

Smudging: Smudging is a sacred traditional Indigenous ceremony and it can be led by any Indigenous person who has the permission to do so. It is used to begin all ceremonies as well as a place to begin all things in spirit. For example, we begin the day, circles, events or gathering. From a parallel perspective it is similar to a call to order.

Sun Dance: A Sun Dance is a very sacred ceremony practiced by many Indigenous nations across North America, particularly the people of the Great Plains in Canada and the United States and takes place over several days during the summer. Participation in and attendance at Sun Dances may be for healing, connection, or celebrating life, among others, and is a deeply spiritual process.

Supervised Visits/Access: In a child welfare context, this refers to visits that are supervised, by a third party, between a child/youth and their parents/extended family.

SFAA (Support and Financial Assistance Agreement): In Alberta, this is an agreement entered into by a child welfare authority and a young adult who has had significant involvement with a child welfare authority. Under a SFAA financial and emotional support can be provided to a young adult to help with their transition to adulthood.

Sweat Lodge: A Sweat Lodge ceremony is a very holistic ceremony and is about healing spiritually, emotionally, physically, cognitively; and relationally. This ceremony is performed by traditional knowledge keepers such as an Elder. Sweat Lodge ceremonies may have slight differences dependent on the nation.

TGO (Temporary Guardianship Order): In Alberta, a Temporary Guardianship Order refers to a court order where the government is shared guardianship/custody of a child. A Temporary Guardianship Order is granted when it has been determined that a child cannot return to their guardian(s) or parent's care at the current time given concerns for a child's safety/well being, but that it is believed that in a reasonable amount of time that a child can be returned. The name of such an order can vary between provinces, territories and states.

Trick: Refers to a sex worker's client. A sex worker typically refers to an individual who receives money or goods in exchange for consensual sexual or companionship services. Non consensual sex and sex with an individual under the legal age of consent is considered sexual assault/exploitation.

Two-Spirit: Two-Spirited is the energy that we all carry of male and female. We believe that people are born knowing exactly who they are and are not defined by the Western perspective of gender. Two spirited individuals often have the role of healers within our community. Two-Spirit identities are represented by the '2S' in LGBTQ2S+ communities, and this has traditional significance in Indigenous ways of knowing and being.

YSO (Youth Speak Out): Refers to a youth in care group supported by the Adoption Council of Canada. Youth Speak Out groups exist throughout Canada. Youth Speak Out groups typically focus on representing the interests of youth in care, the importance of permanency and the sharing of experiences growing up in care to help inform practice, policy and legislation.

Youth Worker: Refers to a worker who works with young people to help develop their capacities through mentorship.

[1] First Nations & Indigenous Studies Program. (n.d.). *Bands*. Indigenous Foundations. https://indigenousfoundations.arts.ubc.ca/bands/

Acknowledgement

In order to follow cultural protocol Elder Kerrie Moore with the University of Calgary was asked to advise on all terms related to Indigenous ways of knowing presented in this glossary.

Thank you for reading our stories and supporting this project. All proceeds from the sale of the Youth In Care Chronicles will be used to fund other projects that will benefit youth in care and the people who work with them.

We are looking at creating future volumes of stories and artworks so if you are a former youth in care or know someone who is, please contact:

Penny Frazier
Project Coordinator
780-221-6124
penny@pennyfrazier.ca
www.pennyfrazier.ca

Made in the USA
Middletown, DE
24 December 2020